Self-Esteem

FOR

DUMMIES®

A Wiley Brand

by S. Renee Smith
and
Vivian Hart

FOR

DUMMIES®

**Self-Esteem For Dummies®**

Published by: **John Wiley & Sons, Inc.,** 111 River Street, Hoboken, NJ 07030-5774, www.wiley.com

For general information on our other products and services, please contact our Customer Care Department within the U.S. at 877-762-2974, outside the U.S. at 317-572-3993, or fax 317-572-4002. For technical support, please visit www.wiley.com/techsupport.

Wiley publishes in a variety of print and electronic formats and by print-on-demand. Some material included with standard print versions of this book may not be included in e-books or in print-on-demand. If this book refers to media such as a CD or DVD that is not included in the version you purchased, you may download this material at http://booksupport.wiley.com. For more information about Wiley products, visit www.wiley.com.

Library of Congress Control Number: 2014948541

ISBN 978-1-118-96709-6 (pbk); ISBN 978-1-118-96710-2 (ebk); ISBN 978-1-118- 96711-9 (ebk)

Manufactured in the United States of America

10 9 8 7 6 5 4 3 2 1

# Contents at a Glance

# Table of Contents

# Introduction

**S**elf-esteem is a personal journey to understanding yourself and the value you bring to the world. We are delighted to have this amazing and humbling opportunity to guide you on this dynamic path of self-discovery. As a teacher and a coach of self-esteem building, we have combined our unique styles and experiences to bring you an engaging, life-changing, interactive reading experience to help you improve your self-esteem.

From the beginning, it has been our intention and commitment to meet you where you are. If you're struggling with the past, we help you conquer it. If you're greatly accomplished but recent circumstances have shaken you to your core, we help you rebuild. If you're a parent, leader, teacher, mentor, or friend who desires to help others build their self-esteem, we also have you covered.

*Self-Esteem For Dummies* is comprehensive, covering everything from where low self-esteem comes from to how to build and sustain self-esteem throughout your life journey. Because "self-esteem," "self-worth," "self-regard," "self-respect," and "self-assuredness" are similar in meaning, you'll notice that we use these terms interchangeably. What's most important is what you get: We want you to feel good about being you!

We've also included guided visualization exercises in various chapters. These exercises help you to envision yourself doing fabulous things before you do them. Seeing yourself succeed before you're in the situation helps to improve your performance because you already know that success is achievable.

We are grateful that you've given us this opportunity to take a deep dive with you into your most treasured personal space. There isn't an ounce of doubt in our minds that by reading *Self-Esteem For Dummies,* you'll discover what you've always known deep inside — you're magnificently brilliant!

## About This Book

Everything you want and will ever dream of is locked behind the door of your self-esteem. Since the beginning of time, human beings have struggled with understanding, affirming, and owning their personal power. Despite the many technological, social, and political advances, there is still buzz about our continuous struggle to know and experience ourselves fully.

This isn't just a book; it's a process. It's designed to guide you to and through the door to your self-esteem. We help you through this process, step by step:

1. **We help you understand what self-esteem is and how it impacts your life.**

2. **We show you how to pinpoint where you are.**

3. **We give you the tools to overcome mistruths that are holding you down and back.**

4. **We support you as you set goals and start feeling good about achieving greater success because of your increased self-esteem.**

5. **We assist you in quickly recognizing and dealing with internal barriers that challenge you when you least expect it.**

6. **We help you to better understand and stabilize your personal and professional relationships.**

7. **We know you want to share your good fortune of increased self-esteem with others, so we show you how to spread the love.**

The great thing about this book is that we share stories that remind you that you're not alone. We also include exercises that have helped others get unstuck and moving in the right direction.

# *Foolish Assumptions*

Before writing each chapter, we had you on our minds. Brilliant one, here are the assumptions we made about what you really know:

- ✔ Feeling funky is no longer fun. You're tired of feeling less than and you're ready to own your power.

- ✔ Change comes with choice. You've made the decision that it's no longer an option to remain as you are in your current condition.

- ✔ Nothing separates us. Your struggles aren't any different from ours and our students' and clients' — we understand where you are, and because we've developed the tools to combat those "crazy" moments, we can guide you to where you want to be.

- ✔ Success doesn't determine self-esteem. You live and work with people who've achieved success, but whose treatment of others makes it evident that they don't feel good about themselves. Because you have to endure them, you want to learn how to deal with them.

- ✔ Real power is empowering others. You understand as a leader, teacher, mentor, and friend that nothing is more powerful than helping others see and own their power.

# Icons Used in This Book

To make this book engaging, interactive, and easy to use, we created the following icons to guide you from start to finish.

This bull's-eye highlights important words of advice to increase your self-esteem.

This icon is used to emphasize a crucial point to keep in mind.

The text next to this icon cautions you to take special care of yourself concerning the topic under discussion.

Here we share stories that provide a foundation for teaching, inspiring, and helping you to better understand the lesson in the text. These anecdotes aren't meant to directly represent any particular situation or client.

This icon is used for exercises. Exercises are used to help you work through the principle we're teaching so you can see where you are and how to apply it to your life and daily interactions with others.

This icon is used for guided visualizations that help you create body/mind alignment and assist you in experiencing what we're teaching you at a deeper level.

# Beyond the Book

As if all the great information in this book weren't enough, you can go beyond the book for even more! Check out www.dummies.com/cheatsheet/selfesteem for a quiz to help you assess your level of self-esteem, plus info on how to identify and stop negative self-talk, how to become better friends with yourself, and more.

You can also check out some free bonus articles at www.dummies.com/extras/selfesteem and listen to guided audio visualizations at www.dummies.com/go/selfesteem.

## ɔm Here

ɔy the reading and learning experience that *Self-Esteem* ides and share what you liked and learned with all those ʋe who will benefit from its teachings. Keep it as a reference ŋ engaged in your self-development by joining S. Renee (`www.` insideyou.com) and Vivian Harte (`www.self-esteem-` ) at any of our free online webinars and teleseminars.

# Part I

# The Lowdown on Self-Esteem

# In this part . . .

✔ Begin to understand self-esteem by looking at the foundations of self-esteem and comparing high with low self-esteem.

✔ Low self-esteem has many consequences. Identify the negative influences that low self-esteem has on your life and appraise the consequences of not making the necessary changes that can lead to a life of healthy self-esteem.

✔ Where does low self-esteem come from? You're not born with it, so how do your experiences from the past affect you? Discover how your self-esteem was both cultivated and injured by people you knew in your early years and how the beliefs you formed in childhood may be influencing you even today.

✔ It's difficult to know what needs to change until you know where you are now. Assess your self-esteem at this point and analyze where your strengths and weaknesses are.

*Self esteem in how I feel about myself as a person*

# Chapter 1

# The Nature of Self-Esteem

............................................................

## In This Chapter

▶ Understanding the difference between healthy self-esteem and low self-esteem

▶ Developing your self-awareness

▶ Improving your relationships at home and at work

............................................................

*Believe in your self*

**B**elieve in yourself! It's such a short sentence, but its impact is crucial to having happiness and success in your life.

Self-esteem is how you feel about yourself as a person. Many people base their sense of self-worth on external factors, such as how much money they make, how many material possessions they have, how good-looking they are, and how many friends they have. But any of these can change, and if they do, self-esteem can take a nose-dive.

REMEMBER

Real self-esteem comes from an inner knowing that you are competent, confident, and worthy of a good life. It's recognizing that you can accomplish what you desire to do and be, that you have the ability to be successful in relationships, and that you are happy with who you are.

## Defining Self-Esteem

*Self means: 'One's own person'*

*esteem:*

Like everyone, you have a self-concept, a sense of who you are. It's the perception you hold in your mind about yourself, how you feel about yourself, and the opinions you hold regarding what you can attain in life and how well you can manage everyday demands.

The dictionary says that "self" means "one's own person" and that "esteem" means "having high regard, respect, admiration." So people with healthy self-esteem have great respect and admiration for themselves. They hold themselves in high regard.

Conversely, people with low self-esteem have little regard for themselves, don't respect themselves, and certainly don't admire themselves. They have little or no confidence and belittle themselves with their own thoughts.

What are the consequences of having low self-esteem? We describe many negative outcomes in Chapter 2. You feel insignificant and lonely. You feel that you don't matter and that no one cares about you. You have little purpose in life and no reason to dream about doing anything worthwhile. Because you're not worthy of other people's love or friendship, you find it difficult to have an open, honest relationship. Most likely, you feel stuck at work, do a mediocre job, and are less likely to get promotions or raises.

# Understanding the Foundations of Self-Esteem

As we explain in Chapter 3, the foundations of your feelings of self-esteem have come from your past. The sources are many — your parents and siblings, the neighborhood children you played with, the children you attended school with, your teachers, and religious authorities. All of these people have helped establish how you've felt about yourself.

Many of your notions of self-esteem have come directly from how you were treated in your family. If you were given loving attention and praise and if you were spoken to in a polite manner and listened to, these experiences have helped you form a strong sense of self-worth. On the other hand, if you were put down, neglected, or disregarded, or screamed at and disciplined harshly, your sense of self-worth has been diminished or extinguished altogether.

If that weren't enough, you have also received messages from society about who you should be. These messages can come from movies, television shows, and magazines. They tell you to act a certain way and look a certain way. They tell you how successful you should be and what a great relationship you should have. They tell you that you should have a perfect life, so if you don't, you feel something must be wrong with you.

All of these factors work together to create core beliefs about yourself in your mind — how you see yourself and how you interpret what takes place in your life. Even as an adult now, you still have the core beliefs you formed as a child.

TIP

Throughout this book, we show you how to change those beliefs and become the person with healthy self-esteem that you desire to be. First, you begin to understand yourself more fully by measuring your self-esteem in Chapter 4. Then in Chapter 5, you discover the power of using affirmations and visualizations to create new beliefs.

# Healthy Self-Esteem versus Low Self-Esteem

*Beliefs are opinions & opinions can be changed.*

The core beliefs that formed your sense of self-worth as a child are just that — beliefs. They're not necessarily true or accurate. They're only your opinions. As opinions, they can be changed.

Healthy self-esteem and low self-esteem are two sides of the same coin. They both activate certain rules for living that either help you or hurt you.

If you have healthy self-esteem, you

- ✔ Learn from past successes and look forward to future successes
- ✔ Care for yourself physically, emotionally, and mentally
- ✔ Create goals in your life and work toward them
- ✔ Appreciate your positive qualities
- ✔ Accept responsibility for your actions
- ✔ Have confidence that you can accomplish things, even if it takes more than one try
- ✔ Feel capable of meeting life's everyday challenges
- ✔ Are happy and sure of yourself

On the other hand, if you have low self-esteem, you

- ✔ Compare yourself negatively with others
- ✔ Are anxious, stressed, and worry a lot
- ✔ Need others' approval
- ✔ Fear speaking up at meetings
- ✔ Fear confrontation with others
- ✔ Are shy to talk with others you don't know

✔ Focus on your shortcomings in the past

✔ Have doubts about your worth

In this section, we explain how negative self-talk is damaging to your self-esteem and how positive self-talk can uplift you. We also describe what happens if you have too much self-esteem. Too much? Yes, you can actually have too much self-esteem, so much so that it becomes intolerable to other people.

## Taking care of yourself

Because caring for yourself is one of the characteristics of having a healthy level of self-esteem, in Chapter 6, we give you numerous ways to nurture yourself to create more happiness in your life and raise your self-esteem. We describe how to take care of your body by eating healthy foods, doing enough exercise, and getting regular, deep sleep.

We also teach you how to focus on positive emotions by shifting negative feelings that drain you to feelings that uplift and encourage you, and we give you many tips to turn around a bad mood. Finally, we share how to change your thoughts by talking to yourself in a loving manner.

As a bonus, you discover how to speak up in an assertive manner, including how to confront another person using this four-step process:

1. **Expressing what the other person is doing that you want to see changed**

2. **Explaining how that person's behavior negatively affects you**

3. **Identifying your emotions**

4. **Describing exactly what you want the other person to do instead**

Confronting another person may be one of the most difficult things for you to do, and we show you how to do this assertively and calmly, but firmly.

One of the most common ways people experience low self-esteem is in the way they consider their body image. In Chapter 7, we help you reconnect with the positive aspects of your body, while emphasizing the importance of appreciating the real beauty that is on the inside.

# Looking at positive and negative self-talk

Your sense of self-esteem is expressed through your inner thoughts. The statements you make to yourself determine how you value yourself and how successful you are in your life. This internal voice inside your head influences everything you experience.

Take a look at the difference in Table 1-1.

| Table 1-1 | Negative versus Positive Self-Talk |
|---|---|
| *Negative Self-Talk* | *Positive Self-Talk* |
| I am stupid. | I have strong abilities. |
| I can't do it, so why try? | I know I can do it. |
| I can't speak up. | I'm speaking up more all the time. |
| I'm too nervous to focus. | I'm remaining calm and relaxed. |
| I'm never going to get a good job. | I have confidence that I'll get just the right job for me. |

Your mind deceives you in several ways to make you believe you have little value. In Chapter 8, we discuss these ways and how to refute each one:

- Mind-reading
- Predicting a negative outcome
- Overgeneralizing
- Labeling yourself
- Blaming yourself
- Focusing on the negative and discounting the positive
- Using "shoulds"

Do you use any or all of these in your everyday thinking? If so, it's time to transform your thoughts into optimistic and positive ones. We show you how to do this step by step.

## Discarding unsuccessful strategies for improvement

You may feel you can improve your self-esteem by seeking approval from others. You seek reassurance that people like you, and you try to please others by doing everything they ask, even if you don't want to. You feel insecure and may try to counter these feelings by becoming the center of attention.

You may use your education and workplace achievements to try to improve your sense of self-worth. You may earn more academic degrees or strive to get a better job at a more prestigious company. Both of these may lead to greater competence in the workplace, but if you haven't dealt with the underlying causes of your lack of self-esteem, you'll find that once in the workplace, you may not believe you deserve the job you have, or you may procrastinate and belittle yourself if you make any mistakes, no matter how small.

In fact, if you're like many people who have low self-esteem, you may feel you must be perfect at everything. If you aren't, you criticize yourself mercilessly, and your productivity actually decreases over time. You suffer from perfectionism, frequently using negative self-talk that says you must do things perfectly all the time and that you're not worth anything if you don't do everything flawlessly. In Chapters 9 and 10, we analyze how perfectionism begins, what the characteristics of a perfectionist are, and how to be a healthy high-achiever instead.

## Considering whether you can have too much self-esteem

Is it possible to have such a strong self-esteem that your confidence and pride are detrimental? Yes, this can happen. Pride can result in a large ego, one that demands that you're always right and must be obeyed.

When you have a sense of self-worth that is too strong, you interrupt others when they're speaking, try to impose your position on others, make decisions for others, and find fault with others without regard to their feelings. You'd rather cause harm or inconvenience to others than bring harm or inconvenience to yourself.

You may even use threats, such as "You'd better" and "If you don't watch out," as well as sarcasm and put-downs like "Oh, come on, you must be joking" and "You should have." Your body language includes leaning forward with glaring eyes, pointing a finger, and using a raised or haughty tone of voice. You may even go so far as to humiliate others. Your aggressive manner encourages others to treat you in a fearful and defensive way.

Obviously, you don't want to go this far. Having healthy self-esteem means being respectful of others and expressing what you want in a kind manner.

# Enhancing Your Self-Awareness

An important step in moving into greater self-esteem is to become more aware of who you are, why you are here, what's important to you, and what you want. Appreciating every phase of your life and what it's teaching you, listening to yourself, and knowing, loving, and accepting yourself are crucial. In Chapter 11, we take you on a deeper journey into your inner self to get ready to embrace the new changes you're about to make.

We help you understand your feelings, why you feel the way you do, what's keeping you from living life to the fullest, and what you're missing by hanging on to unconstructive notions about what life can be and what you can become.

We know that being stronger and living your dreams can be scary and create anxiety. Questions can lay heavy on your mind: Will I fall short? Will people like me? Am I prepared? Most people have these apprehensions, so don't feel alone.

Fear comes from many places, such as uncertainty as to what will happen, past bad experiences, lack of information, and possible mistreatment by others. But beneath all of these is mistrusting yourself. Fear is a mindset that takes control of your life when you can't reassure yourself that you're going to be fine no matter what happens.

Interestingly, statistics show that 90 percent of what you worry about will never happen. To live a life with strong self-esteem, dealing successfully with your fears is necessary. We've found that there's only one way to prevail over fear and develop inner strength, and that's to face the fear. In Chapter 12, we take you through a number of exercises to uncover your core fears and deal with them by flowing with your fears or navigating around them.

After you have a deep understanding of your fears and how to be triumphant in dealing with them, we give you the steps to replace these apprehensive thoughts with words of faith in yourself. This resilient faith supports you in moving forward.

# Designing and Attaining Your Goals

People who experience success have an unshakable faith in themselves, can visualize their accomplishments, and are determined and persistent in reaching their goals. In Chapter 13, we help you focus on some of the most important questions you can ever ask yourself:

- ✔ Who do I want to be?
- ✔ What do I want to do?
- ✔ What do I want to have?
- ✔ Who do I want to help?
- ✔ How will I help them?
- ✔ Who do I want to spend time with?
- ✔ What do I want to spend my time doing?

After you respond to these questions honestly, we direct you on how to set both long-term and short-term goals in your life that will lead to the results you desire as indicated by your answers. Creating these goals has many constructive effects — it generates confidence, encourages interest, inspires hope, and initiates enthusiasm. These qualities are all necessary to achieve your goals, and we give you some additional "secret weapons" you can use to give you the edge to reach your objectives.

# Creating Healthy Relationships

Did you know that you're physically, emotionally, and mentally healthier when you have meaningful and fulfilling relationships? When you're ill, you'll get better more quickly if you have a loving support system. If you're broken-hearted from a romantic breakup, you'll get back to normal more quickly if you have someone to talk to and pour your heart out to. Relationships are crucial to having a balanced, happy, and healthy life.

What makes a relationship meaningful? It's all about sharing. It's opening up to share your true self and having the other person share his true self with you. The more self-esteem you have, the more likely you are to be sincere in relationships. You don't try to be an image of what the other person wants you to be; instead, you think, speak, and behave in a manner that is genuine and easy for you.

When you have a sense of strong self-worth, you have a healthy balance between happiness that comes from yourself and happiness that comes from your relationships. Although you're not totally self-sufficient and happy only to be with yourself, you're also not dependent on people you're in relationships with to fulfill you. When the relationship is going well, much of your contentment comes from that. When the relationship is not going well or when you have no relationship at all with a particular person, you experience joy from within.

As you're developing a stronger sense of self-esteem, you'll be able to have satisfying and fulfilling relationships without the need to be completely dependent on others to define who you are. You can share with others, and you can be contented by yourself too. Both are important.

Before you can develop a healthy relationship with another person, it's best to understand yourself. First, you need to consider what internal barriers you have to being in relationships. In Chapter 14, you find the seven steps to tracking your behavior in order to change those internal barriers. Then, in Chapter 15, you assess what you like about yourself and discover tips for making friends with yourself.

An important exercise in Chapter 15 helps you understand the lessons of ten pivotal moments in your life. If you only hold onto the feelings of these moments without learning the lessons they have to teach you, the feelings stick with you, causing you to unconsciously create more situations to validate the beliefs you have. By bringing the thoughts and feelings you had in these important moments to the surface and seeing when similar situations returned, you're able to identify the lessons you need to learn. This exercise helps release you to have deep and enduring relationships.

Falling in love with the right person is difficult if you don't know what you're looking for. What you need is different from that of anyone else. Here are some questions to consider:

- What do you want in a romantic love relationship?
- What are your core requirements?
- What worked well in past relationships?
- What were your unmet needs in those relationships?
- What is your ideal profile of a partner?

In Chapter 16, you go in depth to break through the fantasy of romantic love and identify truthfully and honestly what your core yearnings are. After you've met someone, we help you explore the essential questions for you and your potential mate to answer about yourself and your relationship before moving forward.

From romantic relationships, we dive into personal relationships with family and friends in Chapter 17. At the core, everyone wants to be loved, accepted, and appreciated for who she is and what she does. But every person needs to receive these expressions in a different way. Understanding your unique needs is the foundation for understanding the dynamics behind your relationships with people you're close to.

There are some family members whose behaviors seem intolerable. Is dealing with difficult family members something you're faced with? If so, the key is to maintain respect and address the behavior instead of criticizing the person. We provide a three-step strategy to preserve your composure while you interact with them:

1. **Live according to how you want people to respect you.**

2. **Immediately address any transgression.**

3. **Show repeat offenders the door.**

If you live in a blended family or have extended family members, you'll benefit from the "ten B's" in Chapter 17, suggestions to help you and your loved ones work together to create the best environment for yourselves and your families.

And where would you be without friendships? We assist you in continuing your journey into relationships by giving you pointers on creating deeper connections and overcoming disagreements and hurt feelings.

# Being Successful at Work

You most likely spend more time working than most things in your life. You get ready for work, travel to work, do your job during the day, have lunch with associates, come home from work, change from your work clothes into more comfortable clothes, and rest to get ready for your next day at work. You may even bring work home with you. So having a solid sense of self-esteem in the workplace is crucial to having a happy and fulfilled life. Chapters 18 to 20 give you astute ways to improve your performance and likability.

You have a brand. Your brand is your reputation. What is your reputation? Building an effective personal brand and presenting yourself in the best image possible creates a presence that draws people to you. They want to talk to you and hear what you're up to.

Most successful people plan their journeys to attain their achievements. To prepare for success, you must

- ✔ Have a vision
- ✔ Have a plan to attain that vision
- ✔ Know what you need in the industry you work for
- ✔ Develop resistance to rejection and affirm yourself
- ✔ Develop a positive outlook on life that is uplifting and inspiring
- ✔ Develop a support network
- ✔ Be strategic with your time and priorities
- ✔ Be confident, but humble

Becoming the go-to person means you know your stuff in a specific area. How can you establish yourself as the go-to person at work? We show you the steps to provide the solutions that your organization, customers, coworkers, and community need. And as the go-to person, you need to grow the awareness of who you are and your expertise by increasing your exposure at work. You do this by engaging three people in leadership and two up-and-coming influencers who would be interested in what you have to offer. Don't be concerned about how to do this, though. We provide a list of 21 different strategies to engage them.

Your relationships with the leaders and your coworkers at your job can make or break your work experience, especially if they're difficult. By understanding others' core needs, you can uncover what they want and how to respond to them. Asking questions, watching their reactions, and listening for the emotion that drives what they say can lead you in the right direction.

The scariest thing for most people is presenting before a group of people. Whether you're an amateur or an experienced speaker, we show you how to present with presence, passion, and power both before an audience and at meetings.

# Cultivating Self-Esteem in Others

Everyone deserves to have healthy self-esteem, including your family members, spouse, friends, and children. Everyone is unique and has his own special gifts to give to the world. Only if you have a strong sense of self-worth can you bring these gifts to fruition so others can benefit.

Chapters 21 and 22 give you the lowdown on nurturing self-esteem in others. To help both adults and children develop their own self-esteem, you first need to believe in them, even when they don't believe in themselves — in fact, *especially* when they don't believe in themselves. Speaking uplifting and encouraging words and supporting others are essential in assisting them.

This is particularly true with children and teens. They need a safe place to share their feelings and to know they're accepted. They need to know you're listening and that you believe in their capabilities. Teach them how to be responsible, prepare them for success, and assist them in making good decisions. You are their model, their example on how to live with healthy self-esteem. Through you, they learn to advance.

Buy a special notebook and put in it only things that celebrate you and the terrific person you are. Find pictures at different ages, mementos of things you've enjoyed doing and places you've enjoyed being, awards and cards you've received, writings you've written, and so on. Open your special notebook often, especially in times when you need to strengthen your self-esteem.

# Chapter 2

# Understanding the Impacts of Low Self-Esteem

*In This Chapter*

▶ Exploring the negative effects of low self-esteem

▶ Looking at the consequences of not making changes

**R**ealizing the many hindrances low self-esteem causes in your life is the first step to identifying why it's so important to make changes. If you're one of the many people who battles a sense of low self-worth, it's helpful to recognize some of the patterns you live with every day.

This chapter describes the many impacts of living a life that lacks self-respect. You can see these consequences in the negative attitudes you suffer through, the relationships you either avoid or damage, the promotions at work you miss out on, and even the problems with alcohol and drugs you may be experiencing. By being absolutely honest with yourself and identifying your problems, you'll be able to more rapidly overcome them.

You may not see all these unpleasant impacts in your life. You may recognize only a few. But even those few are keeping you from living a life of fulfillment, accomplishment, and joy. You deserve better!

# Discovering the Consequences of Low Self-Esteem

A feeling of low self-worth is accompanied by thoughts about yourself where you see yourself as "less than" and "not good enough." In order to lessen these thoughts, you try certain behaviors, all aimed at making you feel better about yourself.

But they don't work. In fact, you find that a negative spiral is set into motion: You have low self-esteem, your thoughts reflect an image in your mind of a person who is lacking, you try to be competent and accomplished, but your low self-esteem causes you to fall short, and this then leads you to a feeling of lower self-worth.

## Recognizing what happens when you feel insignificant

If you have a sense of low self-respect, you may feel like you don't matter. Although you may be in a crowd of people, you feel alone and that you don't belong. You feel alienated from others and disconnected even from people you're close to. It's like you're in an audience watching people happily conversing and relating to each other, and you're just observing the show, on the sidelines and feeling lonely once again.

You feel invisible. You always find yourself at the outer edge of groups, where no one really wants to talk to you or be your friend. Even if you have friends, you feel that they take advantage of you and don't see you as being as important as any of their other friends. You feel you give to them, but you don't see that you get the same in return. They don't remember your birthday. They never call you to go out. When there was a death in your family, no one sent you a card or called you to offer condolences.

So you become withdrawn because you're tired of making the effort to be with people. In fact, you're tired of life in general.

In addition, you don't have any purpose to your life. You don't have anything to offer that's valuable. You have no reason to dream because your dreams don't come true. You may have a humdrum job, but that's all. You come home, watch television, and go to bed. You're invisible and insignificant.

Darren is a man in his 30s. He has a college education, but finding a job in his field is difficult for him. He sends out resumes and makes phone calls, but nothing comes through. Very few of the companies he sends his resume to even respond. His wife belittles him about not being able to find a job and offers no compassion or assistance, and she mainly ignores him while they are both home. He talks to a couple of his friends, even cries in front of them. But neither of them hugs him or gives him any encouragement. Darren feels alone, that no one is helping him, that he is invisible to everyone in his life.

## Exploring the negative impacts of low self-esteem

Feeling insignificant can lead you to the point where you don't even want to get up in the morning and face the day. Why make the effort? No one is going to notice anyway. No one cares.

If this describes you, it's time to make the change to have more awareness of your value. You can't wave a wand and take these feelings away in a moment. But as you read this book, do the exercises, understand yourself more deeply, and follow our instructions, you'll realize that inside yourself is a marvelous person who is just waiting to jump out — a person who's excited to be alive, loves to get up in the morning, and enjoys a life of success and happiness. That can be you!

# Becoming Aware of the Consequences of Doing Nothing

If you do nothing — if you continue to have a low opinion of yourself — your life may very well get worse.

The negative consequences of a poor self-image can lead into a downward spiral of lower and lower self-esteem, a less productive life, and even to self-destructive behavior.

You don't want that. That's not who you really are. In this section, we describe the many features of a person with low self-respect, but keep in mind that you don't have to live with any of these. You *can* improve yourself.

## Continuing the feelings of fear and shame

If you continue on your present path, your feelings of fear and shame will continue and, in fact, may become stronger. Fear leads to feelings of helplessness, that you can't control your life.

Sometimes when you're fearful, you may experience shortness of breath, your heart pounds quickly, you feel dizzy, your knees are wobbly, and your stomach is nauseous. It's difficult to have the energy to deal with life in a positive way when your body is reacting this way.

You fear others will ridicule you and laugh at your mistakes. You're mistrustful of others, always watching to see who's paying attention to what you do. You doubt that you can achieve anything, so you don't even try. You fear failure, and you fear rejection. You withdraw as much as you can from others because you don't want to experience their judgment.

Or you feel you must show others how successful you are so they won't judge you. Everything has to look perfect — your career, family, appearance, car, house.

But that's not all. A sense of low self-esteem can lead to a feeling of shame, especially if you're criticized by others. You feel utter humiliation and anguish. Whether the criticism is accurate or not, you have a sense of inadequacy because you feel unworthy.

Shame can also come from feelings about events from your early past, mistakes you've made, or poor social behavior. It makes no difference what events led to your shame; it's a wrenching feeling that's hard to leave behind.

As with feelings of fear, you want to shrink and hide to get away from these painful feelings. To keep others from finding out how bad you feel inside, you wall yourself off from them and create barriers so you don't have to be with anyone. When you have to be around other people, you may belittle yourself first so that others won't say anything hurtful. Or you may put other people down to elevate your own feelings. Either way, it's not healthy.

## *Going into guilt and depression*

You may feel guilty about something you did wrong or some harm you caused another person. Guilt also comes from not doing something you should have done, such as not helping someone enough. You can even feel guilt from doing something better than another person.

If you have a feeling of low self-worth, you'll see yourself as a bad person who needs to be punished. You'll think you can't be forgiven for the awful thing you did or didn't do. Even if you ask for forgiveness, you won't truly believe the other person when it's offered. You'll continue to berate yourself for what you did wrong.

Feeling insignificant and not wanting to get out of bed can be symptoms of depression. Keep in mind that depression can be caused by chemical imbalances that are typically treated with medication. If you feel this may be the case, please consult with your physician. Depression can also be caused by how you think about yourself and the world, so combining both medication and therapy can be the best way to go.

Depression is very common in people who have low self-esteem. If this describes you, you take things personally in a negative way and do everything you can to verify your negative self-concept by seeking condemnation from people you know. You think about your incompetence and inadequacies as well as focus on the negative things people say about you. All of this leads to a dark mood, which encourages others to think poorly of you, so you in turn feel rejected by others.

If you feel depressed, you probably don't feel like socializing. But even then, you're down on yourself for not having many friends.

None of this feels much fun, does it? If you think that, you're correct. Living in this dark world truly affects your quality of life.

## Maintaining social phobias

As we mention earlier, if you lack a sense of self-worth, it's very likely you don't want to be around other people. This is partly to hide yourself from people and partly because you're so anxious about being around others. You're very afraid that you won't do well dealing with other people and that you'll be terribly embarrassed.

You're afraid of being judged, so you either avoid social situations or endure them with an intense internal discomfort. You're worried about what others will think, so you're uneasy being around them to begin with. You may be so nervous and afraid of rejection that you avoid people and social situations as much as possible. You're sure no one will like you, so why put yourself out there?

Now consider this: How are you supposed to make friends and be a friend to others if you feel and act this way? It's not possible. You can't have a life filled with love and companionship if you're so afraid of other people. Low self-respect certainly isn't good for you.

Donna works at a high-powered company, and when she is asked her opinions at her team's meetings, her heart races, her face turns beet red, and she becomes breathless. Her voice becomes very soft, and she shifts around in her chair. Her teammates are hesitant to take her seriously. Outside of work, she feels awkward around people, so she rarely goes out of her house. As a result of her social phobias, over the years, Donna has become more and more withdrawn.

## Not addressing body image problems

Do you think and talk a lot about your body image, your weight, and food? Do you diet or think about dieting most of the time? Are you sensitive to comments about your body? Do you think some part or parts of your body don't look like you wish they would? Do you compare yourself with others and fall short? Do you constantly think your body isn't good enough?

If you answer "yes" to one or more of these questions, your lack of self-worth is harming the way you see your body and deal with body image issues. Having a poor body image means that you see your body in a negative light. When you look at yourself, you see only the flaws and highlight everything you feel is wrong with your body.

You may not see any point in putting time and effort into taking care of your body — eating in a healthy manner, exercising a few times a week, and dressing yourself nicely. In fact, you may have so much loathing for your body that you don't even like to look in the mirror anymore.

This unhealthy way of relating to your body image can lead to destructive eating disorders, such as starving yourself, anorexia, binge eating, and bulimia (binging and purging). This sort of behavior can even be life threatening if treatment isn't sought.

## *Having poor relationships*

Having low self-worth is directly related to creating poor relationships and may even lead to losing close ones. Because you're insecure and doubt that anyone could actually love you, you need confirmation of others' feelings for you, and you need to be totally accepted by them. Even if your partner sees you in a positive light, you greatly underestimate that and devalue your partner's opinion.

You may have dreams of the perfect mate who will make your life wonderful, but even if your partner is loving and loyal, you don't believe the relationship can be good. If you're not good enough, how can you believe someone would choose you? So you test your partner, requiring a demonstration of his or her devotion to you. And even if your partner comes through every time, you belittle your mate because you know the relationship will ultimately end anyway. When it does, you chalk it up as one more indication that you're not lovable.

Because you're not naturally lovable, you may feel you have to claw and fight for a mate, being consumed with the thought of attracting someone. You work hard to snag the object of your affection, intensely pushing to get a relationship going quickly.

In fact, your insecurities may draw you to relationships where chances are good that you'll be left or cheated on. Because it's happened so many times before, you expect it, and you're not at all surprised when it happens again. In order to protect yourself, you hold back from fully committing yourself, or you become jealous of your partner, making accusations and creating emotional scenes.

Having a disloyal partner may actually represent excitement to you. You're bored and indifferent if the relationship is too dependable.

Another thing that you may have experienced is losing yourself in your relationship, being totally submissive. You have such a low sense of self-worth that you depend on your partner to control you. You lean on your partner to tell you what to do, how to think, and who you can see. This type of control can easily lead to abuse since this is what you inwardly believe is all that you deserve.

Or you must have a perfect relationship to show everyone that you're worthy. So you demand complete control over your partner, leading to your partner resenting you.

You desire to have a healthy, fulfilling relationship, but because of your low opinion of yourself, it's not likely. Creating a healthier level of self-esteem will help you find the right person and experience an affectionate, respectful relationship.

## Having low self-confidence

Self-esteem and self-confidence are related, but they're not exactly the same thing. Your self-esteem defines how you feel about yourself. Your self-confidence describes how much you believe you have the ability to accomplish things in the world.

If you have low self-esteem, you probably also have low self-confidence. You don't feel you're worth much, so you don't desire much for yourself or have the motivation to fulfill any goals. The thoughts in your mind — "I'm no good," "I'm going to do a terrible job," and "I dislike myself" — all lead to having little belief in yourself.

## Staying stuck at work

Your low self-esteem can lead to many things that stunt your career:

- You're less likely to do well in interviews.
- You're less successful in your work.
- You're less likely to get promotions.
- You're less likely to get raises.

A lack of self-respect leads to anxiety and apprehension during interviews. Your voice shakes, you can't remember your best accomplishments, and you can't look the interviewer in the eye. Do you think you'll get the job?

And even if you can fake the interview well enough to get the job, you may very well do poorly. You may become a supervisor, but because of your low self-esteem, you don't know how to deal respectfully with your subordinates and coworkers. You may even end up being a bully to people you supervise.

If you think you're poor at speaking up and getting your point across in meetings, you won't be seen as a leader. If you're reluctant to take on challenges and feel you're not up to the task of taking initiatives in your job, you won't get promoted. If you lack confidence in your own talents and abilities, and in fact you downplay your talents, you'll be seen as ineffective. You'll sabotage your success, even when success is possible.

Because of your fear of rejection, you keep to yourself in the office, tiptoe quietly when you have to move about, and speak softly when you're spoken to. You don't have the nerve to make an appointment with your boss to point out a problem with something he did. You keep to yourself, keep your head down, and keep doing your work.

You get a mediocre job and do mediocre work at that job, which ultimately limits your potential in the types of jobs you get and the work you're asked to complete.

And getting a raise? Probably not. You'll get one only if everyone else does. Other than that, don't count on it.

## Relying on alcohol or drugs

Your lack of self-respect keeps you from finding success and happiness because you don't feel worthy of enjoying these rewards. In order to cope with this situation, you may turn to drinking alcohol and/or using drugs to escape your feelings of low self-worth. But of course, this only leads to further unhappiness.

Partaking of alcohol and drugs may at first increase your self-confidence and improve your social skills, at least temporarily, because you're less concerned about what other people think of you. But over time, the following things may very well happen:

1. You develop a tolerance for the substance.

2. You form a dependence.

3. You're addicted.

4. Your feelings of low self-worth become even worse because now you're addicted to something that you can't shake yourself from.

In your notebook, write down the following items, leaving space between each one to note how true it is for you and how you experience it:

- ✔ Feeling insignificant
- ✔ Being fearful
- ✔ Feeling shame
- ✔ Feeling guilty
- ✔ Being depressed
- ✔ Being shy around people
- ✔ Having body-image problems
- ✔ Not being able to form close relationships
- ✔ Losing close relationships
- ✔ Having low self-confidence
- ✔ Being stuck at work
- ✔ Relying on alcohol and/or drugs

Now that you've explored all the negative impacts of low self-esteem, don't you think it's time to change direction and reach for a better life? Change doesn't usually happen quickly or easily, but it can happen. It comes from your desire to turn course and be that person with high self-worth. You're not powerless!

# Chapter 3

# Where Does Low Self-Esteem Come From?

## In This Chapter

▶ Exploring how self-esteem is built up and torn down

▶ Becoming aware of your beliefs

▶ Benefiting from the adversity in your past

*U*ntil now, you may not have given much thought to how low self-esteem is created in the first place. Instead, you may have believed that it's something that appeared on its own in your life. If you're like many people, you feel that you were born having a low self-view. But that's not the case.

Much of your self-worth comes from your past — from the people you knew, how they talked to you and acted toward you, and the experiences you had. These influences then created your understanding of the world, others, and your relationships.

Your childhood and teenage years were influenced by the people who were around you, including your family, classmates, neighbors, teachers, and religious leaders. And if that weren't enough, society at large had a big impact on you. You got messages about what was acceptable and unacceptable through television, radio, movies, and magazines.

In this chapter, we examine where these messages in your past originated and how they led you to develop the attitudes and beliefs that caused your low self-esteem when you were young. You need to understand these concepts before you can make the changes that are necessary for you to develop the amazing self-esteem that will transform your life forever.

You may be thinking, "Goodness! This is overwhelming! How am I ever to overcome everything that happened in my past?" We assure you that it's possible. In fact, because you're reading this book, you're ready to take the plunge, face what happened in your past, accept it, and let it stay in your past. Then you'll be ready to face the future and create an improved you.

As you're reading this chapter, unhappy thoughts about your past may arise. If they do, we want you to relax and try to remain calm. If you feel you need to lay down the book for a short time, do so. You can come back to where you left off after a break. Remember, though, that these feelings are part of the healing process, and it's important to go through the process of understanding your past before you can move on to new possibilities.

Now, take a deep breath — in fact, take several deep breaths. It's time to dive in and take a look at some of those tough situations.

# Understanding How Self-Esteem is Nurtured and Damaged

Understanding your past means digging deep to identify what you experienced and the feelings you had. You may not be fully aware of the impact these experiences had on you.

Have you ever said something like, "I'm *never* going to have a good relationship!" or "I might as well not even try for that promotion. Everyone else *always* gets promoted, not me."

Statements like these are not based on reality, but on what you think reality is. You're really scaring yourself from trying harder to have a good relationship or putting your name in for that promotion. These thoughts hold you back and limit you from creating your life the way you want it to be.

If you see the world as hostile, that's what you'll experience. On the other hand, if you see the world as friendly, you'll experience it that way.

How you think about reality now is directly related to how you lived through your past. If you have healthy self-esteem, your experiences in your past were positive and enriching. If you have low self-esteem from past experiences, you'll interpret what happens to you as an adult as a repeat of your sense of low self-worth as a child. Zeroing in on the factors that caused your low self-esteem is crucial to dealing with them effectively.

In the following sections, we look at the roles your family, your peers, and society play in determining your self-esteem.

## Considering family impacts

When you were a child, you were open to everything that happened, and your mind was highly impressionable. You didn't have control over most of what you heard, saw, and experienced in your life.

Imagine that you are observing what happened in your past. What loving behavior did you experience? How much kind attention did you get? When were you praised for what you did well? Who did you get affection from?

When parents appreciate their children and guide them toward their strengths, their children naturally develop healthy self-esteem and confidence. What helped you in this direction?

On the other hand, certain experiences in the family can lead to low self-esteem. By comparing the two, you can see what experiences you've had that have led to your sense of self-esteem today.

Following are some family experiences that lead to healthy self-esteem:

- Receiving kisses and hugs
- Being spoken to in a polite manner
- Being listened to
- Being praised
- Being given high and achievable expectations
- Being told that effort over time produces results, so obstacles are accepted
- Being told that failure happens to everyone, so disappointments are accepted
- Being valued for who you are
- Receiving attention and care

The following family experiences, on the other hand, lead to low self-esteem:

- Being severely disciplined
- Being screamed at and ordered around
- Being disregarded
- Being belittled and told you do everything wrong
- Being given high but impossible expectations
- Being told that fortune or luck produces results, so helplessness is the outcome
- Being told that if you fail, you're no good
- Being compared unfavorably to siblings or other children
- Being neglected

Think back on your experiences now. You likely see that experiences typically, but not always, can be categorized as either positive or negative, and depending on which they were, you developed either a healthy or low sense of self-worth. Either way, this feeling can carry over into adulthood, leading to an opinion of yourself as being either a success or a failure.

Look at the previous bullets of how experiences in your family can create either healthy self-esteem or low self-esteem, and in your notebook, write down on one page all the things you remember that were done in your family that helped you develop healthy self-esteem. Then write down on one page all the things you remember that led to low self-esteem. Which list is longer? Write down which experiences had the greatest impact.

Think about your parents or the people who raised you. What were their favorite sayings? What things did they say over and over again in relation to everyday events? In your notebook, write down the language of your childhood to identify the beliefs that were communicated to you.

Now, don't fall into the trap of blaming your parents or other people from your past. If you find fault with others instead of taking responsibility for your own life, you'll wait for others to change. That's not going to happen! The change must come from within you, and we show you how to make those changes throughout this book.

## *Looking at the influence of your peers*

How you related to your peers often determines your self-image. All children compare themselves with the other children they're around. And especially during the teen years, peers can be more important than family to the opinions children form of themselves.

When I (coauthor Vivian) was in junior high, I felt that something was wrong with me. I would go home to my mother, crying that a popular girl was having a party and I wasn't invited. My mother told me I was smart and had a lovely singing voice, but I was so focused on not being invited to the party that I could hardly hear her. Even though I had friends, I thought the most important people in my class at school didn't like me and that I had little worth because of it.

Many experiences with our peers can affect our self-concept. Here are the most significant ones:

✔ Your physical appearance may have had a lot to do with your sense of self-worth. Were you considered pretty or handsome and complimented often for your looks? Were others easily attracted to you as a teenager?

Or was your face not the prettiest? Your size too small or too large? Did you have skin problems that made you feel ashamed? Were you too tall or too short? All of these may have led to a sense that you weren't good enough.

✔ Family financial and social positions also influence people's views of themselves. Children and teenagers commonly compare their house and clothes to those of other people in their classroom. How did yours compare?

✔ Did you have a lot of friends, or were you a loner? Did you have an active social life, or did you stay home most of the time as a child?

✔ Were you bullied? Did children taunt you in school or chase you down to hurt you? Now, children torment other children over social media, email, and texting. All of these can affect one's sense of self.

✔ How did you do in school? Did you get good grades and thrive? Were you congratulated by your parents or teachers, or did you win awards? Or did you lag behind other children? If so, you may have felt you were stupid and couldn't keep up.

In your notebook, write the answers to the questions regarding your relationships with your peers and at school. At the end, answer this question: Overall, did your experiences with peers and in school lead to a sense of healthy self-esteem or low self-esteem?

These may be difficult experiences to face. In the next section, we give you two exercises to help you put your past into perspective. Yes, you have most likely experienced some things that have hurt you and led to a sense of low self-worth, but you can overcome them, leaving the past in the past.

## Recognizing how society affected your self-esteem

In addition, you received messages about yourself from society at large. And these messages were more than happy to emphasize that something was lacking in you.

You may not realize how deeply these products and their messages registered in your mind. Even if you don't eat fast food, when you pass the golden arches, you know a McDonald's is located there. When you hear a jingle for a product, you picture that product in your mind. If you're like many people, you experience a strong desire for the food or drink you see in a television commercial.

Here's something interesting. A study done in 2010 in Australia found that preschool children between the ages of 3 and 5 knew exactly which logo corresponded with brands such as McDonald's and Disney. They could pair logos with products even when the products had nothing to do with children, such as ABC News and Toyota. Imagine that!

So how does this affect self-esteem? Well, think about the commercials you see and hear. Beautiful women and handsome men are unhappy until they use a product that then brings an attractive person to their side. They tell you that their products will make you better. They do this by making you first think that something is wrong with you. Only if you buy their products will you feel better and attract other people.

Take a moment to recall magazine ads you've seen. Did you know that airbrushing techniques are used on most of the models because this beauty is unachievable? These techniques change such things as the model's hair, waist, and hips. In fact, a study by the beauty brand Dove found that more than two-thirds of women suffer from low self-confidence about their bodies. Ads made them feel self-conscious about their appearance and inadequate. And who can blame them? The advertising industry makes people feel inadequate so they'll buy its products. That's specifically its purpose!

We go into this in more detail in Chapter 7 on body image, but for now, realize that the ads you see can very well have a negative effect on your sense of self-worth.

And you can't get away from these messages because they're all around you. You hear them on the radio in your car, and you see them on billboards, on television, in magazines, and on social media. It's easy to believe that you're not good enough and that something is missing in you that only the advertiser's product can fulfill.

In your notebook, draw a line down the middle of a page. On the left, write "What I experienced from the media" and on the right, write "How I reacted." Think about the types of messages you've received over the years and how you responded to them with the way you thought, talked, or acted. After you've made your list, write down on the bottom of the page how you intend to change the way you respond to any messages you know are damaging to your self-esteem.

| *What I experienced from the media* | *How I reacted* |
| --- | --- |
| | |
| | |

Now it's time to put your past into perspective and create a new point of view about what happened to you in your younger years. You can't change the past, but you can look back and draw strength from your victories and obstacles that you overcame. In your notebook, write about situations that you handled well in your childhood and what strengths you gained. Concerning things that led to low self-esteem, what did you learn about how to do things differently? How are you living your life now? Are you treating your children differently than the way you experienced life when you were a child? How are the past and the present similar?

## A magazine's influence

Every week, 13-year-old Kim would go to the grocery store with her mother to shop. When they got to the checkout counter, Kim always picked up *16 Magazine* for her mother to buy. Inside the magazine were pictures of celebrities and advice to teenagers. Kim excitedly looked at the magazine all the way home and rushed to her bedroom to read it cover to cover. She loved taking the quizzes about friends and school, and she learned new ways of dressing by looking at the girls in the magazine.

But one thing always made her sad. Kim didn't have a boyfriend, and no boys were interested in her at school. It made her unhappy to read the stories in the magazine of how girls should treat their boyfriends. She purposely didn't do the quizzes about relationships because they made her even more depressed.

Kim felt as though something was wrong with her, that she didn't fit in, that she wasn't pretty enough, and that no boys would ever like her. It didn't matter that she got good grades and was in two clubs at school. She should have a boyfriend — the magazine told her so every week — and she wasn't complete without one.

# Examining the Truth of Your Core Beliefs

The preceding section shows how your past experiences shaped your attitudes about yourself. Now it's time to understand how these attitudes turned into your core beliefs. As we have certain experiences and hear the same messages over and over again, they take shape in our minds, and these form our core beliefs.

Your core beliefs affect everything about your life: how you see yourself, how you see other people, how you interpret events that take place, and how you react to other people and experiences.

## Identifying common negative core beliefs

Negative core beliefs are connected with a sense of low self-worth. The following harmful core beliefs are held by many people:

- I'm not intelligent.
- I'm a disappointment.
- There's something wrong with me.
- I'm not good enough.

✔ I'm not as good as other people.

✔ I can't do anything right.

✔ I make so many mistakes.

✔ It's hard for me to understand things.

✔ I can't speak up for myself.

✔ I'm a victim.

✔ I don't blend in with anyone.

✔ I'm always left out of everything.

✔ No one likes me.

## Becoming aware of your core beliefs by listening to your inner voice

Your core beliefs can be helpful or harmful. You heard specific messages from your family, your peers, and society as you grew up. That inner voice now constantly repeats the original messages of childhood. It's important to recognize that the core beliefs and this inner voice are completely different for people with healthy self-esteem than those with low self-esteem.

People with healthy self-esteem have an inner voice that repeats messages that are positive, reassuring, and uplifting. They are resilient even when they make mistakes because they have learned positive ways to interpret reality, constructive ways to explain difficulty to themselves, and helpful ways of interpreting events that happen differently than they had hoped. Here are some examples:

✔ "I am a capable person and learning more new skills all the time."

✔ "It's time to find a new job. I'll talk to my friends and scan the online ads."

✔ "I'm sure I can handle the finances and be treasurer of the PTA."

People with low self-esteem have an inner voice that repeats messages that criticize, punish, and belittle them and their accomplishments. They are timid about life, reluctant to do new things, and avoid taking risks. Here are some examples:

✔ "If I go back to school, I'm sure I'll get D's and F's in my classes."

✔ "I should tell her no, but I'm afraid she won't like me if I do."

✔ "I don't even want to go to the party because I don't know how to talk to people."

# One core belief that was formed from one sentence

Jerry was very excited when he tried out for the band as a young teenager. After he auditioned with the trumpet, he overheard the music director tell someone else that this teen could never play an instrument and that he had no musical talent at all. He was crushed! He believed what the music director said, he didn't join the band, and he didn't touch a musical instrument for a very long time. After 20 years, Jerry decided to try the piano. At first he was fearful, but he told himself he enjoyed listening to the piano and he wanted to learn to play. He made a plan and interviewed and hired a teacher. He practiced often, and to his delight, he loved playing the piano and became good at it. But he was also dismayed that he had lost 20 years because he'd believed a denigrating comment from an adult he trusted.

*driving I can drive*

> It doesn't matter whether your beliefs are true or not. You accept what others say and create a picture of yourself based on what you hear. This picture is the foundation of your mental programming that directs you today.

**EXERCISE**

On one page in your notebook, write down all your positive core beliefs. On the next page in your notebook, list your negative core beliefs. Answer these questions: Which core beliefs are most prevalent in your mind? Which negative core beliefs would you like to change? On the next page, list the negative core beliefs you would like to change, and after each one, write the positive core belief you will replace it with. For example:

**Negative core belief:** "If I go back to school, I'm sure I'll get D's and F's in all my classes."

**Positive replacement:** "When I go back to school, I will study hard, talk to my teachers, and get tutoring to make sure I get good grades."

**Negative core belief:** "I should tell her no, but I'm afraid she won't like me if I do."

**Positive replacement:** "In the future, I'll tell her no if I truly don't want to do it. If she doesn't like me for telling her no, that's okay because I'm being true to myself."

**Negative core belief:** "I don't even want to go to the party because I don't know how to talk to people."

**Positive replacement:** "I'll go to the party and ask people about themselves. I know it will take courage, and I have that courage!"

# Which woman becomes president of the club?

This story is about two women who were both given the opportunity to be president of their club — first Marilyn, and then Ava. Notice their automatic thoughts and then see the decisions that followed these thoughts.

Marilyn is asked to be the president of a club she is a member of. She is very hesitant to agree to do so because she automatically feels she's not competent to do a good job in that position. Her automatic thoughts are that she's failed in the past, she can't lead people very well, and no one would follow her as president. So she quickly says no because she doesn't want to take the chance that everyone will see her as a failure once again.

In fact, Marilyn has led people well before both in her family and with her friends, but she doesn't remember those occasions. All she thinks about are the times her classmates made fun of her in high school when she was the leader of the Future Teachers of America Club. She felt humiliated and defeated, and she hated their criticism of her. When she spoke to her parents about it, they told her they weren't surprised since she had failed at other things as well.

Ava, on the other hand, accepts immediately when she is asked to be the president of the club. When she was the features editor of her high school newspaper, other students also criticized her. When the criticism began, she made an appointment with the faculty advisor. They discussed changes she could make in her writing. When she talked to her mother about the situation, she encouraged Ava to work hard to implement what she and the faculty advisor had discussed, noting that she had done well in other writing assignments in school. When her mother told her this, she put her arm around her daughter and told her that she had great faith that Ava would do well at the newspaper.

Ava knew she could lead the members of the club. She was certain that she had the skills to hold great meetings and lead the club in implementing projects. Her healthy self-esteem helped her make the decision to be the next president of the club.

## Tuning into your resulting automatic thoughts

In your everyday life, you have *automatic thoughts* that come into your mind when things happen or people behave in certain ways. Automatic thoughts are the very first thoughts that dart into your head when you encounter an experience or a problem. They are formed in reaction to your core beliefs.

Certain feelings occur along with the automatic thoughts. They may be feelings of anxiety or defeat, or they may be feelings of strength and determination. Actions that demonstrate your underlying core beliefs and feelings also accompany your automatic thoughts. You may be assertive because you know that you can make your wants and needs known, or you may be passive because you feel there's no use in rocking the boat.

# For females: Paying attention to familiar core beliefs

Girls are generally taught to be "less than," to act in certain ways that make them not as competent or as good as boys. These are the common core beliefs that many girls receive:

- Don't be too smart or boys won't like you.
- Get along with everyone and do what others want you to do. *me*
- Be nice and sweet to everyone all the time. *me*
- Don't explore doing something new — it could be dangerous!
- If you speak up, you could hurt other people's feelings, so keep your thoughts to yourself. *me*
- Be well mannered at all times. *me*
- Take care of your family before taking care of yourself. *me*
- Don't be confrontational or aggressive. Accept what happens and make the best of it.
- Marry a rich man. Personality and compatibility are secondary. *me*

*These were beliefs I was taught*

*I would never of chosen these*

*NO. WAY*

# For males: Looking at customary core beliefs

Boys, too, have been taught to be a certain way. They are taught to be the opposite of girls. They should be "more than" all the time. Consider these core beliefs that boys hear most often:

- Being a star in athletics will make you popular, so find your sport and be the best.
- You have to make a lot of money and be rich.
- You can be angry, but you can't show any soft emotions.
- You need to have expensive possessions to be better than other men.
- You must have broad shoulders to be attractive.
- If you're not good-looking, no girls will go out with you.
- Only tall boys are good enough.

✔ You better be tough or the guys will think you're a wimp. If you cry, they'll call you a sissy.

✔ Marry a beautiful woman. Personality and compatibility are secondary.

## Realizing how your core beliefs create your life

Even though your core beliefs were created in your childhood, now, as an adult, your core beliefs affect your life on a daily basis in numerous ways. Consider the following:

✔ **Making sense of things around you.** Your core beliefs determine what you pay attention to and how you interpret things in a way that reinforces these beliefs. So you tend to remember only those things that are consistent with your core beliefs and disregard those that are inconsistent.

✔ **Choosing which activities you take part in and which to avoid.** If you have low self-esteem, you'll avoid certain activities because you feel you'll do poorly or others will see you in an unfavorable light.

✔ **Following your aspirations and dreams.** People with healthy self-regard can aspire to do great things because they have the confidence that they can achieve them. Even if they make mistakes, they know they can learn from these mistakes, adjust what they do, and make their dreams come true. People with low self-regard have very small dreams or don't have any aspirations at all. They don't feel they can attain much, and if they try, they'll only show people how incompetent they really are.

In your notebook, write the numbers 1, 2, and 3 down one page, leaving space between each one. Under #1, write "Current core belief → Automatic thoughts → Resulting actions." Leave some room, and write "Changed core belief → New thoughts → Resulting actions." Write in one of your most difficult core beliefs, the automatic thoughts that come with it, and the actions that come from your belief and thoughts. Under that, write your new, changed core belief, the new thoughts that flow from it, and the actions that result from the new core belief and thoughts. Here's an example:

**Current core belief:** "I'm not good enough → I don't like my job, but I won't look for another one → Stay in the same job and be unhappy."

**Changed core belief:** "I'm skilled at my work → I don't like my job, but I know I can get another one if I take time to look → Look for another job and get one I'm more satisfied with."

Do this for three of your main negative core beliefs.

| #1 Current core belief | Automatic thoughts | Resulting actions |
|---|---|---|
| #1 Changed core belief | New thoughts | Resulting actions |
| #2 Current core belief | Automatic thoughts | Resulting actions |
| #2 Changed core belief | New thoughts | Resulting actions |
| #3 Current core belief | Automatic thoughts | Resulting actions |
| #3 Changed core belief | New thoughts | Resulting actions |

# Learning from Past Adversity

You can benefit from facing the negative experiences of your past. You can see them as positives.

You can choose to be depressed, immobilized by grief or sadness, or you can choose to take the most from your past and <u>develop the strength to create an attitude of being grateful for gaining the knowledge of who you have been</u>. Only then can you leap forward.

## Facing and overcoming difficulties

Many people who develop healthy self-esteem have had tough childhoods. They have discovered how to deal with their past experiences by facing them directly and making changes.

They identify their negative core beliefs and the causes and then create core beliefs that serve them in a more positive manner.

## Developing empathy for yourself and others

When you realize how your core beliefs have affected your life, you can have compassion for yourself. You grew up with your family, your peers, and in your society, and you had to adjust to all of them. You did the best you could under the circumstances, and you can feel sympathy for yourself as that little child and as the adult you are now.

In addition, opening your mind to your past experiences helps you have more consideration for others. They too may have had negative experiences when they grew up, and they also have core beliefs that are limiting them now.

# Trusting your ability to handle problems

Because you were able to cope with the challenges in your past, you can trust that you can transform your beliefs and thoughts to make a healthier life for yourself. You did it in the past, and you can do it now.

You are in the process of becoming more aware of your past in order to create a better future. Believe in yourself and have confidence that your life is improving.

## Releasing muscle tension and relaxing

The following visualization can help you relax fully and release any tension that has built up within your body. Take your time and enjoy!

Put your body in a comfortable position. Either sit or lie down. Adjust your arms and legs until you are comfortable. Find just the right position so you feel at ease. Uncross your hands and feet and close your eyes. Breathe in deeply and exhale. Breathe in deeply again and exhale.

Focus your attention on the tip of your nose where the air is entering into your body. Notice your breath as it goes into your nose and out of your nose. Notice your breath entering and leaving your nose several times.

Tensing your muscles and then relaxing them will help your body totally relax and help you be calm and peaceful. Begin with your feet. Tighten your left foot . . . and now relax your left foot. Tighten your right foot . . . and now relax your right foot. Enjoy the sensation of completely relaxing your feet. Tighten your left calf . . . and now relax your left calf. Tighten your right calf . . . and now relax your right calf. Tighten your left thigh . . . and now relax your left thigh. Tighten your right thigh . . . and now relax your right thigh. Feel your feet and legs being totally relaxed.

Tighten your abdomen . . . and now relax your abdomen. Tighten your chest . . . and now relax your chest. Deeply relax your entire torso.

Tighten your left hand . . . and now relax your left hand. Now tighten your right hand . . . and

now relax your right hand. Tighten your left forearm . . . and now relax your left forearm. Tighten your right forearm . . . and now relax your right forearm. Tighten your left shoulder . . . and now relax your left shoulder. Tighten your right shoulder . . . and now relax your right shoulder. Enjoy the feeling of relaxing your hands, arms, and shoulders.

Now tighten your neck . . . and now relax your neck. Tighten your entire face . . . and now relax your entire face. Fully relax your entire body.

Now breathe in deeply and slowly through your nose into your abdomen, your lower chest, and your upper chest. Totally relax, allowing all the tension to flow out of your body. Feel yourself getting more deeply relaxed with each breath.

Now think about a happy experience you had recently. See that experience taking place and think about how you enjoyed it. Focus your attention on your heart and experience the pleasure and contentment you had with that experience. Smile within yourself and deeply feel peace.

It is now time to come back. Begin to wake up; come back now easily and gently. As you wake up, notice that you have a greater sense of peace and calm. Come back gently now. Breathe in deeply and exhale. Breathe in deeply again and exhale. Become aware of your hands and feet. And when you are ready, you may open your eyes.

# Chapter 4

# Measuring Your Self-Esteem

*Y*our sense of self-esteem is a mind-set that you hold within yourself about who you truly are. It affects every part of your life. In order to get the most from your life, your self-esteem needs to be strong enough to enable you to do what you want and be the person you desire to be.

Before we begin to explore the various ways to develop your self-esteem, it's important for you to assess exactly where your sense of self-esteem is right now and to understand the mechanism of change. In this chapter, you do a number of exercises to examine your life up to this point and determine the degree of self-respect you have at this time. Then you find out about the four stages of change and get tips for going through these stages most successfully.

## Identifying the Indicators of Self-Esteem

Everyone's self-esteem has been shaken by one experience or another. Unfortunately, you can't just wake up one morning to find that your sense of self-worth has skyrocketed overnight. You have to work on yourself daily so that having healthy self-esteem becomes natural and comfortable. By understanding where your sense of self-regard is already healthy and where it needs some improvement, you'll be much better able to focus on the areas that need work.

In the following exercises, you concentrate on several indicators of self-esteem:

- ✔ **Success:** People with healthy self-esteem are eager to imagine a wonderful future and take the steps to achieve that future. Setting goals and reaching them come naturally. Because they have so much confidence, they find it easy to reach out, learn new skills, and stand strong to follow their aspirations.

- ✔ **Competence:** Along with success, competence is taken for granted. Those with strong self-esteem know they have talents and skills they can use in their work and for pleasure. They can ask for help and accept help from others. If they're unfamiliar with something, they speak up and let others know and/or research until they find the answer. Although they listen to suggestions from others, they maintain their power and decide on their own how to act. Even if they're criticized, they evaluate what is said and come to their own conclusions.

- ✔ **Self-love:** You can't go around with negative thoughts about yourself all the time and have a strong sense of self-worth. Those with a healthy sense of regard replace demeaning thoughts about themselves with constructive ones that build their self-confidence. In addition, they are adept at graciously accepting compliments. They know they can do things well, so they are happy to hear others acknowledge this, and they allow themselves to feel good about this recognition.

- ✔ **Appearance:** People with a healthy degree of self-esteem appreciate their appearance, even if they're not what would commonly be considered good-looking. They take pride in their appearance and do their best to be clean and appropriately dressed.

- ✔ **Relationships:** Those with strong self-esteem depend on themselves for their opinions rather than others. They don't worry about the reactions of others, and they can express their opinions with ease. How they feel about themselves is dependent on their own thoughts, not on what others say about them.

- ✔ **Assertiveness:** Being served food that is cooked incorrectly or the wrong food in a restaurant can be frustrating. Getting home and finding out that the clothes you just bought don't fit you as well as you thought can also be annoying. People who have healthy self-regard find it easy to deal with these situations. They're not shy; they speak up and get their needs attended to.

# Considering Your Life As It Is Now

It's important to measure your current degree of self-esteem because when you understand where you are and how you feel, you can make the right changes. Assessing your self-esteem helps you pinpoint the areas where your self-esteem is strong as well as determine where your self-esteem needs your attention.

We include two separate exercises in this section for you to assess your life and your level of self-esteem now. Before doing these exercises, sit down in a comfortable position where there are no distractions. These exercises don't take very much time, but you need to focus your attention on them.

In your notebook or on a blank sheet of paper, beginning at the top, write all the significant events of your life from birth until the present. Include such things as starting and ending school, moving to a different location, a sibling being born, turning points in your life, key people who influenced you, jobs you held, and relationships with those closest to you.

When you're finished, write your answers to these questions:

- ✔ What repeating patterns do you see?
- ✔ What positive outcomes can you see in any negative events?
- ✔ What would you want to do again?
- ✔ What would you prefer to have avoided?
- ✔ What were the most important turning points?
- ✔ What in your life increased your self-esteem?
- ✔ What in your life decreased your self-esteem?
- ✔ What were the main events that affected who you are now?

Now review your answers and write a short summary of the factors and experiences that have shaped your self-esteem. Write about how your self-esteem has evolved over the course of your life.

This exercise is a questionnaire about your level of self-esteem. When you select your responses, do so on the basis of how you usually are, not just how you are at this moment in time. To get the most accurate picture, be honest with yourself. Don't think long and hard about your answers. Just take a few minutes to go through each question one at a time.

You're probably used to taking tests that ask for the "right answer." That doesn't apply here. This isn't a test; rather, it's a private assessment to help you discover your level of self-esteem. There are no right or wrong answers.

1. When you look into the future, your dreams are

    a. in the process of coming true.

    b. something you rarely think about.

    c. never coming true, no matter what you do.

2. When an item of clothing from a store doesn't fit you, you generally

    **a.** take it back to the store and exchange it for one that does fit you.

    **b.** cut it up and make something else from it.

    **c.** put it in the back of your closet and never wear it.

3. Your feelings about yourself when you look in the mirror are

    **a.** satisfaction with the way you look.

    **b.** indifference because you look so average.

    **c.** disgust because you're so unattractive.

4. When there are difficult times in your life, your main belief is

    **a.** the bad times are only temporary and that they'll pass soon.

    **b.** difficulties are natural but they happen to you often.

    **c.** you have the worst luck in the world and things will never change.

5. When other people in your life tell you what to do, you

    **a.** consider their opinions but don't always follow them.

    **b.** argue with them and tell them you're the one who's right.

    **c.** do what they want you to do because you want to be nice and not ruffle any feathers.

6. When you receive a compliment, you're most likely to

    **a.** say, "Thank you. I appreciate it."

    **b.** look the other way because you feel you don't deserve it.

    **c.** say, "That's just a fluke. I'm really not that good."

7. When you observe your thoughts about yourself, they're mostly

    **a.** very confident and helpful. You are upbeat about yourself and have eliminated those thoughts that are critical.

    **b.** somewhat supportive, although you still have many self-defeating thoughts.

    **c.** almost entirely critical and belittling of yourself. These thoughts never seem to stop.

8. When you are criticized, you

    **a.** value what the other person says and determine whether he is accurate. If so, you make a change. If not, you continue doing things your way.

    **b.** get defensive and criticize the other person in return.

    **c.** take it personally, get upset, and feel you're worthless.

9. Your closest relationships are with people who

   **a.** nurture you and help increase your self-esteem.

   **b.** What relationships? You stay home and play video games or watch TV most of the time.

   **c.** take advantage of you.

10. When you think about your career,

    **a.** you're excited about it and feel you can be very successful.

    **b.** you're mainly going through the motions.

    **c.** you have a bad feeling in the pit of your stomach that nothing will work out and you may very well end up poor.

11. When it comes to expressing yourself and communicating your thoughts and feelings about issues, you

    **a.** do so easily.

    **b.** do so on occasion with your best friends.

    **c.** don't do it at all if they're different from what the others in the group think.

12. When you don't understand something, you

    **a.** speak up and ask someone who does know, or you do research to understand the topic more fully.

    **b.** ignore it and hope that someone else understands it better than you.

    **c.** find it difficult to admit that you don't understand it and actually feel you're not very smart because of it.

13. When you're in social situations, you

    **a.** can easily converse with anyone you choose.

    **b.** can talk only to people you already know.

    **c.** clam up and stay in the corner by yourself.

14. When you have a decision to make, you

    **a.** consider all the possibilities, ask for input from others, and make the best decision you can.

    **b.** choose one option quickly because you don't want to think about it very much.

    **c.** ask others for their advice and do what they think is best.

**15.** When you think about your life and achievements, you

**a.** feel very happy about them.

**b.** try to stop thinking about them because they're not as great as you'd like.

**c.** feel depressed because your life isn't going well at all and you're not achieving anything, only living day to day.

After you've noted the most accurate answer to each question, score your answers to find out your level of self-esteem. Give yourself 3 points for each first answer you chose (a), 2 points for each second answer (b), and 1 point for each third answer (c).

**If you scored between 15 and 29 points, your self-esteem is fairly low.** You most likely find that you think of yourself poorly and are having difficulty reaching your personal goals and being happy and satisfied with your life. This book gives you many skills so you can develop your self-esteem and make it stronger and more positive.

**If you scored between 30 and 37 points, you have some sense of self-worth.** However, you need to make some changes in order to improve your self-esteem and achieve the life you've dreamed of.

**If you scored between 38 and 45 points, you are well on your way to having healthy self-esteem.** You feel confident in yourself and feel you can accomplish whatever goals you have in life. In this book, you discover more techniques that can sharpen your sense of self-respect and help you become even more self-assured.

# Creating a Personal Profile

Most of us tend to be stronger and more confident in some areas of our lives than in others. You may have a greater sense of self-worth at your workplace accomplishing your job and relating to your coworkers but find that it's much more difficult speaking with strangers in social situations. Or you may find you can easily speak up and express differing opinions when you're with your friends, but it's impossible for you to tell a waiter that your soup is cold.

In this section, you write a summary of your strengths and weaknesses. Consider how each one works for you and against you. After you see how each aspect of who you are adds or takes away from you, you can work toward designing your new identity.

## Seeing your strengths

Your strengths are the areas of your life where you already have a strong sense of self-esteem. You truly like yourself and acknowledge what you're good at. These are the areas you can build on and in which you can increase your self-regard even further.

Review both the timeline of significant events in your life and the questionnaire. In your notebook, write down the most noteworthy events relating to your self-esteem and the areas in your life where you marked the first answer in the questionnaire. These are the specific spheres where you can pat yourself on the back, accept compliments for your accomplishments, and continue to achieve.

## Seeing your weaknesses

Your weaknesses involve the areas in which you need the most work. They're the areas you avoid; they cause you to think the most belittling thoughts about yourself.

Write down those events from the exercises in the previous section that were most devastating to your self-esteem. Also note those areas of your life in which you marked the third answer in the questionnaire. These are the areas you need to concentrate on most intensely. Look at the different chapters of this book and identify the ones that are most helpful to you in addressing these specific areas.

One more thing. We suggest that you take this questionnaire again in the future. Wait perhaps six months, then another six months. Notice the changes in your answers as well as the changes that have taken place in your life.

# Making a Commitment to Transform

Now is the best time to get started in transforming your life. Your self-esteem can change if you focus on what we show you, do the exercises in this book, and have the confidence that things can improve. You can change for the better!

Being passionate about becoming the person you desire to be includes changing your attitude, increasing positive thoughts about yourself, and eliminating those pesky negative ones. It means nurturing yourself and being kind to yourself. It means standing up for yourself and expressing your thoughts and feelings. How are people supposed to know what you want and need if you don't tell them? They can't read your mind, so expressing how you see things and what you want and need are the most effective ways to inform others about you.

Make a commitment to be focused on your growth, to do the things you need in order to make your self-worth stronger, and to take the next step in your journey to healthier self-esteem.

# Developing the Power to Make Changes

You've decided to take the bull by the horns and actually make those necessary changes to transform your life. You realize that you need to change. You can see that your life will improve dramatically if you make the needed changes.

So how does change happen most effectively? There are four stages of change that will help you make the transition to having higher self-esteem. They follow one after the other, although sometimes they overlap. The following four sections outline those stages.

## Recognizing that you need to change

In this first stage of change, you have not yet formed your new identity. Creating a new identity can be very frightening because although you accept and admit that you need to change, you're in the process of dissipating your old identity. Even though you know it's not working for you, having low self-regard is comfortable and making the needed changes is still uncomfortable.

Here are some tips for getting through this stage:

✔ Realize that it's time to take this important step in your life. Be willing to do whatever it takes to increase your self-esteem.

✔ Rather than being worried about what is going to take place in the future, focus on what is happening in the present moment.

✔ Give yourself permission to mourn the passing of your old self. Experience these feelings; then allow them to fade away. At the same time, recognize that it's time to create your new self.

## Imagining being different

In the second stage, you begin to concentrate on your new personality. You visualize and sense what it's like to start to feel and act as though you have healthier self-esteem. You can see yourself developing the characteristics of this new personality.

You may feel the urge to make changes with your body or home, such as buying new clothes or painting a room. This is perfectly natural, so go ahead and do it!

There are several ways you can use your imagination to visualize the person you desire to be:

- Daydream about how you'll feel when your self-esteem is completely developed and you can easily accomplish what you want and live your life fully.

- Use the guided visualizations in this book often to take you on inner journeys to help you acquire the characteristics you desire.

- Create a collage of pictures, words, and phrases that represent having healthy self-esteem. Look through magazines to find images and text that reflect the new you, cut them out, and paste them on poster board you can purchase from department stores or art supply stores. Put your collage up where you can see it often, perhaps in the hallway or on your dresser — anywhere you pass frequently and are likely to take notice of the concepts and images.

## Taking action

After visualizing what it takes to have a stronger sense of self-worth, you're ready to enter the next stage, which is taking those actions that lead you in that direction. Start with small steps first. Keep in mind that you may try and stumble, and things may not go smoothly at first. But realize that this is normal. You must be persistent and continue to take steps to increase your self-esteem.

Some things that can help you succeed in this stage include the following:

- Continue to visualize and daydream in order to keep in contact with who you are becoming. Spend time by yourself thinking about the benefits of having healthier self-esteem.

✔ Expect that you'll make mistakes and won't be perfect every time. But do eliminate those thoughts in your mind that you're a failure and weren't meant to improve your sense of self-worth and replace them with confidence that you're on the right path.

✔ Keep working on it. It takes time and effort to make these changes. If one technique doesn't work well for you, try another one. Keep being persistent and determined. Eventually, you'll find what works best for you.

## Maintaining your new identity

Over time and with practice, you'll find that having healthier self-esteem is easy. In fact, you'll discover that it feels natural. You'll have honed the techniques we present, and being self-assured will seem simple and comfortable.

The following strategies can help you sustain this stage:

✔ Take time to feel gratitude for making the needed changes.

✔ Congratulate yourself and take deep pleasure in having made this transition. Give yourself some special treat, such as going to a play or taking a much-needed vacation.

✔ There's a chance that you'll relapse into being that person you were before with low self-esteem. If this happens, think about what happened and why you did what you did, and then turn it around as quickly as you can. Even if you have to stop what you're doing mid-action or stop in mid-sentence when you're talking with someone, do so!

Even if it's a bit scary, it's time for a change! Becoming stronger and more self-confident is something that can be mastered. You're capable of living your life in a whole new way and re-creating yourself. You can push through and learn to think in a different manner by seeing greatness in yourself. You can learn to appreciate your talents, skills, and capabilities. You can find that person with healthier self-esteem within yourself, no matter who you are or where you start from.

# Part II

# Expressing a Positive Attitude

| Being Assertive: Creating Your Confrontational "I" Statements | |
|---|---|
| **Parts** | **When Used** |
| 1. Describe the specific behavior of the other person that you want to see changed. | Every time, at the beginning of the "I" statement. |
| 2. Describe why this person's behavior is harming or hurting you in some way (or how it may hurt or harm you in the future). | Use either this one or Part 3 every time; you may also use both. |
| 3. Describe your negative feelings. | Use either this one or Part 2 every time; you may also use both. |
| 4. Describe exactly what you want the person to do instead. | Every time, at the end of the "I" statement, after Part 2 and/or Part 3. |

Head to www.dummies.com/extras/selfesteem for a free article where you can select constructive and encouraging words to use in creating your affirmations.

# In this part . . .

- ✔ Changing your inner script can be a challenge. Get tips for creating and using affirmations and visualizations to generate new beliefs.

- ✔ People with strong self-esteem hold themselves in high regard and care for themselves. Find ways to nurture yourself and discover the four-part process of assertively speaking up to express your opinions as well as your needs and wants to others.

- ✔ Most people want to change something about their bodies. Become more aware of your body image and find out how to improve the way you relate to your body.

# Chapter 5

# Affirming and Visualizing Your Better Self

*T*he way you presently think is a compilation of mental habits you've been practicing for many years. Many of these were formed during your childhood and were acquired from other people. Some of them are not very accurate or helpful to you.

Affirmations and visualizations can help you build new mental habits and beliefs about yourself. They are effective in increasing your motivation to enhance your self-esteem and opinion about yourself. When you can do this, you will respond in different ways to everyday situations.

In this chapter, we discuss the various ways you can benefit from repeating positive affirmations that encourage your sense of self-respect and why they are effective. In addition to providing a list of common positive affirmations for improving your self-esteem, we show you the tricks of writing your own affirmations.

Visualization goes hand-in-hand with affirmations. When you add a detailed picture to the words in your affirmations, you double their power. This chapter explains how visualizations work and how to get the most out of them. Finally, we encourage you to tap into your passion to make the most of these techniques.

# Benefiting from Repeating Positive Affirmations

Affirmations help you shift your thoughts from negative to positive. They are based on the principle that you can be who you want to be only if you have the thought and idea that it's possible for you to be that. It's changing the thought, "I am not good enough" to "I am more than enough."

Affirmations also affect the amount of energy and vigor you feel during your day. If you start your day with positive messages and experience being lively and powerful from the minute you wake up, you'll have a vibrant feeling all day long. You'll also be more upbeat in all the other positive aspects of your life.

In addition, affirmations help you reach your goals. Instead of being hesitant and filled with doubt, your thoughts will be focused on your strengths, capabilities, and talents.

## Understanding why affirmations are effective

To a large extent, your accomplishments and happiness in life are a direct result of the thoughts you repeat in your mind. Positive affirmations are potent statements that build an internal dialogue reinforcing a new vision you have of yourself and your life. They replace the negative thoughts that have been in your mind about yourself and your past. As you believe and feel differently about yourself, you can shift your life in a new direction.

Wherever your thoughts are, your attention follows. If your mind is warning you about the times that you tried to do something but failed, it will dictate your future and limit what you can do now. But if your mind is focused on succeeding, you'll be more apt to try new things and have confidence that you can achieve them. So affirmations deliberately focus your mind on what you want to be and do. They move you from where you are to where you want to be.

What are the most effective ways to use affirmations? Here are a handful of helpful hints to maximize the benefits of using positive affirmations:

 ✔ **Use your affirmations frequently.** It's best to use them every day, saying your affirmations out loud for a few minutes at least twice a day. The truth is that the more you say and think your affirmations, the more readily your mind will accept them. Focusing on your affirmations a couple minutes at a time several times a day is better than saying them only once in a while. Think about the times that work best for you, such as

- In the morning when you wake up
- In the evening before you go to sleep
- When you wash your hands
- When you're driving
- When you're cleaning the house
- When you're relaxing in your bath
- When you're taking a walk or run
- When you're fixing a meal

✓ **Write out your affirmations on sticky notes and put them in places you see often, such as**

- On your bathroom mirror
- On the refrigerator
- On a cupboard in the kitchen
- On your car dashboard
- In your wallet
- On your computer or desk at home
- On your computer or desk at work
- On your cellphone (set your cellphone to beep a few times throughout the day; also, if you have a smartphone, you can download free apps that are completely dedicated to affirmations)

✓ **Actively reject the negative thoughts you have.** If these negative thoughts dominate your mind, your positive affirmations will have little effect. When you find yourself thinking a negative thought that decreases your self-esteem, consciously eliminate it and replace it with the positive affirmation that is most like its opposite.

✓ **Associate colors with your affirmations.** Your brain and memory link things together. Linking colors to your affirmations helps you remember them and bring them more to life. Use colored inks to write your affirmations or write them on colored paper with black ink. Then when you see that color during the day, you'll be reminded of the affirmation. For example, if you write the affirmation "I expect good things to happen in my life" on blue sticky notes or cards, when you see the color blue, you'll be reminded to think of this affirmation and look for good things taking place. Even if it's only a smile you get from a coworker or a hug from your child, you'll notice these happy occurrences and acknowledge that your life is full of them.

✔ **Relax when you say or think your affirmations.** You can use soft music to enhance your relaxation even further. Relaxation helps your mind open to the positive course your affirmations supply. If you're not doing an activity, find a quiet place, sit down, close your eyes, and listen to soothing music. You can also record your affirmations with soft, slow music behind them and listen to the recording. This technique is especially effective before you go to sleep at night.

✔ **Sing your affirmations to yourself.** You can use rhythm to make them easier to remember and repeat.

✔ **Add strong emotions while you're saying your affirmations.** Be excited about achieving them! Imagine what emotions you'll feel once you attain what your affirmation is about — happiness, satisfaction, joy, a sense of accomplishment, and so forth. Really feel them as though you're living them right now.

✔ **Understand that your affirmations may not ring true at first.** When you start using a new affirmation, the statement will most likely seem to be untrue. Realize, though, that once your thoughts are directed in this fashion, you'll start to look for situations in your life that match your thoughts, and you'll begin to discern the many opportunities that can help you reach what you desire. In other words, when you focus on who you want to be, you begin to notice openings to make this happen. As you think about the possibilities and look for them, you'll see new ones that you were completely closed to before. So be sure to take advantage of them. What you think about, you become.

✔ **Determine three action steps to make each affirmation come true.** These don't have to be large or overreaching steps. They may be small, such as reading a book about the topic, researching more about it, or practicing one small thing. For example, one of your positive affirmations may be, "I choose to do things that support my well-being." You may have three action steps such as 1) eating more fruit, 2) researching gyms in your town, and 3) writing down forgiving thoughts about someone who has done something you didn't like. And, of course, as you accomplish these, write three more.

If you'd like, you can ask a friend or relative to hold you accountable to doing these three steps. Keep that person updated on your progress. When you have to tell another person whether you're accomplishing these steps, you'll be much more likely to actually do them. This accountability acts as a powerful motivator to keep you focused on truly living the affirmation.

✔ **Realize that your affirmations are not set in stone.** You can continue to modify or change them as you like. You may find that an affirmation is no longer appropriate or that you've accomplished it so well that you no longer need it. Or you may find that changing the wording or even the intention serves you better. Feel free to revise them. Keep in mind that affirmations are here to serve you; you're not here to serve them.

## Reviewing common affirmations

There are many powerful affirmations to help you increase your sense of self-worth. Here are some of the most common ones:

- ✔ I feel good about myself.
- ✔ I'm happy being who I am.
- ✔ I am calm and relaxed.
- ✔ Every day my trust in myself increases.
- ✔ I expect good things to happen in my life.
- ✔ I now think positive thoughts about myself.
- ✔ I choose to be optimistic about my life.
- ✔ I am in charge of the thoughts in my mind.
- ✔ I am more confident and happy.
- ✔ I choose to do those things that support my well-being.
- ✔ I am at peace with myself.
- ✔ I now appreciate my talents and skills, which are _____.
- ✔ My life is meaningful.
- ✔ I am more than enough.
- ✔ I deserve to be loved.
- ✔ I am lovable.
- ✔ I am competent at many things.
- ✔ I find it easy to stand up for myself.
- ✔ I can express my thoughts and opinions to others.
- ✔ I am a winner.

Identify the preceding affirmations that you feel will be most helpful to you. In your notebook, write them down with three action steps for each one. Begin saying these affirmations out loud to yourself at least two times a day, five minutes each time. If you can, say them more often and for a longer period.

## Discovering the tricks of writing your own affirmations

You can write effective affirmations fairly easily when you know how. Find a quiet place where you can be alone and can focus on writing statements that will improve your self-esteem. Keep the following in mind:

✔ **Choose one negative thought you have about yourself and write down the positive opposite that counteracts that belief.** For example, you may often think, "I make so many mistakes." In this case, you would write an affirmation like, "I am capable and experienced."

✔ **Make your affirmations short so they're easier for you to remember.** Even statements as short as four or five words can be powerful.

✔ **Start your affirmations with "I" or "My."** Because you're making a statement about yourself, it's most effective if it starts with you. "I choose to be positive" is much better than "Positive thoughts are coming into my mind."

✔ **Write your affirmations in the present tense.** Write as though you're experiencing what you desire right now, not in the future. For example, "I easily see my own worth and value" is superior to "I will easily see my own worth and value." It's also better not to put a time frame on your affirmation such as a certain date or "within three months," because doing so limits when what you desire can happen.

✔ **Don't begin your affirmations with "I want" or "I need."** You don't want to affirm that you're wanting and needing. Rather, write your affirmations as an expression of being grateful for already having and being what you want.

✔ **Make sure all your affirmations are positive statements.** If you tell yourself you are discarding negative behavior and thoughts, your focus will be on those rather than on what you want to do and be. Don't include words like "don't," "won't," "am not," "can't," "not," "doesn't," or "am stopping." Instead of "I'm eliminating my miserable thoughts," create an affirmation such as, "I'm happy being who I am."

✔ **Add emotion to your affirmations by inserting, "I am [emotion] about . . ." or "I feel [emotion]."** For example, you could say, "I am excited about being able to express what I think."

✔ **Create affirmations that will work.** If you don't believe your statement, you'll take timid actions and be hesitant, sure that you won't be able to succeed. If you write an affirmation that is truly difficult for you to believe, write another one that starts with, "I am open to . . ." or "I am willing to believe I could . . ." You can also create an affirmation that is close enough to your current situation to be realistic and achievable, such as, "I am speaking up one or two times at future meetings I attend."

Now it's time to write a few of your own affirmations. Take a look at the list of common negative core beliefs in Chapter 3 and select a few that you tend to use often. Write their opposites in positive terms, using the preceding list. After you've finalized them to your satisfaction, write them on sticky notes or note cards and put them in various places you see frequently. Say them to yourself out loud at least twice every day. Only by repetition will they sink deeply into your mind. You can also record them to play during the day or when you go to sleep at night.

## The science behind affirmations

The first person to note how effective affirmations are was the French psychologist and pharmacist Emile Coue. In the early 1900s, he noticed that when he told his patients how effective a potion was as he gave it to them, the results were much better than if he said nothing.

In the 1970s, two neuroscientists from the University of California, Santa Cruz — John Grinder and Richard Bandler — studied the behavior of the most successful psychotherapists. Using the work of linguists Alfred Korzybski and Noam Chomsky, Grinder and Bandler discovered that language patterns can limit behaviors and, conversely, can enhance them.

# Visualizing Your Growth

While positive affirmations provide the words to create new beliefs, visualization provides the mental imagery to see yourself actually living these beliefs. Your mind then records the mental pictures as real and valid. You can see yourself speaking confidently and acting confidently. You can see yourself being a stronger person in your everyday life.

Your brain is divided into two parts: the left, logical side of the brain and the right, creative side. Most of our lives are spent using the left side, logically and rationally solving problems and performing tasks, using words and concepts. The right side sees the world in pictures and is associated with emotions. Visualization uses images and emotions to get training for actual performance.

In this section, you find out how visualizations work to help you create your desires. We also explain the fundamentals of visualization so you have the most successful experience possible. When you combine affirmations and visualizations with enthusiasm, changes happen more rapidly.

## Discovering how visualization works

Visualization is seeing bright, colorful, and vivid pictures of how you want to be. Your mind records these mental pictures as real and valid. Because your mind supports the images it has and wants the mental images on the inside and the physical images on the outside to be consistent, it will try to match your outer reality with your new mental reality.

VISUALIZE

# Developing the picture of your ideal life

Sit or lie down in a comfortable position. Uncross your hands and feet and close your eyes. Now breathe in deeply and exhale. Breathe in deeply again and exhale. Completely relax.

Imagine you are walking along a path in a meadow. There are flowers on all sides — red flowers, blue flowers, and purple flowers. You smell their wonderful fragrance. You can hear the birds singing in the trees. Along the path, you see stones of various colors.

Ahead of you is a white building. The path takes you to the building. You go up the steps and open the white door. You enter into a beautiful room with a table and chair in the middle. As you approach the table, you see a large marble box. You open the lid of the box, and you see a piece of paper that has details about your ideal life. You sit down on the comfortable chair and begin to read about your ideal life.

Where are you? What are you doing? What are you wearing? What are you saying? Who is with you? How do you feel as you see your ideal life? Fill in as many details as you can.

Develop a perfect picture as if it were already a fact. See yourself in that picture actually doing exactly what you want to do as if it were already happening. Concentrate on making this image complete. You do not know how or through what channels your desire is to come true. Just hold fast to the image itself, and the details will be filled in later.

Now imagine that it is ten years from today. You have given yourself permission to be all you can be. You have believed in yourself and trusted that you could live your ideal life. You have taken the appropriate steps to follow your desires. How do you feel about yourself and your life? See a vision about your successes during the last ten years.

You know when you are on the right path. Doors open, people appear, coincidences happen. When you are following the right path and your energy is flowing, your life works easily and well. Like a butterfly that breaks out of its cocoon into a new life, you too are ready to fly into your new life.

Stand up and put the paper back into the marble box and put the lid back on the box. Walk out of the building, down the steps, and onto the path in the meadow.

Throughout your day, recall the picture of your ideal life. Keep the image in your mind, thinking of it often.

Now it's time to come back into your body. You begin to come back into your room and into your body. You are coming back with a new level of understanding of your ideal life. You come back easily and gently. Breathe in deeply and exhale. Breathe in deeply again and exhale. Become aware of your hands and feet. And when you are ready, you may open your eyes.

As you say your affirmations and visualize actually being that person with healthier self-esteem, your mind records the image as happening in the present moment. It seems to your mind that you're living it right now. When your vision is clear and certain, your mind is then alert to what you need to do to accomplish that.

# Getting the most out of your visualizations

To gain the most benefit, combine each of your affirmations with a visualization. For example, say you decide to concentrate on the affirmation, "I am competent at my job." Before your visualization, identify a few areas where you know you're competent and a few areas where you're in the process of becoming more knowledgeable or need to become more competent.

In this visualization, you see yourself being proficient in those areas you've already mastered, feeling positive and pleased with yourself. Then you move into seeing yourself in those areas where you are somewhat adept and becoming more skilled. Finally, you visualize tasks that you need more expertise in and you see yourself doing those well and with ease. You may visualize yourself getting training from a coworker or reading materials to learn more about these tasks, taking note of the steps you need to take to become better informed.

Here are some tips for having a successful visualization experience:

- ✔ Find a quiet, comfortable place. Have no distractions, if possible, including the television, radio, and cellphone.

- ✔ Say your affirmation a few times as you relax your body and release any thoughts or tensions of the day.

- ✔ Visualize yourself in a scene where you're acting out what your affirmation says. Don't watch yourself in the scene. You're not the audience. Rather, imagine being in the scene, seeing through your eyes and acting through your body. Hold this mental picture as if it were occurring right at that moment. Be the star!

- ✔ You may sit or stand. Either way, you may move your body slightly or make gestures with your hands to be in the scene.

- ✔ Imagine the scene in great detail. Engage as many of your five senses as you can. Add bright and beautiful colors as well as sounds. Where are you? Are you outside or inside? Who are you with? What are you wearing and what are the other people wearing? What do you smell? What do you hear? What are you feeling? What would your life really be like if this happened? The more realistic images you create, the deeper the impression is made on your mind.

- ✔ Let the visualization unfold and play with it until you feel very good about everything you're experiencing, until the mental image feels complete.

✔ If part of your visualization is performing a task or activity, focus clearly on the image of the action you are about to make. Then be in the scene achieving the activity successfully and being proud of yourself for doing it so well.

✔ Think about the qualities that will assist you in being successful in your visualization and incorporate these into the mental picture you create. These could be communicating well, speaking up, listening to others, deflecting criticism with skill, and persuading others to do as you wish. Focus on what you want and what you are.

✔ If you have trouble believing you can do what you're visualizing, picture yourself doing it the best you've ever done it.

✔ After your visualization is complete, write down the details, the thoughts that came to you, and any sensations you had. When you read it later, this will help you reenter your visualization state. Then, at your next visualization, take it deeper with more detail.

✔ When you first start to visualize, it may feel strange to see yourself in a new way, and it's perfectly natural to feel this way. It may feel weird and maybe even a little odd. You may even feel uncomfortable acting in this new, self-confident way. Realize that if it doesn't feel unfamiliar, you're probably not doing the visualization correctly. What you need to do is go through these feelings and keep on visualizing. As you do so, over time, you will get more comfortable.

✔ It's crucial that you take action to make your visualization come true. Don't expect it to materialize only because you're imagining it. Look at the steps you wrote down for the first practice exercise in this chapter. These are the ones to concentrate on accomplishing.

The guided visualization in the nearby sidebar, "Developing the picture of your ideal life," takes you on a journey to help you imagine your ideal life.

# Finding Your Passion Within

Are you passionate to live a life of healthier self-esteem? Do you have an intense desire to be a stronger person who accomplishes what you want to accomplish and be the person you want to be? If so, that's the basis of the passion you need to go forward.

The deeper you know yourself and the more clarity you have about how you want to be, the more easily you can create what you aspire to in your life. Successful people fulfill what they believe are the most important parts of their ideal life. You can do this too!

VISUALIZE

# Feeling the energy of the rainbow colors

Sit or lie down in a comfortable position. Uncross your hands and feet and close your eyes. Now breathe in deeply and exhale. Breathe in deeply again and exhale. Completely relax.

Feel yourself getting lighter and lighter. Feel yourself being wrapped up in a white, fluffy cloud. It starts at your feet and comes up your body, supporting you under your arms. You are feeling lighter and lighter.

Gently rise up with the cloud and start floating up to the sky. You feel warm and comfortable and totally safe. Keep gently floating up until all you see are big fluffy clouds. As you go through the clouds, you see a rainbow start to form. The rainbow gets brighter. You gently approach the rainbow and enter into the light of the rainbow while you are still being supported by your cloud.

Feel and see the colors as you go into the red light of the rainbow. Let this red light fill you. Feel the energy of the color red. Let it warm you, feel it go through every molecule, every atom of your body. It is warm and healing. This warmth relaxes you and makes you feel more peaceful.

Gently float into the color orange. Feel the color orange go clear through your whole body. Become aware of its vibration. Let it push through any fears or anything that is bothering you. Let the orange color push it all out of you.

Now gently float into the color yellow. Let it soak into your whole body. Your body feels lightened by this color. Feel it light up your whole body inside. Feel the gentle vibration of this beautiful yellow color. Notice that the color yellow helps you see more clearly.

Gently float into the color green. Let it bathe through and around your entire body. Feel its healing vibration as it melts away any aches and pains. Let your body soak up the green light and send it wherever it is needed. Enjoy the feeling of this green light.

Now gently float into the blue light. Feel its calming and healing vibration. Let the blue light soak into every molecule and every atom, calming and soothing your whole body. Feel and embrace the feeling of this blue light. Feel its calmness. Let it push out any anxiety or troubles you may have. Feel calm and smooth.

Now gently float into the violet light. Let the violet light cleanse your whole body and your mind. Let it purify your very essence. Feel any negativity flow out of you. Feel yourself filled with this beautiful violet light. Concentrate on the feeling of the vibration of the violet color.

Feel all the colors of the rainbow come together and fill you with a brilliant white light. Feel yourself being cleansed by the white light and yet still relaxed and calm. You feel this white light as a calm, clear, crisp energy that smoothes the energy around your entire body. The white light purifies your body and your mind. Feel clean and pure.

Now feel yourself gently going back through the rainbow, down through the clouds, gently back into your body. Keep this feeling of calmness and smoothness, feeling totally cleansed and purified. Hold onto this feeling as you gently begin to wake up.

Come back now, easily and gently. Breathe in deeply and exhale. Breathe in deeply again and exhale. Become aware of your hands and feet. And when you are ready, you may open your eyes.

With enthusiasm and excitement, you can master the skills we show you in this book and live the life of your dreams. Think of the next few months as your golden opportunity to be that butterfly and enhance your sense of self-worth fully.

The guided visualization in the nearby sidebar "Feeling the energy of the rainbow colors" takes you up into the clouds and through the colors and qualities of the rainbow, assisting you in feeling energized.

# Chapter 6

# Nurturing Yourself to Create Happiness

*O*ne of the most important aspects of having healthy self-esteem is treating yourself like a prince or princess, caring for yourself so much that you want only the best for yourself and doing what needs to be done to attain this.

Throughout this book, we show you how to increase your confidence, improve your relationships, create more success at work, and reach your goals. But underlying all of these is the ability to live your life from a feeling of happiness. Without this ability, you'll just be going through the motions and not living your life to the fullest.

Many people believe that material possessions will make them happy, but studies have found that beyond having enough money to meet basic needs and live above the poverty line, money and material possessions do very little to elevate happiness. The happiest people are those who are physically healthy, experience positive emotions, have strong social relationships, and have a meaningful life. They realize their full potential, cope well with everyday stresses, work productively, and make contributions to their neighborhood, city, or community.

This chapter details the many ways you can cultivate personal happiness. We think of happiness as "thriving" — your body is the picture of health and vigor, your emotions are contented and cheerful, and your mind encourages you and helps you achieve your highest ambitions. Remember, when you're thriving, your self-esteem is unstoppable!

Review this chapter regarding what's healthy for your body, emotions, and mind as well as how to be assertive with other people in speech and body language. Detail in your notebook which one of these to tackle first in terms of making changes and what you'll do to implement those changes. After you've mastered that one, move on to the next, and the next, until you've mastered all of them. You'll be nurturing yourself, creating more happiness, and developing your self-esteem all at the same time.

# Taking Care of Your Body

How can you be happy and thriving if your body is sick? It's impossible. In order to be physically vital, it's essential to eat foods that keep you in good physical shape, exercise often, and get enough deep sleep.

To set yourself up for success and live a healthier life in your body, feelings, and mind, believe that you can do what it takes and use the resources available to you. Be persistent, and happiness will be around the corner.

## Eating healthy foods

Society seems to use weight as the only indicator of health or sickness. But there's much more to having a fit body. Many people wait until there's some sign that their body is damaged before they start to live a healthier lifestyle. They think they'll make changes only when their blood pressure is sky high or their joints and muscles are in pain. It's smarter to treat your body well to begin with so these difficulties don't even start.

There are numerous benefits to eating well:

- Higher energy and vitality
- A stronger immune system to fight infections
- An improved ability to focus and concentrate
- Easier sleep
- Avoidance of muscle and joint pain
- A healthier heart
- A stable mood
- Less chance of disease

The typical Western fare centers on red meat, whole-milk dairy products, sugar, salt, and saturated fat. A balanced diet includes foods from all the major food groups: fruits, vegetables, proteins, whole grains, and healthy fats.

One of the keys to eating a healthy diet is to consume a rainbow of fruits and vegetables every day. Fruits like berries, apples, bananas, and mangos provide fiber, vitamins, and antioxidants. Bright and dark greens like lettuce, kale, and mustard greens are full of vitamins and minerals. Sweet vegetables such as corn, squash, carrots, sweet potatoes, and beets add flavoring to your meals and help satisfy your sweet tooth.

You may think that taking a daily vitamin and mineral pill or powder will provide all the nutrition you need, but that's incorrect. In fact, the health benefits of fruits and vegetables derive from the many vitamins, minerals, and chemical compounds working together. If these are broken down, they aren't as effective. So eating fresh fruits and vegetables is the best way to get their healthy nutrition.

Protein is one of the main sources of energy. It gives you stamina and strength. The healthiest kinds are beans, nuts, seeds, tofu, fish, and chicken.

The best grains to eat are whole grains, including brown rice, quinoa, buckwheat, barley, millet, and whole wheat. We suggest that you try different ones until you find two or three that you like. If using whole-grain flour is new to you, try mixing some in with what you normally use and gradually increasing the amount until you're using 100 percent whole-grain flour.

Use only monounsaturated fats from plants, such as olive oil, canola oil, and peanut oil. Or eat avocados, nuts, and seeds for healthy fats.

Here are some simple tips for eating in a healthier manner:

- ✔ Eat only when you're hungry. If you think it's time to eat, drink a glass of water first to determine whether you're thirsty instead of hungry.

- ✔ Stop eating before you feel full. It takes about 20 minutes for your brain to tell your body that your stomach is full, so take your time and don't stuff yourself quickly.

- ✔ Eat smaller meals throughout the day to keep your energy high.

- ✔ Eat when you're most active and steer clear of eating at night. Try not to eat for 14 hours between dinner and breakfast.

- ✔ Change your eating habits slowly. For example, add a salad once a day or change from eating red meat to eating chicken or beans every other day.

✔ Instead of concentrating on the number of calories you eat, add a variety of foods with freshness and bright colors.

✔ Focus on finding foods that are tasty and making easy recipes that include some fresh ingredients.

✔ Drink a lot of water throughout the day.

## Getting enough exercise

Exercise can do so many things. It can improve your overall health, reduce stress, help you feel more energetic throughout the day, sleep better at night, and lift your mood.

Fortunately, you don't have to do hard labor for hours in the gym for all these wonderful benefits to occur. You can start with five- or ten-minute sessions and slowly increase the amount of time you exercise. The key is to commit to doing moderate exercise at least every other day.

Moderate exercise is defined by your breathing and the way your body feels. You breathe a little heavier than normal, but you're not out of breath. Your body feels warmer but not exhausted or very sweaty.

You can start by doing more movement in your everyday life. Doing housework, gardening, washing the car, mowing the lawn (as long as it's a push mower), and sweeping outside will all get your blood moving. During breaks at work, take a brisk walk around the block. When you're shopping, park away from the store and walk quickly up to the door. If you take public transportation, get off one stop early and walk to your destination.

Go walking or jogging with friends or take a water aerobics or dance class. Play tennis with a partner or join a soccer, basketball, or volleyball team.

You can get your children in on exercising too. Go bike riding as a family on the weekend. Play games outside that involve running or play exercise video games indoors.

Whatever you do, here are some pointers for starting an exercise program:

✔ Talk to your doctor first, especially if you have a health condition.

✔ Do some gentle stretching before and after your session.

✔ Do only exercises you enjoy. You're not going to stick with it if you dislike what you're doing.

✔ Go at your own pace. If you're in a class with others, make sure it's with people whose fitness level is similar to yours.

✔ Commit to exercising every other day until it becomes a habit. Then you can increase the number of days you exercise.

✔ Drink water before, during, and after your session.

✔ If you miss a few days, don't get discouraged. Rather, build up slowly to where you were before.

## Sleeping deeply

Sleeping has become a dilemma for many people. Over half of adults say they have problems sleeping, and prescriptions for sleeping pills number over 50 million. These medications also have unwanted side effects, such as dependence, memory loss, sleepwalking, and changes in brain chemistry.

Being able to have a restful, deep sleep is absolutely essential for the health of your immune and digestive systems, your bones and muscles, and your glands. In addition, a good night's sleep helps reduce stress, keeps your mind clear, and boosts your mood. Even if you're eating a great diet and exercising frequently, if you're not sleeping well, it's difficult to be healthy and happy.

There are many ways to naturally improve the quality of your sleep:

✔ Don't drink coffee after 2 p.m. because it stimulates your body.

✔ Have the same schedule throughout the week, getting up and going to bed at approximately the same time.

✔ Don't be too hot or too cold. Research shows that 65 degrees Fahrenheit is optimum for most people. Use a lighter or warmer blanket and pajamas, turn on a fan or heater, and set your thermostat.

✔ Don't eat a lot of food before bed or go to bed hungry.

✔ Put shades over your windows to make your room pitch black.

✔ Use a sleep mask over your eyes.

✔ The light emitted by devices such as televisions, computer screens, and cellphones has a short wavelength and suppresses melatonin, which is the major hormone that controls sleep and wake cycles. So don't use your computer, television, or cellphone for one hour before going to bed because the light that is emitted may keep you awake.

The following visualization can help you sleep. Read it over, lie down, and imagine you're in the warm water.

# Don't become a statistic

In this case, statistics don't lie. Fully two-thirds of Americans are overweight or obese because of the foods they eat and overeating. As many as one-third of children and teenagers are overweight. An estimated 300,000 people a year die from obesity. Although about 75 percent eat their dinners at home, almost half of those meals are fast food, delivery, or takeout from restaurants or grocery delis. About 40 percent of Americans either always or often watch television while they eat dinner.

Only 20 percent of Americans get enough exercise. As much as 25 percent of adults don't get any exercise at all. It's easy to see how exercise and weight are related. About 26 percent of underweight or normal-weight people exercise, 22 percent of overweight people do, and only 13.5 percent of obese individuals do. Eating poorly and lack of exercise are both related to a propensity toward having a heart attack. Every year, almost 800,000 Americans have their first heart attack, and 470,000 have a second, third, or fourth heart attack.

More than one-third of Americans have trouble sleeping every night, and 51 percent say they have problems sleeping at least a few nights a week. And over 9 million people take sleeping pills for insomnia.

VISUALIZE

# Relaxing into the warm water

This visualization is best done when you're ready to go to sleep. Lie down on your bed and close your eyes. Breathe in deeply and exhale. Breathe in deeply again and exhale. Completely relax.

Feel the gentle support of your bed. Feel your body relaxing into your bed. See and feel your bed gently turning into a small, private, warm pond of water. Feel yourself gently floating in this warm water, while the water supports and caresses you. Get totally comfortable. Smell the fragrance of lavender and violets. The water helps you feel at ease. Feel totally supported by the water. It is totally safe.

Feel the warmth of the water and think about the things that have gone on during your day. As you think about them, let them all flow out into the water. Let the water carry away all your troubles, worries, fears, and emotions. Let them float away from you and be dissolved into the water. Let it all go.

Remove any memories of fears or troubles that you hold within your body. Let them float out into the warm water. Let them all go and be dissolved back into the water.

Feel your muscles begin to relax, releasing any tension and negative emotions. Let them flow into the warm water. Release any aches or pains from your muscles. Let them all flow out.

Now concentrate on your spine. Feel any tension in your spine. Let that release into the warm water. Feel your spine relaxing and realigning itself into a perfect position. Release any pain, any troubles. Let it all float into the wonderful, warm water.

Feel all your bones and joints relax. Any pains, any inflammation, any negativity within your bones float into the water. Feel the warm water calming and healing your bones. Your joints are lubricated by this water, refreshing you. All your bones and joints are in perfect working order.

Now let the healing water cleanse your heart and lungs and all your other organs. Pull any negativity out. Feel any negativity you have, and let it all be dissolved into this water. Go through your kidneys, your liver, and all your other organs. They are now in perfect working order. Now let any memories of negativity float out into the water to be dissolved; let them all float away. You remember only perfect health.

Go into your mind and release anything that is troubling you. Allow these thoughts to be released into the water. Completely calm your mind. No more worries, no troubles. All you are left with are the lessons you have learned and the pleasant memories you wish to keep. Feel your whole body, mind, and soul being totally relaxed and totally at peace with the world. Feel all the tension melt away.

Let your mind relax and get sleepy, preparing for beautiful dreams, relaxing sleep, and a long, healing night's sleep. Feel the warmth from the water and its cleansing. Feel the water now as it gently and slowly disappears, leaving you back on your own bed, feeling totally relaxed and cleansed, ready for a wonderful night of deep sleep. Sweet dreams. Good night.

# Focusing on Positive Emotions

Emotions are a natural part of life. They are an indication of how you feel about a situation, so you can take the needed actions to deal with it most effectively.

Emotional wellness is the state where you normally radiate joy and feel positive about life, both your life and life in general. It's the degree to which you feel secure and have a relaxed body, an open heart, and a calm mind. The higher your level of emotional health, the more self-worth you have. Instead of reacting in an anxious and upset manner to events that happen in your life, you are composed and tranquil, ready to deal with situations in a beneficial way as they arise.

## Acting to increase uplifting emotions

In order to elevate your emotions, the first step is to become aware of which emotions you have. Become aware of what triggers you — what sets you off and gets you upset and what gets you very excited. One trigger is watching certain television programs and allowing the emotions of these programs to permeate your mind. For example, people who watch crime shows believe there is a lot more crime taking place than there actually is, so they're much more fearful. Another trigger may be a certain person who brings either loving emotions or emotions of strong dislike. A third trigger is a situation that reminds you of something that happened in your childhood or other experience in your life.

Become aware of what's going on in your body. Notice changes in your body temperature, heart rate, and breathing pattern. With both highly negative and positive emotions, these will change.

As you become more aware of your emotions, you'll see what you're automatically reacting to. When you can identify that, you can begin to work through the emotion and think about the best way to act, identifying the different options to deal with the situation. Contemplate how your response will impact both yourself and others, and consider what the consequences will be.

Keep in mind also that any particular event can evoke different emotions in different people. So it's not actually the event that creates the emotions, but rather, the perception of the event that triggers the emotion within you. Your emotions are also connected to your thoughts; in fact, your emotions are guided by your thoughts. By understanding this, you can start to have more control over your emotions.

The ideal is to consciously shift from emotions that drain you to emotions that invigorate you. These are some of the emotions that lead to real happiness:

- ✔ Delight and joy
- ✔ Acceptance and gratitude
- ✔ Enthusiasm and zeal
- ✔ Peacefulness and harmony
- ✔ Understanding, caring, and compassion

In your notebook, write down ten emotions: rage, anger, dejection, worry, frustration, contentment, hopefulness, enthusiasm, passion, and ecstasy. Then follow these steps:

1. **Imagine a short story that would evoke each emotion.**

   Make up ten different stories exemplifying the emotions from rage all the way through ecstasy.

2. **Experience these emotions in the same order without the stories.**

   Pay attention to what is happening within your body with each emotion. Without thinking of the stories and only feeling the physical sensations, bring each of the ten emotions to mind one at a time.

3. **Switch from one emotion to the next, experiencing first a negative emotion and then a positive one, until you've experienced each one.**

   Do this several times until you become proficient and deeply understand that you create your emotions.

This exercise should be done over a period of time. It can be emotionally draining, so don't try to do all the steps at once. It's important to do only one step at a time. Allow some time to pass between the different steps of this exercise, perhaps days, in order to reap the most benefit.

## Taking control of a bad mood

Life can be full of irritations — the Internet is down, you're stuck in traffic, you spill water on your keyboard, your flight is cancelled. When things just don't seem to be going your way and you can't shake a bad mood, there are several ways to brighten your outlook:

- Call someone you're close to and whom you trust to talk about the difficulty.
- Put on some soothing music or put on fast music and dance.
- If you're an introvert, read a book or concentrate on doing a project you started in the past or would like to start now.
- If you're an extrovert, call a friend to go out.
- Do some exercising like jumping jacks for a couple minutes.
- Think about a funny incident and smile.
- Take a couple deep breaths and think about something you really like, such as your family members, friends, or an activity you enjoy.
- Go out in nature and quiet yourself.
- Do something creative like drawing or crocheting.
- Go for a drive or take a walk.
- If the problem is complex, look at all parts of the problem and then try to see the entire picture, looking for a solution that will work for you and everyone concerned.

# Fostering a Healthy Mind

Changing your thoughts is a powerful way to increase your self-esteem. Your thoughts can make you feel like a helpless victim or a strong, confident success.

There's more than one way to look at life and focus your thoughts. A person with healthy self-esteem can take control of those untamed thoughts that seem to come from nowhere and aim them in a positive direction.

## Talking to yourself the way a loving parent or best friend would

One of the best ways to nurture yourself is to talk to yourself the way a loving parent or your best friend would talk to you. Even if you feel that your parents or the people who raised you weren't very loving or you don't have a best friend, imagine how they would talk to you. This is the way you should be talking to yourself.

Consider each of the following traits of people who love you and feel them deeply. Then write in your notebook how you can express them to yourself. A loving parent or best friend would

- ✔ Care about you very much
- ✔ Support you in expressing yourself
- ✔ Value and respect who you are
- ✔ Appreciate your talents and skills
- ✔ Be patient with you
- ✔ Remind you about some triumph that makes you feel good about yourself
- ✔ Give you inspiration to take on the world
- ✔ Love you unconditionally, no matter what you do
- ✔ Commend you for your achievements, even if they're not perfect
- ✔ Always be there for you

## Finding positive meaning to events

There's an old story about a farmer whose horse ran away. His friend said, "That's terrible luck!" and the farmer replied, "Perhaps." The next day, the horse returned, bringing with it a wild horse. The farmer's son tried to ride the wild horse, fell off, and broke his leg. Again, his friend said, "What an awful thing!" and the farmer again replied, "Perhaps." The next day, military officers came to the village to draft every young man into the army. Because he had a broken leg, the farmer's son didn't have to go. The farmer was very happy and saw how these events led to this outcome. Even though they seemed negative at the time, these events ended up being positive.

Reality is actually looking at what happens around you and assigning meaning to it. You interpret what happens, emphasizing some things and disregarding others. You then assign either negative, neutral, or positive meaning to events and situations.

 Interestingly, studies show that your brain highlights negative interpretations more than positive ones, so you tend to focus on the negative. And what you pay attention to increases. So when you focus much more on negatives, they strengthen in your mind, whereas when you focus on positives, they intensify in your mind.

Finding an alternative, more positive meaning to negative events that happen in your life helps you be more upbeat and optimistic. We know it's often difficult to see the silver lining in a challenging situation. Asking yourself these questions helps:

✔ How can this experience teach me something I need to learn?

✔ How will this situation strengthen my character?

✔ Can I interpret this as an indication to change course?

✔ How can this negative experience affect me in a beneficial way?

✔ What can I smile about concerning this event?

✔ Will this matter in a week? A month? A year?

✔ What areas of this situation do I have control over to influence even a small change?

 It's healthy to be an optimist. Optimists tend to explain positive events as having happened because of their own talents or actions and believe that positive things will continue to take place in the future and in many parts of their life. Optimists see negative events as coincidences that won't affect their future or other areas of their life.

If you think in this way, you won't focus on negative events, and you'll see positive events as sustaining your belief in yourself and the goodness of life as well as your confidence that good things are happening to you now and will continue to happen in the future.

# Making Assertive "I" Statements

Are you afraid to tell others your opinions or express your needs and wants? Do you want above everything else to be liked? Are you afraid you'll be seen by others as being aggressive?

This is ultimately not a healthy way to live. If you answered yes to these questions, you're generally not getting the respect you want. Your mind goes a mile a minute and you hold your emotions inside, never sharing what you're really feeling. Not only does this hurt your relationships, your physical body is harmed by clinging to those negative emotions.

In this section, we show you a wonderful method for asserting yourself and making yourself heard. We introduce you to the "I" statement technique that you can use to tell people the truth.

## Disclosing your opinions, wants, and needs

With self-disclosure, you share details about your life: what you like or don't like, what your attitudes and opinions are, what you believe, what you feel, and what interests you have. You open up about who you are: "I really enjoy water skiing. I went water skiing with some friends recently at Lake Fallon, and we had a great time." "I did not like that movie at all." "I certainly hope that my candidate wins his election in the fall."

You can also tell people about your wants and needs. "It's important to me that my car gets fixed today." "I would prefer to go out for Italian food tonight." "You know, I need to rest this evening. I've had a long day."

## Saying no to others' requests

Does this describe you? Others are used to you saying yes to everything they want you to do. You feel you don't want to do it and you ache inside every time you say yes. You want to shout, "No, no, no!" But you say yes with a smile on your face anyway, feeling angry at yourself and them too. But, of course, you never let them know your true feelings.

As a person with healthy self-esteem, you need to understand that your own wants and needs are just as important as anyone else's. Of course, there are situations, like having a sick relative, in which this principle may need to be adjusted. But generally, you should respect your own wants and needs first.

So if someone makes a request of you, consider the request, and if you truly want to do it, then respond, "Yes, I'd be happy to." But don't say yes just to please the other person or to keep her from getting angry at you.

If you don't want to do as others ask, tell them so. You can do this in several ways. You can give them a detailed reason: "I'm sorry, but I won't be able to go shopping with you on Wednesday because I'm going to my son's play then." If you feel the person will argue with you about your plans and try to talk you out of them, you can be vague. "I'm sorry, but I have other plans that day." Even if you don't have plans and you just don't want to go, you have plans to be by yourself or with your family. If the other person demands to know each and every thing you'll be doing to determine whether or not you'll have time to go shopping, don't provide any details at all. Say, "I'm busy that day" the first time, then "I have plans, so I won't be able to make it" the second time, and then "I have other commitments that day" the third time.

## Requesting cooperation or support

People can't read your mind, so you must tell them if you want cooperation from them or support in some manner.

The best way to ask for cooperation or support is to share what your need is and the reasons for the need. That way, others will have a fuller understanding and will be more likely to meet your need. "I need to take a walk to calm down after work. Would you please make dinner?" "I would like an extension on this project because I don't have all the information I need to report the correct figures."

## Confronting a person when there's a problem

For most people, confronting another person is the scariest thing to do. However, it's important to confront people when their behavior interferes with your needs. Even though telling others that their behavior is causing you a problem is very difficult, doing so is necessary in order to maintain open, honest communication.

Many people say nothing and keep their anger inside, just under the surface; then they explode and become very aggressive at the least little thing. The other person is completely confused about why this is occurring. It's much more effective to speak honestly and openly about the situation and see whether the two of you can come to a win-win agreement on it.

Confrontational "I" statements are created in three or four steps, summarized in Table 6-1. Steps 1 and 4 are always included. Steps 2 and 3 may both be included, or only one of the two may be included.

| Table 6-1 | Being Assertive: Creating Your Confrontational "I" Statements |
|---|---|
| **Steps** | **When Used** |
| 1. Describe the other person's specific behavior you want to see changed. | Every time, at the beginning of the "I" statement |
| 2. Describe why the behavior is harming or hurting you in some way (or may harm or hurt you). | Use either this step or Step 3 every time; you can also use both |
| 3. Describe your negative feelings. | Use either this step or Step 2 every time; you can also use both |
| 4. Describe exactly what you want the person to do instead. | Every time, at the end of the "I" statement, after you've described why |

1. **Describe the specific behavior.**

   Begin a confrontational "I" statement with the word "when." Tell the person the specific behavior that's causing the problem: "When you drive 85 miles an hour on the freeway when we go to your cousin's house . . . ,"

   Be careful to state only facts. Don't put the other person down or moralize. For example, don't say, "When you act in a thoughtless way . . ." If you blame the other person, he's much more likely to take offense and not cooperate with the change you request.

2. **Describe the tangible effect.**

   Explain why the behavior is hurting you in some way by explaining what effect it's having on your life: "When you drive 85 miles an hour on the freeway when we go to your cousin's house, I don't want to ride with you . . ."

3. **Describe your feelings.**

   Describe whatever negative feelings you experience because of the behavior and the tangible effect: "When you drive 85 miles an hour on the freeway when we go to your cousin's house, I don't want to ride with you because I'm afraid we'll have a crash . . ."

4. **State exactly what you would like the other person to do instead.**

   It's important to state exactly what you want his behavior to be instead. Don't use "we," as in, "I think we should sit down and talk about it." Specifically describe only what you want him to do. This request should always come at the end after you've described the behavior that's causing the problem and why it's a problem for you. Only then will the other person be open to hearing your request. Don't put the request at the beginning. It always belongs at the end.

Here's how this entire "I" statement sounds: "When you drive 85 miles an hour on the freeway when we go to your cousin's house, I don't want to ride with you because I'm afraid we'll have a crash. Please drive at 70 miles an hour. I'd feel much safer."

Be careful not to include what you believe the other person is thinking or feeling, such as, "I feel you don't care about our relationship" or "I know you're trying to hurt me." You don't know the other person's thoughts and feelings as well as he does. If you say this, the other person may seize upon such a statement and argue that you're wrong, and he would be correct because he knows his own thoughts and feelings better than anyone else in the world. Unfortunately, this is an excellent way for the other person to start an argument (that you would lose) so the two of you won't be able to talk about the issue you brought up in the first place. State *only* your own thoughts and feelings about the situation. Also, don't use "we," such as, "I'd like us to see a financial counselor" or "I would appreciate it if we spent more time together on the weekend." Doing this weakens your request. It's better to state what you want the other person to do instead.

You may want to include more than one suggestion for resolving the situation and ask the other person which one he'd prefer. You can also point out any benefits to him with your suggestions. For example, in the preceding scenario, you can suggest that you drive, with the benefit that he can rest while you drive.

There may be some give and take so that the two of you can make this a win-win situation. Stay open to suggestions on what could work better for the other person and still meet your needs.

## Dealing with aggressive people

When you make confrontational "I" statements, many times the response is positive and the person is more than willing to make the change you request. But sometimes aggressive people respond with even more aggressiveness, wanting you to back down.

One effective way to deal with this is to state what you want more than once, either in the moment or over time. Use slightly different language but say the same thing. Aggressive people often need to hear the request a few times before they'll respect you enough to do as you ask. "Tom, this is important to me. When you don't put your dirty clothes in the hamper and they're on the floor, I'm really afraid that I'll trip. I could hit my head or break my arm. I don't want to do that. Please put your dirty clothes in the hamper as soon as you come home. I'll feel much better if you do that."

You may feel like shouting, but don't get loud, irritated, or angry. At all times, keep very calm and speak in a matter-of-fact and kind voice. Stick to the point while at the same time respecting the rights of the other person.

## Using body language to complement your assertive speech

Your body posture is important in order for other people to take you seriously. Stand (or sit) as tall as you are, square your shoulders, and straighten your back. Face the person and stand or sit at an appropriately distance. Look him in the eyes. You don't have to look straight-on continuously. You can take your eyes off him some of the time you're talking, but look at him as much as possible. Maintain a calm and firm expression on your face.

While you're making your "I" statement, speak in a conversational tone. Don't talk in a harsh or shrill voice. Speak in a smooth, well-modulated voice at an even volume that is slightly loud. In order to make your words sound more serious, take your time and talk a little more slowly than the average rate of speech. Don't use a monotone in your voice; instead, make your voice go up and down with different words. If you can, speak in a lower pitch. If you have a high-pitched voice, practice speaking in your lowest pitch.

Pronounce your words clearly so the other person clearly understands what you're saying. Speak naturally. Emphasize words that describe the harm the behavior is causing you and the details in your request.

To show your self-confidence, feel free to take up some space. Uncross your arms and legs. Spread out your arms, putting them over the arms of a chair if you're sitting. If you're sitting on a sofa, you can stretch your arm along the back of the sofa. Lean your arms across a desk. All of these actions help you seem more assertive.

# Chapter 7

# Creating a Healthy Body Image

• • • • • • • • • • • • • • • • • • • • • • • • • • • • • • • • • • • • • • • • • • • • • • • • •

## In This Chapter

▶ Examining what body image means

▶ Seeing how body image is formed at a young age

▶ Considering how businesses make you feel bad about your body

▶ Relating to your body in a healthy manner

• • • • • • • • • • • • • • • • • • • • • • • • • • • • • • • • • • • • • • • • • • • • • • • • •

*O*kay, ladies, tell the truth. You've looked in the mirror and thought you looked too fat, or you've looked in the mirror and thought you needed to put on weight. You've emphasized that flaw on your face — a mole is in the wrong place; your nose is too large; your lips are too small. Or you don't want to look in the mirror at all because it's too tough on your emotions. You put yourself down, so you certainly don't want to see yourself any more than you have to.

And men, you do the same thing. Your shoulders aren't broad enough; you're too short; your stomach is starting to be a pouch. When you look at your face, you think it's not manly enough, your jaw isn't strong enough, or you have sagging jowls. Even though you hate to admit it, you're concerned about your appearance just like women are.

Body image is something almost everyone has to contend with. And as we get older, our bodies change and become even more of a challenge.

This chapter helps you understand what body image means. We look at how businesses make you feel as though your body isn't good enough in order to sell you their products. Then we discuss ways to reconnect with your body and personality so you enjoy and take pride in both.

## Pinning Down What Body Image Means

You may think that your body image is related to what your body actually looks like. But it's not. It has more to do with your personal relationship with your body — how you think about it, how you feel about your body, and what your beliefs are about what is good-looking.

In this section, we look at the various ways people relate to their bodies, first in an unhealthy way and then in a healthy way. It is possible to feel good about yourself and to love your body.

## The way you see yourself

Your body image is directly related to how you see your body in your mind's eye. It's not what is physically true; it's what takes place in your mind that's important. Consider this: Almost all women overestimate their body size, and about half of *underweight* women consider themselves to be overweight.

Having a perfect body is a myth, but many people see an image in their mind and that's what they strive for. They're so engrossed in becoming this image that they spend excessive amounts of time trying to change their appearance. Some people even put their lives on hold. They think, "I'll do such-and-such when I finally look the way I want to." They miss out on life for years because they're waiting to have that ideal body.

If, instead, you see your body as the outer form that holds within it the marvelous personality that is you, your mind's eye will hold a different picture. You can become a stronger, more confident version of yourself, and your body will reflect this.

## The way you feel about your body

If you're dissatisfied with your body, your poor body image will lead to a feeling of general unhappiness in your life. If you try over and over again to change your body, disappointment and frustration are sure to follow.

For a healthy body image, you don't have to enjoy every little part of your body. It's important though to like your body overall. In addition to how your body looks, you can appreciate how your body functions. If you can walk, run, move, and accomplish tasks, you can appreciate your functional body that serves you in many amazing ways.

## The thoughts you have about your body

People typically engage in negative self-talk about their body. Have you ever thought something like the following?

- ✓ I'm so fat!
- ✓ I have to start losing weight now.
- ✓ I need to work out harder.
- ✓ My mouth looks terrible.

✔ I need to fix (whatever you don't like).

✔ I'm so skinny, it seems like I'll blow away.

✔ I'm such a shorty, no one will ever go out with me.

✔ My eyes are too close (or too far apart).

✔ My nose is too long (or too short).

✔ I can't stand my stomach because it sticks out so much.

✔ My hips are so big you can hardly see around them.

✔ I am so ugly! Yuck!

These are the thoughts of a person with a very poor body image. They can lead directly to low self-esteem if you think that your body is the only thing that's significant. As the frequency of these types of statements increases, the less you value yourself and the more likely you are to take action to solve this "problem."

If you have a poor body image, every negative comment someone else makes becomes a blow to your sense of self-worth. And every compliment is interpreted as being insincere. You feel you deserve to be rejected by other people, and that your worth is totally tied to how your body looks. Only if you become the "ideal" will others start to accept and respect you. So it makes sense to fixate on your perceived flaws, which inevitably leads to a poor body image and decreased self-esteem.

On the other hand, you can use positive self-talk to tell yourself how very awesome you are. Even if you don't believe these words literally now, using statements such as these can turn your thinking process around. Try these out:

✔ I'm a strong, confident person and my body shows it!

✔ My body is beautiful (or handsome) in its own unique way.

✔ I love the way I look.

✔ I think my body works in a marvelous way.

✔ I am intelligent, and I intelligently take care of my body.

✔ My body can do so many things, and I'm grateful for everything it can do.

✔ Attractiveness comes in all shapes and sizes, and my body is attractive.

✔ I know that nobody's physical body is perfect, and I still love my body, even with its imperfections.

✔ I am worthy of love.

✔ I enjoy feeling good about myself.

✔ I choose to be healthy, both inside and out.

✔ I deserve to be treated with love and respect. I treat myself like this, and I treat others like this.

## The things you do as a result of your body image

Having a poor body image compels you to go to drastic lengths to make changes. You may try radical diets, starve yourself, exercise several hours a day at the gym, or have cosmetic surgery. But ultimately, these don't seem to work very well, especially if they're not accompanied by changing your thoughts, feelings, and beliefs at the same time. And dieting away those extra pounds and having a facelift aren't a guarantee that your self-esteem will increase. Although others may see you differently, you may not see yourself as being more valuable.

Plastic surgery has been used by many people for the wrong reasons. It can help you feel better about your body, but only if your motivations are healthy. If you have the surgery out of a desire for self-improvement and enjoyment of your body, that's one thing. But if it's out of fear, a desire to be approved by others, or pressure from someone in your life, that's not healthy. Understanding that you are worthwhile whether you have the surgery or not is crucial. In fact, you're valuable just the way you are.

Other behaviors that commonly accompany a poor body image are inadequate grooming and hiding parts of the body. Interestingly, not looking in the mirror or at store windows to avoid looking at the body and doing the opposite — frequently checking one's appearance in the mirror and over-grooming — are all activities that belie an attitude of poor body image.

With a healthy body image, you accept yourself as you are and are comfortable and happy with the way you look. You may want to improve, but you do so with an attitude of liking yourself first. Your lifestyle revolves around nourishing eating habits, healthy exercise habits, and positive self-talk that helps you set focused and beneficial goals.

# Analyzing How Body Image Is Formed in Your Youth

Think back to your younger years. How closely do the following statements describe your family?

- ✔ No one exercised.
- ✔ The car was used even for short trips.
- ✔ Heavy, fattening food was the usual fare.

✔ No one drank water.

✔ Dessert was served at the end of every dinner.

✔ You were told that something was wrong with your body.

✔ Most activities revolved around food.

✔ Celebrations were based on having sweet foods.

✔ Your family went to restaurants with unlimited buffets.

✔ Your parents complained about not being the right size.

✔ Your siblings and/or parents made fun of your body.

✔ Everyone watched television or was on the computer during most of his free time.

Generally, what you experienced with your family when you were growing up had a direct effect on the thoughts and feelings you had about your body. If your family members had poor health habits, and were obsessed with their bodies and felt disgust toward them, you probably disliked your body too. And if you had positive role models and the people in your family were happy about their bodies, you most likely grew up liking yours as well.

Especially for a girl, body image is influenced heavily by watching her mother. Seeing her mother in front of the mirror or going through the hardship of dieting and making critical comments about herself influences young girls to do the same things. One study found that girls as young as 7 years old mimic their mother when she says how fat she is, how old she is, or how bad she looks.

Keep in mind, however, that the messages you received from your childhood family do not necessarily transfer into later life. Some people who grew up in homes where they got strong negative messages about body image do not carry these same messages into adulthood. They're happy with their body no matter what it looks like. Conversely, some people whose family didn't address body image at all are obsessed with what their body looks like as they grow older.

Here's an exercise to help you identify the body messages you received in your youth. In your notebook, answer the following questions. After you finish answering these questions, write a summary of what messages you got about your body and what it should look like when you were younger and also how these messages affect you today.

✔ When you were growing up, how did you feel about your body?

✔ How did this change or stay the same when you entered school?

✔ How did you feel about your body when you were a teenager?

✔ What did your parents say about their own bodies?

✔ What did your parents say about your body?

✔ When you were a teenager, did you subscribe to magazines? If so, what images did you see in them? What stories were about body image, dieting, cosmetics, and fashion?

✔ Did you diet when you were younger? If so, what was the outcome?

✔ Did you go swimming in the summers? How did you feel about getting in a bathing suit?

# Examining How Businesses Convince You to Buy Their Products

Almost all commercial media aimed at women get their advertising revenue from the food, beauty, diet, and fashion industries. Just the diet industry itself is a $33 *billion* a year commercial enterprise. And, of course, these industries needs customers on a continual basis in order to keep being successful. It's in their best interest to create a fantasy of what being attractive is. Unfortunately, only 5 percent of the population has the fantasy body they show us.

As we discuss in Chapter 3, the media survives because it makes us believe that we have problems that don't exist in reality. People in the media business are responsible for urging consumers to adopt limited notions of beauty. They airbrush photographs in magazines and online so that women look smaller and prettier and men look larger and more handsome. They hire professionals to do the models' hair, makeup, and clothing to make people fit an ideal image in television commercials. Only when you feel bad about your body image will you buy their products in hopes of changing your body to look like the perfect body they tell you is a must. And if you look closely, you'll see that the media praises some people and insults others.

On top of that, the media links such things as thinness and beauty in women and strength and good looks in men to having a social, happy, and desirable lifestyle. They tell you that you must invest great importance in your body to be valuable — and of course, purchase their products to fix or conceal your numerous imperfections so you can have this enviable lifestyle.

In addition, the media business makes women feel bad about aging. Have you ever noticed when you watch television commercials that older men are always with younger women? Almost none of the women in commercials have gray hair if they're married, while many men with gray hair are with women with brown or blond hair, indicating the women are younger than they are. And never do you see it the other way around in commercials — a younger man with brown or blond hair married to an older woman with gray hair.

Being older, especially for women, is considered unacceptable in media. Comics make jokes about older women, and gray-haired women are rarely seen in roles that are complimentary or strong. This is another way the media industry makes people — especially women — feel there's something wrong with them as their bodies naturally age.

For a week, jot down every media message you see about bodies in your notebook, whether it's on television, the Internet, newspapers, magazines, or elsewhere. Mark whether you believe the message is true or not.

# Evaluating Whether You Judge Yourself Accurately

So now you know how poor body images are formed and the damage they do. Negative beliefs about your body can hold you back from what you want out of life. Do you believe that if you're too overweight, no one will be attracted to you, so there's no reason to go out or be open to a new relationship? Or that having an unattractive body will keep you from getting that promotion, so you might as well not even put in for it? Or that having some physical flaw will prevent you from starting a new business, marketing yourself as a consultant, or selling your new product, so you'd be wiser to drop any dreams of doing those things?

How accurate are these beliefs? One way to realize that this thinking isn't based on reality is to think of a person who has what you want but also has a body that is not the ideal. For example, say you believe that being overweight eliminates the possibility of ever finding true love. Think about a friend who is overweight and has been married for over 20 years or a successful person at work who's overweight and just recently started a new relationship.

Imagine that what you don't like about your body isn't keeping you from what you want. Visualize getting exactly what you want out of life with the body you have at this time. You may choose to make changes to make you healthier, but you don't need to make changes to be happier. It's your personality, your inner magnificence, that will attract the life that you want.

# Reconnecting with Your Body

You don't need to continue to dislike your body. You can pivot and turn another direction. In this section, we introduce you to several techniques you can use to relate more deeply and more constructively with your body. Feeling a stronger attachment to the body you have now can lead you to take the steps to improve it, if you desire. Or if you prefer to appreciate your body as it is, that will also lead to having healthier self-esteem.

## Stopping the comparisons with others

When you believe that you come up short as you look at other people's body types, certain parts of their bodies, or their clothes, or even look to see whether they seem more confident or happier than you, you've entered into a form of self-loathing. You belittle yourself because you don't measure up. Of course, this comparing doesn't happen just with people you see in person. It may occur when you look at models, movie stars, sports stars, and body-builders too.

It's better to recognize that every person is unique, and the differences we have make us distinctive. And believe it or not, the flaws you see in yourself that you think are so important are generally not even noticeable to other people.

Most people look average, so wishing you had someone else's body, someone else's face, or someone else's physique is a waste of time. It's healthier to feel comfortable in your own skin, to observe and appreciate others without comparing yourself with them and putting yourself down.

I (coauthor Vivian) inherited thick, wavy dark hair from both of my parents. I've received many compliments about my hair, and I've even had people stroke my hair in admiration. I've observed that most of the people who've complimented my hair have had straight, thin hair. They would love to have hair like mine. But you know what? When I was a teenager, all I wanted was straight, blond hair. I worked as a carhop at a drive-in, and the carhop who made the most tips was a girl who was a senior in high school (I was two years younger) who was pretty with straight, blond hair. Boys from her class would come to the drive-in and leave her very large tips, and I got much less. I figured it must be her hair. One day, I accompanied my mother to the beauty parlor and tried on several wigs of straight, blond hair. I looked absolutely terrible! With my olive complexion and dark eyebrows, there was no match at all. I gave up the idea of having blond hair during that visit, and I've never wanted it again. Ever since then, I have loved my thick, wavy dark hair.

## *Eliminating concentrating on a negative body image*

Changing your attention from a negative body image to a positive one makes an enormous difference in your life. Seeing your body in a positive, affirming, and accepting way frees you from remaining unhappy and stuck.

Here's the fastest and most efficient way to change from having a negative to a positive body image: When you notice you're giving attention to any of the thoughts, feelings, or actions on the left side of the following chart, immediately and consciously replace them with those on the right side.

| *Negative Body Image* | *Positive Body Image* |
|---|---|
| You have a false view of your body. | You have a clear, accurate picture of your body. |
| You feel uneasy in your body. | You feel relaxed and self-assured in your body. |
| You allow your inner critic to run rampant in your mind. | You take control of your thoughts and use positive self-talk. |
| You either obsess over your body and go overboard to improve it, or you feel you don't deserve to take care of your body and ignore it. | You respect your body and care for it in an intelligent manner. |
| You feel embarrassed, awkward, and apprehensive about your body. | You feel proud of your unique body. |
| You believe that others are good-looking and that your body is an indication of individual failure. | You appreciate your body and know that your physical body isn't as important as your personality and value as a person. |

## *Focusing on what you like about the way you look*

Don't feel guilty about taking pride in your body. And don't try to hide your body and ignore your physical self because it's not exactly the way you want it to be. Concentrate on what you like about your body; then imagine expanding that empowering feeling to the rest of yourself. You can have pride in your body by recognizing what you appreciate and enjoy.

People with healthy self-esteem and a healthy body image don't believe they're the best-looking people around. Instead, they recognize their physical flaws, but at the same time, they place their attention on what they like about the way they look.

It's important to eat correctly and exercise enough to be physically healthy. In Chapter 6, we look at how to do this in detail.

This exercise prompts you to describe the parts of your body you appreciate. In your notebook, draw a line down the middle of a page. Stand in front of a mirror and look at every part of your body. On the left side of the page, write down each and every part of your body that you like, even if it's as small as "freckles on the bridge of my nose." On the right side, record why you like it, such as, "They give my face an interesting coloring and they come from Dad." Continue to do this for as many parts as you can. When you're done with your list, read it out loud and announce, "I love [feature from the left side] because [reason from the right side]" while looking at it with fondness. If you have a negative body image, do this exercise at least once a day.

## Making the best of your good features

No matter how you look, you can have the attitude that you are attractive. You dress in an attractive way and move in an attractive manner. You feel attractive. Everything about you is attractive. You care about yourself, and others can see that just by looking at you.

Don't wait until you're the perfect size to buy that new wardrobe or that new dress or suit. To emphasize your best features, don't wear drab, plain clothes. Instead, wear bright colors like red, blue, yellow, and green. How about adding some smart pieces to your wardrobe to liven up your clothes? You can enhance your look by wearing nice scarves, jewelry, belts, cuff-links, and shoes.

Too many people slavishly follow the latest fashion trend, no matter what it looks like on them. Your clothes and accessories can be a statement about yourself and who you are. Don't wear anything that you don't feel great in. Your goal isn't to look like stick-thin models or muscular men. Rather, dress in ways that make you feel good about yourself, that fit you now but that are also comfortable and that you enjoy wearing. Don't try to squeeze into clothes that are too tight or try to camouflage your body by wearing clothes that are too loose.

## Making the most of your skin tone

Wearing clothes that flatter your skin color is one way to feel good about your appearance. Take three tests to determine whether you have a cool or warm skin color:

✔ Look at the underside of your arm in the outdoor sun. If your veins are blue tinted, you have a cool skin tone; if your veins are green tinted, you have a warm skin tone.

✔ Hold up gold and silver cloths or jewelry to your face. If silver looks better next to your skin, your skin tone is cool; if gold looks better, your skin tone is warm.

✔ Drape two pieces of cloth around your neck, one pink and one orange. If the pink one complements your skin, your skin tone is cool; if orange is your best color, your skin tone is warm.

Now you're ready to choose your colors. If your skin tone is cool, choose royal blue, sapphire blue, gray, black, lemon yellow, soft white, purple, pink, and deep emerald green. If your skin tone is warm, choose light yellow, sage green, olive green, dark brown, ivory, camel, red, and orange.

## Promoting a healthy and happy lifestyle

You can take an entirely new approach to your body. It's one where you concentrate on the notion that your most important focal point is on being healthy and happy.

How do you do this? Take these measures:

✔ **Realize that your body is not an indicator of your self-worth, so accept yourself for who you are and what you look like right now.** Look around you and you'll see that people are different sizes and shapes. Appreciating the diversity of different bodies is important. Not everyone can be rail thin; in fact, it's not necessarily healthy. And what if you're a petite or tall woman? Or a short man? Your body is individual and unique. Instead of hating it and trying to be something different, love and enjoy it.

✔ **Change your self-talk.** Compliment yourself for what you admire about your body. If you do want to change, use affirmations and positive self-talk to motivate you to do what's needed.

✔ **Eat when you feel hungry and enjoy the foods you eat. Get in touch with your appetite.** When are you not hungry? When are you the hungriest? When you're the hungriest, can you drink more water so you don't overeat? Get in touch with when you're halfway full and when you're full.

Stop eating somewhere in between those two. Eat a variety of foods that offer you full nutrition and balance. Choosing foods in a variety of colors helps you get the vitamins and minerals your body needs.

The other day, I (coauthor Vivian) began eating a bowl full of cherries. They just started being in season, and they were *so tasty.* I ate the entire bowl, so I got another full bowl. I was about halfway through the second bowl when I realized I was full. But because I had the cherries right there in front of me, I continued to eat them until the bowl was empty. My stomach felt heavy and stuffed. I realized then that I should have stopped after one bowl or, at most, 1½ bowls. It was an important insight.

- ✔ **Enjoy some sort of physical activity at least every other day, but make sure you like the type of physical activity that you choose.** If you find that following a specific exercise routine keeps your enthusiasm high, by all means do that. But if you discover that you get bored over time or you don't enjoy the routine any longer, look for various physical activities that you like. Most people find that changing exercises every few weeks or even within the week helps them to stay motivated. And if you enjoy sports, play them often.

- ✔ **Schedule some time to pamper your body.** Take a soothing bath, get a massage or facial scrub, dry brush your body with a skin brush, or put good-smelling moisturizing lotion all over your body.

- ✔ **Stand up straight, look straight ahead, walk with a spring in your step, and smile.** Be that confident person you want to be.

- ✔ **Develop supportive relationships with your family and friends.** Spend time with people who have a positive effect on you, who energize and invigorate you. If one of your family members or friends wants to improve her health too, you can exercise together, swap recipes, have each other over for dinner, and encourage each other in your healthy endeavors.

- ✔ **Show yourself that you're worthy.** Create a beautiful environment at home and at work. Surround yourself with your favorite colors, put fresh flowers with a wonderful fragrance on the table or your desk, play your favorite music, and place lovely artwork on the walls.

- ✔ **Make a list of things you've always wanted to do but that you've held back on while you were waiting to achieve a perfect body.** Start right away to go out and do them!

- ✔ **Realize that all the tips in this list contribute to a healthy lifestyle, no matter what your weight is today.** Focus on being healthy overall physically, mentally, emotionally, and in your relationships.

# Giving Yourself Credit for Your Entire Personality

If you judge yourself only by your body, you reduce your focus to only the form side of yourself and completely ignore the substance within that form. What about the other parts of your personality? Don't they matter too?

Real beauty is defined by who you are on the inside — your excitement for life, your concern for others, your joyful personality, and your friendliness toward others. All of these attributes make you who you truly are. They are the real you.

Here's an interesting fact. Some people whose appearance is the opposite of the "ideal" are very happy, and some who look just like the "ideal" are unhappy. So is it really how perfect your body is that makes you feel good about yourself? Obviously not.

A French term applies here: *jolie-laide,* which means beautiful-ugly. This word describes people who don't fit the typical portrayal of beautiful or handsome but who develop into being beautiful or handsome by the way they present themselves, by who they are on the inside.

Pay attention not only to your physical health but also to who you are as a person. You aren't just your body. You're so much more!

In your notebook, list at least 15 positive qualities you have outside of your physical body. Here are some topics to get you thinking:

- How you relate to family members
- How you relate to friends
- Volunteer work you do for various organizations
- How well you do at your job
- What you do well as a parent
- Sports you participate in or watch with friends or family
- Artistic abilities — painting, sculpting, singing, dancing, acting, and so on
- Natural talents and skills you either were born with or developed

These are the qualities that you need to focus on. Carry this list with you and look at it often so you concentrate on these aspects. And develop these characteristics fully to become the person with healthy self-esteem you desire to be.

# Part III
# Changing Your Negative Thoughts and Coming to Grips with Being a Perfectionist

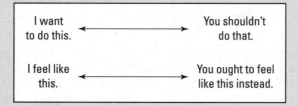

# In this part . . .

- ✔ Negative thoughts are directly related to experiencing low self-esteem. Identify the types of negative thought patterns you normally use and discover how to turn them into positive ones.

- ✔ A special type of negative thinking is perfectionism. Become familiar with the characteristics of perfectionism and its many drawbacks as well as where perfectionist thoughts, feelings, and actions begin.

- ✔ Transform your perfectionist tendencies to instead become a high achiever who has healthy self-esteem.

# Chapter 8

# Dealing with Your Negative Self-Talk

*Y*our self-talk consists of the thoughts you have in your mind, both those that are fleeting and those you contemplate. Do you realize that you think about 50,000 to 60,000 thoughts every single day? All day, every day, the thoughts you have are directly related to how you live your life. Your thoughts come from many places — people and events from your past, what's going on right now in your life, and visions and concerns about what's in your future. What you tell yourself determines how you value (or devalue) yourself and how successful you are (or aren't). This internal voice inside your head influences how you perceive and feel about every situation you face.

In this chapter, you discover the negative patterns that trap you into self-talk that doesn't serve you and how to get out of those traps. Only by deliberately creating new language that describes a more positive result and using it whenever you find yourself in such a trap will you change your thinking habits.

It takes awareness, the willingness to challenge your negative self-talk, practice, and repetition. After you've mastered these and completely transformed the way you talk to yourself, you'll be thrilled with the result.

Your thoughts direct your behavior, your behaviors form your habits, and your habits create your life!

# Understanding How Self-Talk Can Become Harmful

Some of your self-talk is reasonable. If you need to go to the grocery store after work and you think about what you want to buy, that's fine. If your company gives you an award for a great idea you came up with and you mentally pat yourself on the back, that makes perfect sense.

A small amount of negative self-talk is normal. For example, you forget to call your friend on her birthday, and you think to yourself, "Darn! I wish I hadn't forgotten Joan's birthday yesterday! I'll call her after I get home from work this afternoon." Everyone makes minor mistakes, and recognizing those is normal.

But talking to yourself about yourself in a derogatory fashion often or constantly definitely isn't helpful. When you have negative self-talk, you're actually instructing yourself to behave in certain ways. For example, if you say to yourself, "This is too difficult for me to do," there's a good chance you won't even try to do it. If you think, "I'll always be poor," you'll feel defeated and fail to get more education or work harder to earn more money. What you think is what you become.

Negative self-talk is cruel. It's judgmental and mean-spirited. It makes you feel small, inadequate, ashamed, unworthy, and hopeless. It's constantly looking for proof that you're not good enough. It leads directly to low self-esteem.

However, your negative self-talk can serve a purpose. Common ones include the following:

- **Feeling powerless:** "I'm so weak that I can't do anything about it."

- **Putting yourself down before anyone else can:** "No wonder I didn't get that promotion. I'm not nearly as good as everyone else in this department."

- **Being able to justify yourself:** "I can't control myself, so I'll eat all I want."

- **Getting attention:** "I'm going to cry on your shoulder because my life is so miserable."

Some people imagine this negative voice as their inner critic. It's sitting on their shoulder whispering damaging thoughts into their ear, just waiting to destroy their self-esteem another time.

And what are some of the consequences of thinking poorly about yourself?

- ✔ Frustration
- ✔ Anger
- ✔ Feeling like a victim
- ✔ Anxiety
- ✔ Depression
- ✔ Difficult relationships
- ✔ Alcohol abuse and drug use
- ✔ Feeling hurt
- ✔ Stress
- ✔ Less of an ability to meet life's challenges
- ✔ Difficulty focusing, relaxing, digesting, and sleeping
- ✔ Poor performance

# Challenging the Many Ways You Talk to Yourself

One of the most important things to understand about negative self-talk is that these thoughts only reflect your feelings about yourself, not the actual truth. For most people, these feelings begin in childhood and continue into adulthood. But the fact that you have these feelings doesn't mean that they're an accurate picture of reality.

There are numerous ways your mind can deceive you into believing that you have little value. These are irrational errors that make you feel bad and act in self-defeating ways.

## Using mind-reading to create an unhappy story

*The error:* Your thoughts tell you what other people are thinking, and you believe others are always focused only on your faults. You actually project your own negative views of yourself as though they're coming from other people. You're sure you know what others are thinking, and of course, you always come out in a bad light.

***Example:*** Jane wears a new dress to work, and as she is passing the desk of one of her coworkers, he glances at her but doesn't smile. Immediately, Jane presumes this coworker thinks her dress looks awful and that's the reason he didn't smile at her. She goes to the restroom and looks in the mirror, chastising herself for even buying this dress in the first place. She thinks, "You were crazy to get this dress! It looks awful on you! Ben is right. It was a waste of money."

***How to refute the error:*** Realize that you don't actually know other people's thoughts unless you ask them to tell you. People may look at you or act a certain way for a variety of reasons. Most likely, none of these reasons have anything to do with you. Although people do sometimes make judgments about others, this error either gets it totally wrong or exaggerates what people are thinking.

Don't assume that you're in the wrong. Don't take personally what others say or do. Realize that every person is in his own world and that you're not the center of that person's world. You can ask people whether they're upset about something concerning you, but don't imagine that you are the reason.

***The new way of thinking:*** Jane thinks, "Ben just looked at me without smiling. I have no idea why, but I wish him the best. Now, what project do I start with today?"

## Predicting a negative outcome is inevitable

***The error:*** This error is related to the one in the preceding section. In mind-reading, you interpret other people's actions to make you look bad when there are no facts to support it. This happens in the moment or about something that happened in the past. When you make the error of predicting a negative outcome, you assume that things will turn out badly, much worse than you have reason to. You can even foresee a catastrophe ahead, and this thought causes you great anxiety and apprehension.

***Example:*** Craig has made two mistakes at his job in the past six months. They were small mistakes, and he was able to correct them fairly easily once they were pointed out to him by his supervisor. He has a performance evaluation coming up tomorrow, and all he can think is, "I'm sure I'll get fired! My supervisor had to tell me about those terrible mistakes, so I'm going to get the worst performance evaluation of my career, and then he'll give me my pink slip. I know it!" Craig can't sleep that night and gets into work late. He is anxious and perspires all through the day until he is finally called into his supervisor's office for the performance evaluation. He's so nervous that it's difficult for him to speak clearly in his meeting.

***How to refute the error:*** To challenge this type of negative self-talk, realize that your worst-case scenario is often overstated and melodramatic, even outlandish and implausible. It's important to have an accurate perspective on what could happen. Once you've identified this, reinforce the belief in your own ability to handle whatever comes your way. Also, reverse your thoughts to think about what you've done right in the past.

**The new way of thinking:** Craig thinks, "My supervisor did find those two mistakes. But you know what? They were small, and I've done a terrific job on these major projects we've worked on lately. If he brings it up in the performance evaluation, I'll explain why I made those mistakes and emphasize all the good work I've done. And even if I do get a pink slip, I know I have the skills and experience to find another job in a short period of time. If that does happen, I'll talk to Steve and Al. They'll know of job openings, I'm sure."

# Overgeneralizing about things that happen to you

**The error:** Overgeneralizing involves seeing the world in black and white with no shades of gray. You take one isolated fact or event and believe it will always happen. When this inner critic whispers in your ear, you hear words like "always," "everyone," "never," and "forever." The thoughts in your mind are only about extremes.

**Example:** Arthur got a D– on his first exam in his calculus class in high school. He didn't study very much for this exam and didn't seek out any of his classmates to study with. He read the material once and thought he knew it. He thinks, "What a terrible student I am! I'm sure to flunk this course. I might as well just quit the class because I'll never understand the material."

**How to refute the error:** Consider only the facts. If you do something wrong, admit it and then move on. Don't believe that you're a failure because of one event. Learn from the mistake and make a plan on how to deal with it so you don't make that mistake again.

**The new way of thinking:** Arthur thinks, "I got a D– on this exam. Well, I better start studying a lot more than I have been. Mary said this was an easy class for her. I wonder if she'd like to be my study buddy on this. I'll ask her after class. No matter what, I've got to hit the books a lot more than I have! This is a wake-up call."

# Labeling yourself in a derogatory fashion

**The error:** Labeling is a form of overgeneralizing. This inner critic defines you by using words like "loser," "failure," "stupid," "wimp," "ugly," "not good enough," and "useless" as soon as something doesn't go well in your life.

*Example:* Valerie was part of a dance troupe. She and her fellow dancers practiced for several months to put on a number of performances of *The Nutcracker.* In the first performance, Valerie didn't get her cue right, and she was late coming onstage in one of the scenes. The other dancers had to make adjustments, but after a minute, they were back to the correct dance routine. The thoughts going on in Valerie's head after the performance were, "I sure am a rotten dancer! I can't believe I came in late! I'm just not good enough for this dance troupe. I should drop out now before I cause any more problems." She went to the director after the show and offered her resignation.

*How to refute the error:* Consider the actual facts, both what went wrong and how you also did things right. Out of the many, many times you did something, only once did it go wrong because you made a mistake. Realize that the great majority of the time, things went quite well.

*The new way of thinking:* Valerie changes her thinking, "I sure made a mistake coming out late. But the rest of the time, I danced great! I'm going to pay more attention to when Shirley comes on stage because that's when I know I follow."

## Blaming yourself for things that aren't your fault

*The error:* With this thinking error, you blame yourself for everything, even if you're not at fault or have no control over it. You think it's your responsibility to make sure other people are happy, all your relationships flourish, and everyone has fun at social gatherings. When things don't go the way you expect, you believe it's because of a mistake you made along the way.

*Example:* Jeanine's boss makes some small changes to a report Jeanine prepared. She apologizes for being so inept for missing these in the first place, and she thinks to herself that she's absolutely incompetent.

*How to refute the error:* Although taking responsibility for your life is important, these thoughts take blame to an extreme. Realize that you're not omnipotent. You can't know everything and you're not all-powerful. And your influence goes only so far. When something happens that's different from what you'd like to see, identify ways that you tried your best and give yourself praise for what you did accomplish. You have normal, human inadequacies, just like everyone else.

*The new way of thinking:* Jeanine acknowledges the changes her boss made to the report and appreciates that these improved it. She makes a note to include these topics in future reports and moves on to do other work.

# Focusing on the negative and discounting the positive

**The error:** You have a filter in your mind that allows in only those thoughts that reinforce your low self-esteem and disregards anything that may raise your sense of self-worth. Any negative detail is magnified as you think exclusively about that, and at the same time, no positive detail is even considered.

**Example:** Britney has been dating Kevin for a few weeks. She thought the relationship was going fine, but one day, he said he wanted to date other women and just be friends. Britney went into a tailspin. All she thought about was, "I just got dumped. I must not be marriage material. I might as well get used to being alone for the rest of my life." Britney never thought about the other words that Kevin said when he broke up with her. He told her she was a wonderful person and that he enjoyed being with her during the time they had dated. But he thought they weren't very compatible because they didn't have many of the same interests, so he needed to find someone he was more compatible with. Britney stopped going to parties, and she wouldn't accept invitations from friends who wanted to set her up with a blind date.

**How to refute the error:** Make a determined effort to emphasize the positive instead of the negative. Put your thoughts on what you're doing right or what went right instead of what went wrong. Congratulate yourself for the positive things in the situation.

**The new way of thinking:** Britney's heart is broken, and she cries for a few days after Kevin breaks up with her. But then she dries her tears and thinks, "This was a good lesson about finding a man I have more in common with. Kevin did tell me he enjoyed dating me and that he thought I was a wonderful person. And I am! I really am! I'm kind, helpful, and loving. I think I'll call Janet about going to Sue's party on Saturday. I'm ready to meet someone new."

You can uncover how much you use negative self-talk in various ways. One is to take some time, think back, and consider your thoughts that fit into the different types of thinking errors listed in the preceding sections. You can also take note of what you're thinking at random times during the day. Another way to notice your self-talk is to identify what you're thinking when you experience uncomfortable emotions such as anxiety, stress, and depression. If you do this after the emotion has passed, identify what you were thinking before and during the emotional experience. In addition, detect your self-talk when you're about to encounter a difficult situation. After you've written down a number of negative statements you say to yourself, go to the next exercise.

In your notebook, make four columns, one entitled "Negative Self-Talk," one entitled "Error," one entitled "Positive Self-Talk," and the last entitled "Actions." Under each column, write out the negative thoughts about yourself in your mind, which pattern of error it is, a new thought that reinforces your self-esteem, and what new actions you'll take as a result of changing to more positive self-talk.

# Overcoming the Problem of Using "Shoulds"

A special kind of thinking error is the destructive use of the word "should" and its siblings "must," "ought to," "have to," "got to," and "better." It's one of the most common errors because everyone learns from their parents and from society at large how to be. Manipulative rules slavishly require you to look, act, think, and feel certain ways. When you fail to measure up to these rules, you can feel frustration, anger, and even hatred toward yourself.

Not only that, but your "shoulds" can also express themselves in three other ways:

✔ You can think about how others believe you should be.

✔ You can think about how others should be.

✔ You can think about how the world should be.

All of these can lead to unhappiness and misery. You can feel hurt and confused because you and everyone and everything else aren't living up to your expectations.

Take a look at some common "shoulds" people have that cause criticism:

✔ I should be successful.

✔ I better work hard.

✔ I should get up early every morning.

✔ I should be a loving parent at all times.

✔ I should be ready to help whenever others ask for my assistance.

✔ I should look attractive.

✔ I better get all A's in school.

✔ I should be popular.

✔ I ought to be calm and in control at all times.

✔ I must finish everything I start.

✔ I have to be happy and serene, even during difficulties.

✔ I should put others' needs before my own.

✔ I ought to be able to depend only on myself.

✔ I should be married.

✔ I must own my own home.

✔ I should be a lawyer because my father is and he expects me to be one.

✔ I ought to be happy all the time.

✔ I should never be tired or sick.

✔ I must be more organized.

✔ John should be a nicer friend.

✔ Mary shouldn't talk so much in our conversations.

✔ Henry should go to church more often.

✔ My spouse should know what I'm thinking without me saying anything.

✔ The government shouldn't (or should) be doing this.

✔ The weather should be nicer today.

Do you see how your inner critic can use these thoughts to demand impossible or unhealthy behaviors? When you hold onto these beliefs, your chances of feeling bad about yourself, others, and the world increase dramatically. And when you don't live up to the standards in your mind, it feels like a severe scolding happening in your thoughts.

There are many problems with the "shoulds" in your mind. These rules are absolute and inflexible. They can't be changed and must be followed at all costs. Because they're ironclad and you've been told it's always been like this, you have a duty and obligation to match what they say, and others do too. They lead to blaming yourself for not living up to these expectations as well as blaming others and the world at large when they don't either.

# Recognizing the "shoulds" that make sense

Some "shoulds" are rational and make sense. Mostly, these have to do with cause and effect. Here are some examples:

✔ I should call my friend if I want to stay updated on his new job.

✔ I must do some research to know whether I'm on the right track in this project.

✔ I should stop at every red light and drive forward only on a green light.

✔ I have to study hard if I want to get an A on the test.

✔ I should not cause anyone bodily harm.

✔ I ought to go to the doctor if I'm very sick.

✔ I should treat my spouse well to have a good relationship.

These beliefs are helpful and appropriate. They are based on common sense, so they're fine to have in your mind and serve you well.

## Carrying around learned behaviors

Many damaging "shoulds" are messages you learned from your parents. Some are little things. They may have told you to brush your teeth every night, sit up straight, and take a shower every morning.

But the types of "shoulds" you learned that are most detrimental to your self-esteem are those that go deeper — what kind of job you should have, what kind of person you should marry, what represents success, how you should spend your free time, who your friends should be, and what your religious and political beliefs should be. These are value-laden and deny the reality of how you feel as well as who and what you are.

Now as an adult, you're so used to following others' "shoulds" that you've not allowed yourself to be who and what you truly are. You have feelings of confusion. One part of you says that you want to do something, and the other part says you should do something different, as shown in Figure 8-1.

**Figure 8-1:**
Following others' "shoulds" pulls you in different directions.

| I want to do this. | ⟵⟶ | You shouldn't do that. |
| I feel like this. | ⟵⟶ | You ought to feel like this instead. |

*John Wiley & Sons, Inc.*

Consider a few examples that may apply to you:

- You're afraid. You think you should be strong, but you're still scared.

- You're angry. You think you should be empathetic, but you're still upset.

- You're crying because a friend died. Your inner critic tells you that you should be over your grieving, but you can't stop crying.

- You love to draw. Your inner critic stresses that you can't make enough money doing that, so you become a business major. But your real love is still drawing.

- You have strong feelings toward someone of another race, but your family's and community's messages are that it's wrong to feel that way. But you still have this attraction.

ANECDOTE

## Frank's inner critic of "shoulds"

Frank was told while he was growing up that he must put on clean clothes every day and place his clothes in the clothes bin every night. He feels it's a waste of water (his area has been in a drought for several years, water is more scarce, and the price is rising), and he knows it's costing him more because washing his clothes so often causes his electricity bill to be higher and because his clothes wear out sooner and have to be replaced. He has also noted that on most days, his clothes seem to stay fresh for more than one day.

But that nagging inner critic starts to pound in his mind every time he hangs his shirt up after wearing it for a day. "You should put it in the clothes bin!

It's dirty! Don't wear it more than once! It has to be washed!" Frank knows that his shirt doesn't have to be washed each time he wears it, but his parents' messages are strong in his mind. And if he doesn't wash his shirt, he'll think, "I'm such a slob because I didn't wash this shirt after I wore it!"

Frank can challenge his inner critic by replacing these "shoulds" with other thoughts. He can deliberately say to himself, "My clothes are fresh more than one day, and I don't want to spend money needlessly on new clothes by washing my clothes every day. I'm going to wear them two days instead." Then it's important for Frank to follow through and carry out what his new thoughts direct him to do.

## *Freeing yourself from your "shoulds"*

You can use a number of methods to change this dangerous inner critic of "shoulds":

> ✔ **Accept yourself.** Whenever a "should" message doesn't reflect who you truly are, what you love to do, and what your values are and instead requires you to be different, your authentic self and your freedom are in danger of disappearing. Be open and honest in looking within and finding that authentic self. Be very conscious of who you are and who you aren't, and what you choose to do and what you choose not to do. When faced with a "should" belief, ask yourself these questions:
>
> - Who am I really? Does this "should" belief reflect that? Does it make sense, given who I am?
> - What are my natural gifts and talents that I want to develop? Does this "should" belief enhance these?
> - What do I truly believe? Is this "should" belief in tune with that?
> - What are my physical, emotional, and intellectual needs, and do these "should" beliefs serve them?
> - Where did this "should" belief come from? Is it valid?
> - What will the consequences be if I release this "should" belief?
> - How would I feel if I released this "should" belief?

✔ **Acknowledge and accept things as they are.** Realize that things won't always work out the way you wish they would. You can't change others, so allow them to be themselves too. Don't expect things to be different just because you believe they should be. Instead of thinking, "I shouldn't be upset," think, "I am upset about this." Instead of thinking, "I have to take over the company from Pop," think, "I don't enjoy doing the work of managing Pop's company. I'd much rather be a teacher."

✔ **Change your language to express a preference, a suggestion, a choice, or an aim.** Use words such as "could," "aim to," would prefer," "choose to," and "would like to." Instead of thinking, "I ought to be more confident," think, "I aim to become more confident." Instead of thinking, "I must always look sharp," think, "I would like to look sharp." When you think this way, you'll work on being confident and looking sharp, but if you don't achieve great success with them, you won't beat yourself up and can be more relaxed and easygoing about the situation.

✔ **Set limits on people who impose their "shoulds" on you.** Instead of feeling victimized or upset by other people who believe you should feel or behave a certain way, be assertive with them and explain how you see things and why. In Chapter 6, we explain in detail how to do this. Setting these boundaries will help keep others' "should" requirements silenced.

✔ **Be flexible.** Allow for exceptions to the ironclad rule, depending on the circumstances and situation.

Don't waste your life living by someone else's rules. Don't spend your time and energy on things you don't really care about, while you ignore those things you're most passionate about. Listen to your own inner voice and don't allow others' voices to overrule your own. Be brave enough to understand and live your authentic self, according to what you truly feel and believe. When you do this, you'll be free to become the person you've dreamed of becoming.

Try this exercise to inventory and change the "shoulds" in your life: In your notebook, complete "I should . . . " in each of these areas of your life:

✔ Your appearance

✔ Your relationships

✔ Your home and yard

✔ Your work

✔ Your feelings

✔ Money and finances

✔ Social activities

✔ Political activities

✔ Religious and spiritual activities

✔ Your free time

Identify where each "should" belief came from and whether it's serving you well. If not, write a sentence for each one that either reverses it or reframes it to something that works well for you.

For an entire day, write down each time you think you should be or feel a certain way. Do the same for any of "should's" siblings, such as "must," "ought to," "have to," "got to," and "better." In addition, write down every time someone else tells you how to be or feel. Then complete the exercise like the preceding one, replacing each command that isn't in your own best interest.

# Harnessing Your Power to Change Your Thinking

People who are successful in life — in terms of work, relationships, health, and feeling fulfillment and happiness — predominantly think in terms of optimism, hopefulness, and cheerfulness. They aren't just lucky. They're successful because they have a set of attitudes that bring these positive consequences into their lives.

Studies have found that using your mind to think in a more positive manner has many important benefits:

- **Your health is better.** Being more optimistic reduces cardiovascular disease, even if you smoke cigarettes, are overweight, or are older. Also, your blood pressure is lower and your pain tolerance is higher.

- **Stress is reduced.** People who use positive thinking can cope better with problems that arise, so they have less anxiety and depression.

- **Relationships are more enjoyable.** Optimistic thinkers are more likely to have strong relationships. People are more drawn to others who are happy and cheerful than they are to others who are worried and apprehensive. Because they concentrate on the good qualities of their friends and mates, positive thinkers are more contented in their relationships. They also give more attention to having a fulfilling relationship and are therefore more effective at it.

- **You have better coping skills during adversity.** Thinking in a positive manner doesn't mean that you ignore life's tough situations. It means that you approach these challenging situations in a more constructive, upbeat, and productive manner.

Ask yourself this question: Are your thoughts and beliefs helping you or hurting you? If you're not living the life you desire, it's time to upgrade your internal voice.

## *Identifying all of your positive qualities*

What would a list of all your strengths, positive attributes, skills, and abilities look like? Now that you're changing your negative self-talk, make a catalog of everything good you can identify about yourself. They can be small things or big things. Consider everything about your life and create such an inventory.

Another way to create such a list is to identify the person who knows you best and describe yourself as that person would describe you.

Here are some questions to start the process:

- ✔ What do I like about myself?
- ✔ What are my positive characteristics?
- ✔ What attributes do I have in common with people I admire?
- ✔ What are my skills and talents? What do I love to do?
- ✔ What are some difficult situations I've overcome?
- ✔ What compliments do others give me?
- ✔ What are my major achievements?
- ✔ Who have I helped?
- ✔ What kind things have I done for others?
- ✔ What successes have I had at home and at work?
- ✔ How would my best friend describe me?

When you find yourself being filled with negative self-talk, take a break and bring out your list. Read it over and add to it. Think about all your excellent attributes.

## *Asking yourself whether your thoughts are reasonable*

It's important to test the legitimacy of your inner critic. If critical thoughts impose on you, examine them by asking yourself these questions:

- ✔ What evidence do I have to back up these thoughts? What facts contradict these thoughts?
- ✔ Am I using one of the thinking errors? If so, which one?

✔ Am I coming to negative conclusions needlessly?

✔ What is the worst outcome in this situation? How likely is it to happen? If it did happen, how could I handle it?

✔ What is the best outcome in this situation? How likely is it to happen?

✔ Are my thoughts based on the way I feel instead of facts?

✔ What would my best friend say about these thoughts?

✔ What would I tell my best friend if she had these thoughts?

✔ Are these thoughts helping me to be happy in the long run? Do they make me feel good? Do they help me reach my goals?

After you've tested whether your self-talk is well-founded and justifiable, you'll be able to decide whether to make changes in your life to conform to your self-talk or release the thoughts and carry on with your life in a way that's more satisfying to you.

## Detaching from your negative self-talk

By observing the thoughts of your inner critic, you can distance yourself from them and become more detached. You can think of these thoughts as floating overhead like clouds drifting in the sky. Or you can see them as if they're being said by someone else and not you.

Deliberately fill your thoughts with joy. Also, breathe deeply and allow negative thoughts to fall away. You don't have to pay attention to them. Become immersed in an activity you enjoy or call a friend or relative on the phone. Put yourself outside of these thoughts.

## Being compassionate with yourself

Being compassionate with yourself provides the care, tenderness, and kindness you deserve. Here are some suggestions for providing yourself that consideration:

✔ **Recognize that you're not unique.** Everyone has times when they did something wrong or didn't measure up to what they wanted. If you do make mistakes, accept them without judging yourself; instead, learn from them and aim to do better next time. When you realize that you're just like everybody else in the world, you can calm down and be more at ease.

✔ **Change your voice.** Say to yourself, "It will be okay. I'm okay." Instead of continually criticizing yourself, use a calm and gentle voice to replace those thoughts with more positive ones. You can say "Not helpful!" or "I did the best I could" as soon as you realize your inner critic is attacking you. Repeat these replacements many times so the new sentiments sink in. Even if this voice doesn't originally sound genuine, keep doing this. Gradually, this new voice will become sincere.

✔ **Give yourself a time limit.** Tell yourself that you'll have these negative thoughts for a short period of time, such as 1 minute or 5 minutes. After the time has passed, write in your notebook what you're going to do differently next time. Don't write about what happened or what went wrong; instead, write only about how you'll improve and do better next time. If there won't be a next time or you can't do anything differently, write about your favorite television show, a joke you recently heard, or your greatest accomplishment.

✔ **Be your own best friend.** Treat yourself the way you would treat someone you are close to if they felt like a failure. You can give yourself a hug and gently rock your body. This can soothe you and make you feel cared for.

✔ **Think about something that makes you happy.** Put your attention on your children or grandchildren, your favorite hobby, a fun movie you saw recently, or pretty scenery. If you continue to have negative self-talk, keep thinking about things that make you feel better for as long as it takes to release the inner critic.

✔ **Surround yourself only with people who have an optimistic outlook.** You'll feel stronger and more energized because they will already have a deep-seated sense of healthy self-worth.

✔ **Write two things you appreciate about yourself every day.** At the end of each week, read your list out loud to yourself at least three times. Do this with passion and enthusiasm.

# Chapter 9

# Analyzing Perfectionism

- - - - - - - - - - - - - - - - - - - - - - - - - - - - - - - - - - - - - - - - - - - - - -

*In This Chapter*
▶ Looking at the characteristics of perfectionists
▶ Realizing how perfectionism begins
- - - - - - - - - - - - - - - - - - - - - - - - - - - - - - - - - - - - - - - - - - - - - -

**P**erfectionists use frequent negative self-talk based on core beliefs to tell themselves that they have to do things in a perfect manner and that they're not worth anything if things aren't not done exactly right. In Chapter 8, we describe how negative self-talk tears down your sense of self-worth, and perfectionism is a specialized type of negative self-talk.

Following are some of the statements perfectionists commonly think to themselves:

✔ "If I don't set the highest standards for myself, I'll fail at everything I try."

✔ "I can't make any mistakes at all. Every detail has to be absolutely perfect."

✔ "There is only one best way to do things."

✔ "People won't accept me if I do anything wrong."

✔ "I always have to be busy because I have to do things flawlessly."

✔ "I have to figure out the best way to do this, so I'll wait until the last minute to start."

✔ "I won't let others help me because they can't do it as well as I can."

In this chapter, we encourage you to investigate whether or not you're a perfectionist. We discuss what the characteristics of a perfectionist are and how perfectionist tendencies begin in the first place. (In Chapter 10, we describe exactly how to deal with perfectionism to become a healthy high-achiever.)

# Uncovering the Characteristics of Perfectionism

Here's how perfectionism works: First, you have low self-esteem to begin with. Then in order to deal with this feeling, you set unrealistic and unattainable goals to prove once and for all to yourself and to others that you do have value and that you are competent and important. But because the goals are impossible, you fail. This failure leads to feelings of anger at yourself. If only you had spent more time, if only you had tried harder, you could have reached these goals. This anger turns into even greater low self-esteem.

So you try again. You set even higher unrealistic goals, fail to meet them, experience even more profound anger at yourself, and your low self-esteem takes a deeper nose-dive. Eventually, you may give up and avoid even trying to reach your goals at all because you consider yourself such a failure. Figure 9-1 shows a visual of this cycle.

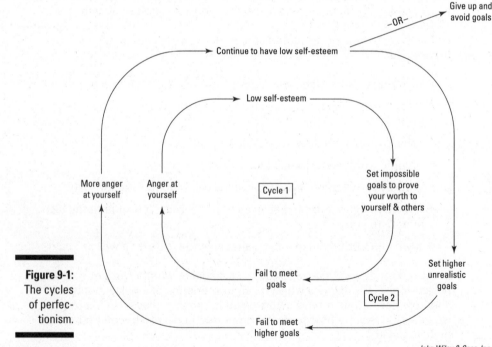

**Figure 9-1:**
The cycles of perfectionism.

*John Wiley & Sons, Inc.*

Perfectionism manifests in many different ways. Take a look at the rest of this section to see which of the traits match up with your own thoughts and actions; then complete the following exercise.

After you read this section, use your notebook to keep track of all the perfectionist tendencies, thoughts, and behaviors you have for a week. Every evening before you go to sleep, review the day and write down each time you felt you hadn't done something well enough, each time you saw yourself as a failure or not good enough, and the thoughts that went through your mind when these things were happening. After a week, look at your list and note which tendencies, thoughts, and behaviors were the most frequent. Then write about how you and those around you are hurt by what you observed about yourself.

## Feeling deeply upset if you make any mistakes

Being a perfectionist means that you believe that perfection definitely can and should be achieved at all times. None of this mamby-pamby "Everyone makes mistakes" for you! Even if the task isn't something you have much interest in, you think that you should be the best at it because you should be the best in everything you do.

Because all you do has to be top-notch, you're very disappointed in yourself and feel that your life has no value if you make a mistake. Even if it's a tiny error, you have a sharp eye and hone in on that one error and then blow it out of proportion. You're extremely critical of yourself and have trouble seeing anything other than this slip-up.

Mistakes are totally unacceptable, especially because they may show other people that you're incompetent. You're anxious about being accepted by others, and as a result, you won't take any risks, which reduces your ability to be creative or do something new and original. Instead, you concentrate on doing only safer tasks. You stick to projects you trust yourself to do an excellent job on and know you can accomplish in the best way possible.

Unfortunately, this regimentation makes it so you're not open to learning new information or taking advantage of new opportunities that open up. This attitude holds you back on your job and keeps you from getting promoted.

Even if you do something well, you downplay what you did achieve and wonder whether you could have done it even better. You're not satisfied with the result, and you're not happy with yourself because you believe your work will never be good enough.

In this exercise, answer the following questions to see whether this type of perfectionism is part of your personality:

- ✔ Do you believe that being perfect is achievable?

- ✔ Do you believe you have to be perfect to be liked, accepted, and viewed as smart and capable?

- ✔ Do you put yourself down mercilessly for any mistake you make? If so, when has that happened?

- ✔ Do you find that you rarely take risks or try something new? If so, how has this affected your career?

- ✔ Do you minimize your achievements?

## Thinking you're stupid if you perform imperfectly

If you're a perfectionist, you believe that something is wrong with you if you do anything that isn't flawless. You must perform at 100 percent in everything you do or you may be considered "average," which is a terrible thing to be.

You have standards that are extremely high — in fact, they're so high that they're practically unrealistic and unattainable. These are inflexible, personal standards that you must meet. Because your yardstick is so high, you feel you must do a great job and you're stupid if you don't. This leads to black-and-white thinking. You have to be a success at everything you do, and if you aren't, you're a total failure.

The reason this level of success is so important is because you want to avoid the shame and guilt you feel when something is not done perfectly. You feel that if you do everything perfectly, look extremely beautiful or handsome, have the ideal job that you do exactly right, and live a perfect life, you can somehow prevent those feelings of shame and guilt.

If you live your life with extreme perfectionism, these feelings of shame and guilt can take you directly to anxiety, which can then lead to performing at very low levels because your anxiety over being a failure is so high. And if you don't reach your goals at all, you can easily fall into depression.

Even when you acknowledge that these unyielding standards cause you stress and may be extreme, you continue to believe that you must have them in order to excel and be productive.

Do you get upset with yourself when your performance is less than what you expected? Find out by answering the following questions:

- ✔ Do you belittle yourself if you think you're just mediocre?

- ✔ Do you create standards for yourself that are impossible to achieve? If so, what are those standards?

- ✔ Do you feel shame, guilt, anxiety, or depression about your performance? If so, how has that affected your performance?

## Rarely letting others help with your projects

Because it's crucial that everything be done to the highest level of attainment, it's very difficult for you to let others help you in anything you do. You must see it through to the end, making sure that every little detail is done correctly.

Delegating work to others is out of the question. They may not do it as well as you, so you've got to do it yourself to ensure it's done the right way.

Your eye is totally on the goal of achieving the end product. You don't care about the process or what happens during the process.

Even though you may believe that striving for excellence is good, you're so eager to please others that you worry about every little detail in your projects and have to check things over many times to be confident that you've done the best you can. You may spend much more time on your projects that anyone else would, but that's fine because if you let others see your flaws, you feel they'll disapprove of you and not accept you because they'll see you as a loser. Your fear of being rejected makes you work harder and longer to do the best job possible.

Unfortunately, because it takes you so long to complete your work, you end up being less productive than other people. You fuss over minute details and ignore other tasks where you could be more useful. You see it's taking you a long time to accomplish one task and that other tasks are piling up. Then you think even more negative thoughts about yourself and feel worse.

In addition, you can take a long time redoing a task, usually many times over, to make sure there are no faults. This also slows down your performance and effectiveness as a student and as an employee. It can lead to poor grades on tests that have time limits and poor performance at work.

Imagine you're working on a report for either school or work. You feel that you must make it have a common look, with matching font types, font sizes, and colors. The formatting has to be faultless. The content must flow easily from one part to the next. You work and work on it because it can always be improved upon. And once you're done, you review it five more times. You have to make sure there are no errors and that it's perfect.

Working so hard and so long also makes you exhausted. You can never get it perfect, but you keep trying. You put in extra hours, working in the evenings and on the weekends, to make sure you achieve excellence. Of course, you can't be "almost perfect" because that would be a sign that you're not a success at all.

Not only that, you may even forfeit your well-being to keep going until it's perfect. You won't get the right amount of sleep or take breaks to relax at work. The idea of having fun is out of the question. You have too much work to do! You eat fast food on the run because you have so much to do. And downing those energy drinks and coffee keeps you awake to continue working. Your body may be run down, but that's insignificant because the only thing that matters is that the tasks are done exactly right.

And your negative emotions don't help your well-being either. You worry about the outcome of your tasks and every little thing that could go wrong. You're frequently anxious, skeptical that you're doing your best, and frustrated that things are not going smoothly. In fact, things go much less smoothly for you than they seem to for other people.

If your project doesn't come out exactly as you'd like, you set a higher bar for the next project. You figure that as long as you put all your time and effort into reaching perfection, you'll attain it. If you don't, it means that you just didn't work hard enough and you should work even longer and harder.

You may have a constant feeling that you're not there yet. Even though you've accomplished many things, you don't feel you've accomplished everything you need to, and you need to outdo yourself by achieving even more. You're like a hamster on a wheel, never getting where you want to go, always having more to get done.

You exhibit positive self-esteem when you welcome and respect the opinions and expertise of others. Answer the following questions to discover whether you fall into the perfectionist category of having to protect your work from others:

- ✔ Do you turn people down when they offer to help you?

- ✔ Do others get upset with you when their help is declined?

- ✔ Are you afraid of being rejected by others if you don't do your work perfectly? If so, who are these other people?

- ✔ Do you have to examine your work over and over again before you feel it's flawless? If so, has this reduced your productivity? How has this affected your grades at school or your advancement at work?

✔ Do you set even higher expectations for yourself if you don't do something well enough the first time? If so, have you been able to meet these higher expectations?

## *Waiting to do things at the last minute — or maybe not at all*

If you have perfectionist tendencies, when you fear you're going to fail, you put off doing what needs to be done. You procrastinate. You're so immobilized with anxiety and dread that something will go wrong, you can't find the motivation to get started on what you need to accomplish.

Another thing you may do as a perfectionist is to make sure you've found the ideal way to approach the project before you begin. Sure, you might fall behind in your work, which could affect your relationships with your coworkers and your reputation in the workplace, but at least you'll feel more comfortable starting the project.

The situation can get so bad that you won't even start a project. Your perfectionism, instead of helping you be successful, can actually be the very thing that prevents you from reaching your goals.

Procrastination and not starting a project can also be switched on because of your anticipation of disapproval from others. If others are going to find fault with what you're doing, it's better to put it off as long as possible or not do it at all. You may even go so far as to hide your mistakes from other people so you don't feel that disapproval.

Perfectionism determines not only how you relate to projects you do yourself, but also how you relate to the work others do. If someone does a task better than you, you feel you've fallen short. There must definitely be something wrong with you if your coworker is more proficient.

Most people procrastinate once in a while, but perfectionists do it often. To find out if this is one of your challenges, answer these questions:

✔ Do you commonly procrastinate and get work done poorly because of it? If so, when was the last time this happened?

✔ Have you not done something important because you were afraid you couldn't do it right or couldn't do it well enough?

✔ What negative things have happened to you because of your procrastination or because you didn't do something you should have that you were anxious about?

## Procrastination leads to a demotion

Sam knew he had to prepare for the presentation to give to his department two weeks before it was due. It was on a topic he was very familiar with because it had to do with the sales statistics and methods of sales he and the other salespeople had accomplished in the past quarter. But he was afraid that he would completely fail during the presentation and disappoint the people in the audience. Something bad would happen — his voice would break, his PowerPoint slides wouldn't be good enough, he would forget what he was saying — something, for sure, would go wrong.

Because of this fear, Sam waited until late the night before the presentation to start working on it. He rushed and did the best he could in the short time frame he had. He made the PowerPoint slides quickly and ended up misspelling several words. He even got some of the statistics on the slides incorrect. He staggered into bed at 3 a.m., exhausted and very worried.

He didn't have time to practice the presentation because it was scheduled first thing in the morning. He put his best foot forward. But he talked fast because he wanted to get through it as quickly as possible. Because he hadn't had time to practice, he stumbled over several of the statistics, and he forgot one of the sales methods his team had used. He sweated all the way through the presentation, both physically and figuratively.

When he was finished, he sat down quickly, giving a furtive glance at his boss. His boss didn't look very pleased.

Two weeks later, Sam was informed that he was being demoted to a sales assistant position. He asked whether the poor presentation had anything to do with the demotion. His boss had to admit that it did. Sam's procrastination had caught up with him.

## *Being defensive if others criticize you*

If perfectionism is something you live with every day, your self-esteem is low and you're basically an insecure person. You have a sense of inadequacy.

These feelings of incompetence lead you to need to prove yourself through what you do. Your desire to be perfect, to show others that you are very capable, is the longing to make a positive statement about yourself.

When you're criticized by anyone, you take it personally. You take that criticism as evidence that your deepest fear — that you're not good enough — is actually true. You're outraged and disgusted with yourself. Because your self-esteem is low, you do your best to defend yourself and even turn the disapproval around so that you criticize the other person.

By answering the following questions, you'll have a better understanding of how you relate to your work and how difficult it is for you to accept criticism:

✔ Do you feel inadequate about your work?

✔ Do you believe you need to prove yourself to others so they see you as being competent?

✔ Do you feel personally abused when someone criticizes your work? If so, when has this happened?

## Handling relationships poorly

You're actually scared of people because they can point out that you're imperfect and incompetent. This doesn't lead to close relationships. It leads to isolation and loneliness.

You have a difficult time opening up to people. You feel deep down that you must remain strong and in control of your emotions at all times. So you can't talk with others about your worries, shortcomings, and frustrations.

In fact, you end up pushing people away because you can't connect with them in a natural way. They feel alienated from you because you keep an emotional wall up that is always there to protect you.

You may even act like a dictator, telling others what they must do to have an ideal relationship with you. You expect your relationships to be perfect too, and when they're not, you cut off the people in your life — your family, spouse, friends, and coworkers. It's easier that way because you don't have to spend your time on relationships. Accomplishing your tasks is much more important.

Just as you're highly sensitive about others being critical of you, you also carry a lot of judgment of other people and readily criticize them when you believe they are not doing the best they can. You feel that if you ease up on others, you may start easing up on yourself, and both of these are totally unacceptable.

Relationships are an important part of life. People with high-quality relationships and positive interactions tend to be healthy both physically and emotionally. Answer the following questions to determine how well you relate to others:

✔ Do you commonly feel alone and that no one wants to be with you?

✔ Do you find it difficult to open up and share your feelings with others, even those people who are closest to you?

✔ Do you try to control others so they do what you think is right? If so, who have you done this with?

# Becoming Aware of How Perfectionism Begins

You weren't born a perfectionist. When you were a baby, you had to try many times before you could get that spoon into your mouth without spilling food. You had to walk first by holding onto a low table, and sometimes you fell. Then you walked a few steps next to the table without touching it, and you fell down. Finally, after many tries, you were able to walk without holding onto anything or falling. In time, you walked faster without tripping, and at last, you ran.

As a child, you found many things interesting, and you discovered that you could do some things well and others not as well.

While you were doing your best to learn to sit up, crawl, walk, and run as well as sing, hop, study, and all the other things you were involved in during childhood, the adults in your life were reacting to you. The way they talked to you and how they acted in response to what you did had an impact on you.

In this section, you discover the ways that perfectionism may have been instilled in you as a child.

As you read all the following examples, realize that your parents did the best they knew how. They related to you based on their own personalities and the way they were raised by their parents. So don't blame them, and don't blame yourself for your perfectionism. The point is just to recognize it for what it is so that you can deal with it.

## Hearing criticism often

If you were criticized often by your parents, you grew up thinking you had to go that extra step to please them and make them proud of you. Some parents never give their child high regard for what they do. Instead of saying, "Good job — I'm pleased with you," these parents say, "Couldn't you have done better?" Their children grow up believing that what they do isn't very worthwhile and that they have to strive to be better. Maybe then their parents will look kindly at them and give them a pat on the back for doing a good job.

Some people grow up in homes where other people are criticized too — people at work, neighbors, friends, and family members who live outside the home. Children in these households decide it's wise to stay on their parents' good side and not be like all these people who are criticized. If they can only be perfect, their parents won't condemn them like they do other people.

## Having things done for you

Imagine you're trying to do something for your family, such as putting away the dishes. Your mother comes up to you and says, "Here, let me do it! I can do it faster. You don't even know where the dishes go." How do you feel? Of course, you're going to feel that you did something wrong because your mother can certainly put the dishes away faster and better than you. You feel you might as well not even try. She's going to push you out of the way and belittle you anyway, so why make an effort?

But then you start to think that working hard to do things perfectly is a good idea. You want to do things well, and if you perform extra well, you can feel that you can accomplish things. In fact, you redouble your effort to learn exactly which dish goes where, so you can jump up out of your seat after the dishes have been washed and start to put them away as quickly as (or even quicker than) your mother. You want to show her that you *can* put the dishes away in an expert manner.

## Being compared to another child

If you heard such things as "Why can't you be more like your sister? She gets such good grades and never gets in trouble," you likely had the opinion that you weren't as good as your sister. In fact, you may have thought you weren't as good as any of the kids in the neighborhood. They all got good grades too and weren't in trouble. You wondered what was wrong with you.

These messages from parents can be very damaging, trampling on your sense of self-worth from an early age. You figured it was hard to live up to the love your parents had for your sister, so you'd better try really hard to get those high grades and be very, very good. Only then might your parents think you were as good as your sister.

## Getting little attention or affection

You may not have been criticized for what you did. In fact, you may have heard nothing at all about your performance at school or at home. Your parents were so busy with their own lives and perhaps other children that they gave you no notice at all.

So you resolved within yourself that you were going to get straight A's and be on the basketball team, just to get your parents' attention. All of your efforts were intensified in that direction. You wanted your parents to notice your accomplishments, and this was the only way you could think of to get them to become aware of you.

Or you may have gotten little affection. You began to notice that the only time your parents gave you any affection at all — when they put their hand on your shoulder or gave you a hug — was when you did a fantastic job in your classes, in sports, or in the play. You worked extremely hard to do that fantastic job, and you got what tiny amount of affection they handed out for doing so. You figured you must be exceptional at everything so they would keep giving you at least a little affection.

# Chapter 10

# Dealing Positively with Perfectionism

*P*erfectionism can harm you in oh so many ways. We're glad to tell you in this chapter exactly how to remedy any perfectionist tendencies you may have.

It's important to realize that perfectionism is really a misconception, something that isn't actually true. It's true only as long as you believe it's true and you hold tightly to perfectionist attributes. Once you see the harm these concepts are creating in your life, it's time to let go and create a new way of living, free from the anxieties, rigidity, and problems that perfectionist characteristics bring with them.

This chapter details how you can strive to do the best you can while letting go of the dictates of perfectionism. When you do this, you'll become more flexible in how you approach tasks to be done as well as in your relationships. We also show you how to make needed alterations so that you can think, feel, and act in a healthier, nonperfectionist manner.

## Being a High Achiever Instead of Being Perfect

If you're a perfectionist, you're probably thinking that if you let go of these attributes completely, you'll do terrible work and lose whatever determination or discipline you have. However, now that you know that perfectionism serves no positive purpose and can actually damage your performance, you can commit yourself to making changes step by step. In this way, you can make speedy progress.

The first step onto a more beneficial path is to understand the difference between being a high achiever and devoting yourself to being perfect. They're similar in some ways but different enough that the first is healthy and the second is not.

When you work at being a high achiever, you push yourself to do your very best, but you don't try to be perfect or put yourself down if your work isn't faultless. And you're not anxious that something isn't just right or that your best isn't good enough. If it goes well, fine; if it doesn't go well, you'll work with it to make it better.

If you make mistakes, you don't beat yourself up about them. Rather, you understand that making mistakes actually helps you learn. You realize that errors help you see where you need to make adjustments until you no longer make those mistakes. So you analyze them to see what you did incorrectly, strive not to duplicate those same mistakes in the future, and keep on going.

Perfectionists tend to worry that they haven't done well enough even when things go well. As a high achiever, when you see you've done some things well, you pat yourself on the back and give yourself credit for doing a good job in those areas. You're pleased with your accomplishments. You recognize that you're improving as you do well more often and make fewer errors.

From a very early age, I (coauthor Vivian) have been a singer. The first time I remember singing was for the Mothers Club that my mother belonged to in my hometown. I was only 4 years old, and I gave it my all. I am blessed with a beautiful singing voice, and I've sung ever since then. A few years ago, I was going to give an afternoon workshop at a church, so I was invited to give a short talk and sing a song during the church service. I was in the middle of the song when my voice totally broke, and I stopped singing. Instead of being mortified, I said, "Well, it happens to the best of us!" and smiled, and then I continued singing until the very end of that song. The people in the church gave me thundering applause because they knew I had made a mistake but had kept right on going and gave a beautiful performance.

Table 10-1 lists some areas in which you can compare being a high achiever to being a perfectionist.

| Table 10-1 | High Achievers versus Perfectionists |
|---|---|
| *Being a High Achiever* | *Being a Perfectionist* |
| You research material for your project, give it your best effort, complete it in a timely fashion, and feel good about what you prepared. | You research material for your project, work on it until it's perfect, check it over several times, turn it in late, and worry that it's not good enough. |
| You delegate work to your coworkers who have expertise and who you feel will do a very good job. | You keep all your work to yourself because you can't trust anybody, and then you feel overwhelmed because you can't get everything done on time. |
| You acknowledge your achievements and feel proud of yourself for accomplishing them. | Although you've achieved many things, you can't feel satisfaction because your work is never absolutely perfect. |
| When you make mistakes in your work, you appreciate them because you learn from them. You evaluate what happened and think about how to avoid having this happen again. | When you make mistakes, you're terribly ashamed, and you try to cover them up so no one knows you made them. |
| You're excited to undertake new things and learn new skills because you know your value in the workplace will improve. | You know there's a big learning curve when you learn something new and that mistakes are common, so you avoid putting yourself in that position. |

# Recognizing the Positive Qualities of Doing the Best You Can

People who strive for high achievement exhibit many positive qualities. Which of these do you feel describe you? Which of these can you enhance in your life? High achievers

- Are prepared to put effort into anything they do
- Are enthusiastic about their work
- Take responsibility for what they've been assigned to do or have volunteered to do
- Pay close attention to details
- Feel their work is important and significant

- ✔ Manage their time and space well

- ✔ Take pride in their achievements

- ✔ Learn from their errors and fairly easily bounce back from challenges and disappointments

- ✔ Make sure tasks are completed and on time

- ✔ Evaluate whether criticism is warranted, and if so, learn from it

Write this list in your notebook and look at it often. Mark which ones already describe you, and identify ways you can improve on the ones that don't describe you now in your efforts to strive for excellence.

# Letting Go of Impractical Expectations

Perfectionists are strongly attached to impractical, impossible, and unreachable goals they set for themselves. To counteract this, consider changing the way you relate to goals and expectations.

- ✔ Set realistic and sensible goals based on what you've accomplished in the past with high standards that are reachable with effort.

- ✔ As you attain a goal, set your next goal only one level beyond the one you've already achieved.

- ✔ Focus on the process of achieving the goal as well as the end result. Recognize that the process is the longest period in achieving your goal, and do your best to get pleasure from it too. Include in your analysis of how successful you were whether and how much you enjoyed the process of reaching your goal.

- ✔ Identify the goals that are a high priority to you and those that are less important. Give more effort to the high-priority goals and less effort to those that are less significant to you.

- ✔ Be happy with any steps that are made in the right direction of your goals.

- ✔ Choose an activity that is not crucial in your life. Deliberately give only 90 percent effort into accomplishing it and feel what that's like. Then give 80 percent and 70 percent until you get familiar with not trying to be perfect at this activity.

# Increasing Your Flexibility

Being flexible in work and relationships is a sign of a high achiever. While perfectionists are rigid and unbending in their work and how they interact with others, high achievers are more open and accommodating.

## Being more flexible at work

Ralph never offered suggestions during brainstorming sessions at team meetings. He felt that his team members might not like his suggestions, and he thought they would probably make fun of him. He knew that he needed to make some changes to become less of a perfectionist. In starting to be flexible, Ralph realized that brainstorming sessions are deliberately designed for team members to consider initial ideas, talk about their pros and cons, and decide which ideas are the best. So he began to give his input with ideas he thought would work, and he was pleasantly surprised that his teammates liked many of them.

Here are some useful ideas for increasing your flexibility at work:

- ✔ Break your goals down into bite-sized tasks.

- ✔ Assess whether each task makes a big difference in the entire project. Give higher priority to those tasks that have the greatest effect.

- ✔ Make a plan to achieve each one of the tasks.

- ✔ Create time limits for each small task and set an alarm. If a task is taking too much time, ask whether it's a high priority. If not, put it farther down on your to-do list.

- ✔ Take regular breaks at work to stretch and walk around. You can also do some deep breathing to help you relax.

- ✔ Check your work thoroughly only once and then deliver it to the appropriate person.

- ✔ Stop worrying about things that are not within your control.

- ✔ Be open to gaining new skills, trying new tasks, and being on new teams.

- ✔ Use affirmations to say positive things to yourself about yourself and your abilities.

- ✔ Approach your work with confidence, enjoyment, and a desire to improve.

## Being flexible in your relationships

Perfectionists are generally not very good at relationships. Just as they try their best to be flawless themselves, they expect everyone else in their lives to be flawless. This is an impossible goal and one that is very frustrating to people with perfectionist tendencies (and the people in their lives).

As you're making changes to stop trying to be so perfect, you also need to pay attention to the way you interact with others.

Here are some suggestions for being more flexible in your relationships with people you work with and people you're close to:

✔ Have faith in your coworkers' abilities and delegate some of your work to them, if appropriate. Exhibit trust and respect for them. If a coworker has difficulty doing a task you delegate, give her guidance instead of taking over the task yourself.

✔ Have consideration for your coworkers. If they make a mistake, speak to them respectfully.

✔ Deal with criticism in a positive manner. If it's feedback based on actual knowledge, appreciate it and do something about it. If someone's opinion is negative and not based on fact, tell him calmly and nicely that you have listened to what he had to say, have considered it, and don't accept it, but that you respect what he thinks. Then ignore anything else he says.

✔ Give your personal relationships the time and attention they deserve. Make sure you don't sacrifice your social life for work.

✔ Allow other people to be who they are without criticizing or correcting them. Learn to appreciate their individual traits.

# *Retraining Your Perfectionist Tendencies*

Perfectionism manifests itself in your thoughts, feelings, and actions. As you recognize that perfectionism permeates your entire personality and that transformation is desirable, you need to concentrate on each of these areas to have the most effective outcome.

Making changes in these three different areas will give you many rewards — your work will be more productive, you'll see better results in the things you undertake, you'll have more satisfaction in your life, and your relationships will be closer and warmer.

## *How you think*

As a high achiever, it's time to treat yourself with the respect you deserve. Realize that you are an individual with abilities and talents and that you are fine just the way you are.

Don't allow your negative self-talk to bully you! It's better to have an honest discussion with your inner critic, listen to what she has to say, and respond honestly to her point of view. You need to get beyond the cruel and unforgiving accusations and concentrate instead on constructive problem-solving. You also need to insist that your inner critic be a positive, respectful voice that is trying to help you and not hurt you.

Check out the nearby sidebar, "Having a conversation with your perfectionist inner critic," to see an example of what such a conversation sounds like.

It's important to replace self-critical and perfectionist thoughts with more realistic and helpful statements to and about yourself. These statements will be most effective if you practice them regularly to crowd out those you don't want anymore.

Try these examples of positive, more accurate statements:

- ✔ "Not one single person is perfect."

- ✔ "My best is good enough."

- ✔ "Everyone makes mistakes. It means I'm human like everyone else. I'm learning from my mistakes and doing my best not to repeat them."

- ✔ "Words like 'should,' 'shouldn't,' and 'not good enough' make me feel guilty. I see these as irrational and destructive words that do me harm. I'm eliminating them from my thoughts now."

- ✔ "I'm an imperfect person who cannot always be the ideal and have no faults. I'm doing my best and working hard to be excellent, realizing that perfection is impossible."

To have a healthier perspective, think about how others might see your situation. For example, if you're working nights and weekends on a report that you know others would be able to finish much more quickly during the workday, ask yourself how your coworkers would look at this situation. Also, if a close friend of yours were exhibiting this behavior, how would you advise your friend?

## How you feel

Feeling anxious, fearful, embarrassed, angry, ashamed, and disgusted with themselves are the hallmarks of perfectionists. As you can readily see, these feelings not only lead to misery, but they certainly can't be physically healthy either.

As a high achiever, you set achievable goals for yourself, viewing yourself with an abundant amount of empathy and understanding. You compassionately see that perfectionist thoughts and feelings are figments of your imagination and are better able to grasp the realities about yourself and your work.

# Having a conversation with your perfectionist inner critic

**Inner Critic:** You certainly did a terrible job on that report! You're so stupid and incompetent!

**High Achiever:** It sounds like you didn't like the report. What didn't you like about it?

**Inner Critic:** It stinks! It's disorganized, the grammar is awful, and it sounds dim-witted. It's got to be the worst report you've ever written!

**High Achiever:** You know, I really want to hear what you have to say, and I promise I'll deal with all your concerns. But please rephrase your criticism, and I don't want you to call me names and be disrespectful.

**Inner Critic:** I don't know how to do that!

**High Achiever:** I'm sure you can do it. Talk to me politely, and I'll listen to what you have to say. Okay?

**Inner Critic:** Okay. The report should be organized so that the history section comes first before everything else.

**High Achiever:** I understand. I agree that's a good idea. It will help my boss understand why we need to do the suggestions I put forth.

**Inner Critic:** And you keep spelling "your" like "you're." That needs to be corrected.

**High Achiever:** That's certainly easy to do.

**Inner Critic:** You need to add some sections to strengthen your suggestions. There's not enough in the report to convince your boss to make the changes that need to be made.

**High Achiever:** I'll reread it and see whether that's something that needs to be done. What do you think about me asking Matt to look it over also to see whether he can recommend additional sections?

**Inner Critic:** Good idea.

**High Achiever:** I think all these ideas will make the report better.

---

You also feel respect for yourself and appreciate your talents and skills. You know you can't do everything perfectly, but you celebrate what you can do well.

Don't say: "There's no way I'm going to be prepared for that talk I have to give on Thursday! Why in the world did I ever tell my boss I'd make that presentation about recycling opportunities? I'm such a bad employee! I'm going to make her look bad too! I better just tell her I'm too overwhelmed and bow out now so she can get someone else."

Rather, have compassion and understanding for yourself and say: "I need to cool down and have a rational talk with myself. I know I'm not prepared for the talk, but I have two hours this afternoon to prepare and some time tomorrow too. I'm a very smart person, and I just have to do a little research to get the information I need. Let's see — first, I'll search three other cities and see how they deal with recycling by businesses. Next, I'll create a matrix of pros and cons of our business recycling. Once I do that, I'll be able to analyze what will work and what won't. I think I'll call the City Recycling Office too in order to get their input. Actually, this won't be as hard as I thought it would be."

In addition, think of yourself as your own loving parent or wise teacher. Use the language you think those people would use with you. View yourself with care and understanding.

## *How you act*

As a high achiever, you act with confidence and poise. You accept responsibility for your actions. You take pride in at least trying to accomplish things. You're a very productive person.

You know you are capable of meeting life's challenges. In fact, you look forward to challenges because you know you have the skills to overcome any obstacles.

You associate with positive people, and you're in the process of becoming more positive and appreciative of others at the same time.

You focus on your past successes and are highly motivated to succeed. You now have the right attitude to succeed and you know you can.

You are in charge of your life. If things are not the way you want them to be, you ask yourself what you can do to tap into your creative side to alter what needs to be changed. You discover what can be done and make the necessary modifications.

Being willing to make the changes that are required is very important. This is the bridge between recognizing you have an issue with perfectionism and attempting to transform it. You also need to be willing to step back from yourself and observe your thoughts, feelings, and actions.

While willingness gets you started on the road to change, having a desire to change motivates you to change. When the going gets tough — when you want to revert back to your old, familiar, perfectionist self — your desire to keep going is what will carry you onward.

You create and attain goals in your life. As you do this, you take command of your life and control more of what happens to you.

You keep a constant focus on making the needed changes and make them a priority in your life. By doing this, you make them actually happen. You think about the new, more confident person you're becoming when you wake up, as you go throughout your day, as you evaluate what happens during the day, and as the last thing you think about at night.

You're happy and sure of yourself, and you have a passion for life.

In your notebook, write down each perfectionist tendency you want to transform. Next to it, write what to transform it into and when you will begin. Keep a log of how these changes are progressing, what victories you experience, which tendencies are more difficult to deal with, and suggestions for handling them in a healthier manner. After you've made these changes in your thoughts, feelings, and actions, you'll have a much more relaxed and even-tempered nature and greater inner peace. You'll be able to say that "almost perfect" is still a job very well done. You'll have a higher regard for yourself, and you'll be able to take much more pleasure in your work, your life, your relationships, and yourself.

# Part IV
# Growing Your Self-Esteem

| Accusations | Factors of Influence | Your Truths | The Truth |
|---|---|---|---|
| I'm good at what I do, but I won't get the promotion at my job. I'm not going to apply. | I don't have enough education.<br><br>Leadership doesn't like me.<br><br>It's about politics anyway.<br><br>I applied for another promotion and they gave it to someone less qualified. | You're making assumptions.<br><br>You're making excuses.<br><br>You're insecure.<br><br>You lack confidence.<br><br>You're thinking negatively.<br><br>A past experience is influencing your current decision. | If you are objective and honest, you have no hard evidence to confirm that any of what you're saying to yourself is true. |

# In this part . . .

- ✔ Uncover the mystery of who you are and develop your ability to hear your own voice.

- ✔ Find out how to stop dreadful worrying and take a leap of faith into possibility.

- ✔ Discover how to create intentional success through clarity of your mind and the understanding of your heart.

# Chapter 11

# Increasing Your Confidence through Self-Awareness

*T*he simplest questions are the hardest ones to answer. Who am I? Why am I here? What's important to me? What do I want? It seems the moment you think you have the answer, you ask yourself again and find yourself once more in a place of bewilderment.

Is it a mistaken belief that you'll ever have answers to these complex questions? We believe they have ever-evolving answers. That when you fearlessly embrace your answers to the questions, life presents you with experiences that confirm your truth and opportunities to grow beyond them.

As you increase your self-awareness, you build the capacity to accept more of your own brilliance. The understanding of how incredible you are is what increases your confidence.

In this chapter, we help you uncover the mystery of who you are. You develop your ability to hear your own voice. Your heart strengthens, giving you the courage to answer. You break through your tendency to believe others more than you believe yourself.

## Getting to Know You

You'll be with yourself for a lifetime. Nothing is going to change that fact. Getting to know, like, listen to, and appreciate yourself is crucial for your sanity. Perhaps getting to the point of loving, accepting, and embracing all of who you are is difficult for you to imagine right now, but if you're open to it, we can help you.

I (coauthor S. Renee) was my own first client. I had to get through and beyond my own craziness and self-doubt. I still have moments when I have to sit myself down and have an executive session. That's why I know you're beyond your experiences. Your greatness runs deeper than your pain. You're mightier than your disappointments. There's a genius buried beneath it all.

## Discovering what you're capable of

You're capable of achieving whatever you want. Does that sound far-fetched? Here's proof. Is there anything in your life that you have now that you didn't have before? What is it? Your "it" could be your job, your home, or family. Your "it" could be the confidence to say how your feel without reservation or the ability to change a tire. Think freely because your "it" is anything that you once thought was impossible for you to have.

Before you had it, it seemed unlikely to happen, right? Now that you have it, it seems it has always been a part of you. It has. It was in you as a thought, an idea, a possibility. Whether deliberately or not, you miraculously did the work that led to its creation. In case you don't remember, this is what you did, which is why we know you're capable of producing anything you want. You just have to do it again.

1. **You decided what you wanted to do.**

   It may have been a thought. Maybe you told a friend that someday you wanted to do it. Perhaps it's so outrageously awesome that you're still in the midst of creating it. Regardless, at some point, you claimed it as your own.

2. **You believed in yourself.**

   Your faith set your feet in motion. You didn't commit time and energy because you thought you would fail. You invested so much of yourself because you believed, maybe ever so slightly, that you would produce the desired results.

3. **You faced criticism.**

   There were people who didn't understand what you were doing or why you were doing it. Some even told you that you were wasting your time. You rose above the criticism and reaped the benefits of doing so.

4. **You overcame obstacles.**

   You faced problems along the way, but you solved them. You walked, climbed, or crawled around the ones you couldn't solve.

5. **You dedicated yourself.**

   It takes effort to succeed. You can't always see how you're going to get there. You may not have understood why certain people or situations came into your life. Despite your uncertainty, you remained dedicated to what you wanted. As a consequence, you got it.

You don't need us to tell you what you're capable of. Time after time, you've proven to yourself how extremely capable you are of getting what you want. Don't stop now. Do what you've done to get what you want.

## Appreciating the good, the bad — and the ugly

Self-esteem comes from within, but it's built on a succession of successes. Success supports your self-esteem development because it says, "Life and people accept me. This feels good."

But what happens when you're in the trenches working toward your success? When no one knows your name and no one cares, you're invisible. This feels bad.

And what do you do when you've built a name for yourself but life still disappoints you? You're highly respected in your job and community. You've worked hard and made many sacrifices to rise to a high level of success. But secretly, you've been battling with private challenges and now your life is falling apart. Divorce, disease, or death snatches you from success and drops you off at the doorstep of devastation. This feels ugly.

The good, the bad, and the ugly are natural changes in everyone's life cycle. Although the good is preferred over the bad and the ugly, each one comes bearing a gift of truth and transformation.

Designed to give you a makeover, the good gives you the opportunity to see the positive impact of your contributions. The bad offers you the opportunity to expand your thinking and find creative ways to face and overcome adversity. The ugly creates suffering, which produces compassion, bringing you closer to yourself and others.

When you learn to appreciate every phase of your life and what it's teaching you, you build a sustainable model for maintaining positive self-esteem.

## Believing in yourself

"Believe in yourself" is the advice everyone in the field of self-development seems to offer for the attainment of success. But what does it really mean to believe in yourself? How do you feel when you believe in yourself? We believe that believing in yourself is trusting yourself with yourself. Just as a marriage represents the entrusting of one person's life to another person, you are two people struggling to operate as one.

## Deep wounds

I (coauthor S. Renee) met a man I'll call Connor during a self-image development workshop. Connor was brutally teased as a child and into his teenage years. At age 16, he attempted suicide. By age 22, he had plastic surgery to "remove the face that caused him so much grief." By changing his looks, he thought he would heal the wounds that deeply disturbed him.

I met him when he was in his early 40s. During the workshop, I presented *The Rock*. He started to cry.

*The Rock* is a visual presentation. I hold up a rock and tell my audience that this is them when they're born — beautiful, brilliant, and whole.

I put the rock in a jar and say, "This represents your body."

I pick up another jar that is full of dirt and say, "There were things that happened in your lives that covered who you really are."

I continue, "When you were a little boy or little girl and your mother said, 'Shut up. Sit down. Get out of my face. I wish you were never born,' you began to get covered by the filth and pain of others."

As I narrate hypothetical, but likely, experiences, the audience watches intently as I pause after each statement and pour dirt over the rock until it's completely covered.

Then I ask, "What has you covered?"

Unable to contain his emotions and new awareness, Connor shared his story. He credits that workshop with changing his life. He has since written a book and launched his own business. He continues to grow, but still battles with feelings of unworthiness. Perhaps one day his deep wounds will be healed by the love he already possesses.

There's the real you and there's your representative. The real you is buried beneath all the experiences that shape the personality and behavior of your representative. You can't trust or believe in your representative because he is inauthentic and you know it. Hence the reason you feel guilt. Deep inside you know you're better than that, whatever "that" is for you.

In Chapters 3 and 5, respectively, we encourage you to process past negative experiences and affirm yourself to create a new mindset. Through this process, you see that nothing you've experienced is worthless. As a result of looking at your life with a new perspective, you expand your love for yourself and others.

As you become more highly evolved and live your new truth, we want you to begin to measure your growth. By doing so, you can identify things that still challenge and hinder you from walking bravely into your life's purpose.

There will be situations that you'll think you've dealt with, but that you later realize require more attention and different skill sets. Don't be disturbed by that. Your self-esteem grows and changes over time. Therefore, it requires different tools to help you best support yourself in that growth.

Some people can heal their wounds through acknowledgement, forgiveness, affirmation, and a shift in their personal belief system. Others are so deeply wounded that after completing that process, they need more. What is the more?

Connor, the subject of the sidebar "Deep wounds," acknowledged his issues with self-esteem. He forgave the people who impacted his life. He affirmed who he was and changed his beliefs about what he is capable of. He even began moving his life in a new direction.

But, like many people who continue to struggle after completing the first part of self-esteem development, Connor has to let go of resentment. You can forgive a person, yet still feel bitter toward them and about your life experience. The second stage of self-esteem development is becoming aware of the internal issues that are still blocking you. We discuss this in Chapter 14.

A shift in your thinking is essential to move you forward. Accomplishing goals builds your confidence, but how you see, think, and feel about yourself, others, and your life's journey stabilizes and sustains you. At the core of the second phase of self-esteem development is learning how to operate from a place of abundance versus lack. This is applicable to everyone, regardless of who you are. Everyone has something nagging at him that he needs to come to terms with. Learning to reach and operate from your highest self is a life-long journey.

Here are a few suggestions to help you manage old wounds and keep new ones at a minimum:

- **Believe in something greater than yourself.** Statistics show and recent newspaper and magazine articles and television segments confirm that people who are religious or spiritual or choose to meditate feel better about themselves. They also have greater control over negative feelings and are better able to process past experiences and current challenges.

- **Perform daily evaluations.** Take a few moments every day to reflect on your day. Celebrate yourself in the areas where you did well. Spend a few moments reflecting on what you did that was out of alignment with the real you. Try to identify what you did and why you did it. Put together a game plan for how you'll show up when a similar situation arises.

- **Become an astute student and teacher for yourself.** When you know, love, and accept yourself, the real you comes forward and directs your life. You began to operate as one — you and your higher self instead of you and your representative. You'll never be perfect, but you'll be in alignment with truth and you'll be gutsy enough to live it.

- **Renew your mind.** Your life is not one seamless line. There are bends, curves, dead ends, accidents, and breakdowns. Don't crash and burn. Don't start off every day where you left off the day before. Start fresh with an optimistic, confident perspective. Smile and say to yourself, "I got this."

## Closer than you think

I (coauthor S. Renee) had been a model and actress for ten years. Since I was a young girl, I'd had a secret desire to be a television talk-show host. Although insignificant, I had some experience in co-hosting television programs.

Despite my minor experience in the industry, I put together a television demo and headed for Philadelphia, the fourth-largest market in the United States. Every television station I called granted me an interview. Unfortunately, after looking at my demo, their responses weren't as promising as their enthusiastic welcomes. I consistently heard, "You look good. You sound great. Get experience in a smaller market and come back to see us."

I thought I was out of options until one day while flipping through television channels, I stopped at a station unknown to me. The host

was talking and instantly something said to me, "You'll host that show."

I waited until the show was over to watch the credits. I wrote down the name of the executive producer and called the station. She took my call, and asked me to send in my demo. I followed up a few times, but she didn't make any promises.

Three months after my initial call, my phone rang and she invited me to audition for a street reporter's position. Within an hour of arriving back home I received a call with an offer to host and produce the show and to be the spokesperson for the United Paramount Network (UPN-Philadelphia) station.

To further assist you, you can find additional information and exercises on how to manage internal conflict in Chapter 14.

# Listening to Yourself

How many times after you've missed an opportunity, made a mistake, or gotten exactly what you wanted have you said, "I knew that was going to happen?" Sometimes you listen and respond and sometimes you don't. Imagine for a moment what your life could be like if you discovered how to listen and respond more frequently to your voice, gut, instinct, feeling, intuition, or God.

The title you give it doesn't matter. The gift of knowing allows you to more confidently express your preferences and live in your own power. Because you're unique in design, how you receive messages is exclusive to your personality.

You can receive a message anywhere and at any time. The ways are countless. Some include sitting silently, reading a book, talking to another person, listening to a song, watching television, clicking a link on the Internet to read an article, or walking in a park.

# Recognizing the sound of your own voice

You're bombarded with messages and voices daily. They never stop. Even while you're asleep, you're receiving messages through dreaming. Living in a complex, hasty society that's always telling you what you want, what your options are, and how you should feel, it's difficult to know what you like, think, or want to do in a situation. Despite the chaos, you can learn how to know, hear, listen to, and respond to your own voice.

- **Know how you receive messages.** You can receive messages in different ways at different times. You're likely more in tune with one way of receiving messages than others. You may hear a voice, have a feeling, see an image, dream a dream, or have a "this is common sense" moment.

- **Know what you're asking for.** It's important to slow down and be aware of what question you're asking. By being aware of the question, you'll know when the answer shows up.

- **Be on the lookout for the answer.** You'll get internal promptings when you see, hear, or feel the answer that's right for you. It may be a sensation in the belly, goose bumps on the arms, a warm feeling in your body, or an "Ah! That's it" moment.

- **Listen to what's right.** Some things are obvious. You already know right from wrong. Your voice is always trying to tell you to do the right thing.

- **Consider past experiences.** Life has taught you many lessons. Take them into consideration, but never let a past experience override a gut feeling telling you should try something again.

  For example, say you're looking for a job. You've called once and the person told you not to call again. You get a nudge to call. Don't let the past dictate your choice — make the call. However, if your child is running in the house, use past lessons, yours or others', as an indicator for your current choice. Tell your child to stop running.

- **Use common sense.** You know the answer, but you want easier, faster results. Don't let being lazy override getting the task at hand done the right way.

- **Trust when you're getting the same message.** There are times when you have to make a decision that'll change the course of your life. Trust what you're repeatedly saying to yourself and don't turn around because you don't get immediate results.

- **Realize that you're still right even if things go wrong.** Success according to society's standards doesn't mean you took the wrong path. Through your decisions, you're creating what you need for your journey. You can psych yourself out by convincing yourself that the other option would've been better, but you'll never know that. When you follow your gut, you're on the right track.

### Trusting yourself with your own life

Any doubt you have in trusting yourself stems from your track record of making bad decisions. The more bad decisions you've made, the harder it is to trust yourself. You don't feel equipped to make decisions to move your life forward.

It's likely you were never taught how to make good decisions. By learning how to make good decisions and establishing the habit of doing so now, you'll gradually build credibility with yourself to be a trusted resource for yourself.

We know you have dreams that, if you trust yourself and pursue them, will move you beyond where you are today. Give yourself a chance and trust that you're serious about changing how you make decisions.

Doing so requires a new level of commitment to yourself — a promise to love yourself regardless of what state you may find yourself in, whether you're rich or poor, moving straight ahead or being pushed four steps back, healthy or sick, happy or sad, on point or out of alignment. No matter what you learn about yourself that may shock or alarm you, be patient and kind toward yourself, trusting that you'll figure out what you need to know.

Here are eight questions to ask yourself before making a decision. They'll increase your trust in yourself when you thoroughly and honestly think about your responses and decide accordingly.

✔ What am I trying to create?

✔ Am I clear on the decision being made?

✔ Have I considered all available choices?

✔ Do I need to seek wise counsel?

✔ Who else besides me will feel the direct impact of my decision?

✔ How will it impact them?

✔ Based on my decision, what will my life look like on the other side?

✔ Is the decision in alignment with integrity?

### Shifting from criticism to self-care

Criticism comes from a place within yourself of unacknowledged shame, guilt, and anger. It causes senseless pain and often creates negative relationships. To begin understanding why you criticize and how to give yourself the care you need — in order to stop being overly critical — ask yourself the following questions:

✔ **Who am I criticizing?** The same eyes I use to look at others, I use to look at myself. Why is this person or group of people the target of my criticism? What did they do or not do to me? Was the error deliberately directed at me?

✔ **What am I criticizing them for?** Whatever bothers me about them likely bothers me about myself. What's at the core of my frustration? What feelings are associated with my frustration? Why is the behavior offensive?

✔ **What do I need that I'm not getting?** Criticism is an action that results from hunger. Perhaps I need attention, acceptance, recognition, or an understanding of where I fit within community.

---

# Senseless pain

I (coauthor S. Renee) had a client I'll call Cheryl. Cheryl called my office because she was on a soul-searching journey. She wanted to understand why she was the target of people's negative emotions and anger.

Cheryl believed her supervisor, colleagues, family, and church friends were all targeting her. If her supervisor walked past her office door, she assumed he thought she was being inefficient at her job. The eldest in the office at 42 years old, she thought her younger colleagues talked about her behind her back and laughed at how she dressed.

According to her, her siblings hated her because she was the youngest and their mother's favorite. Whenever she was in meetings at the office or in church, she felt that people wished she would stop talking because she always expressed her ideas.

Convinced this was not true, I gave her an assignment. She could not think for, judge, or draw conclusions about others for one week. She had to jot down what she was telling herself about herself. This is what she discovered: She was accusing others of what she was saying about herself.

Her supervisor had never given her a bad review in her ten years of working for him. He walked past her office simply to get to his. She was comparing herself to her younger colleagues, thinking they were doing the same. This justified in her mind her right to conceal information from her colleagues to solidify her position in the company.

Her siblings didn't hate her and she wasn't her mother's favorite. At 41 years old when Cheryl was born, Cheryl's mother had been a different person — more patient and loving with a better understanding of herself — than when her eldest child had been born 20 years earlier.

The lack of relationship with her siblings was a result of their being much older and out of the house when she was born. She noticed that when she spoke up in meetings, people were engaged and seemed to appreciate her sharing.

It's not uncommon for your pain to rule your life and for you to be totally unaware that it is. You are not a victim. You are a powerful and wonderfully created human being. Being the victim is surrendering your power to others. Although most often done unconsciously, it is a cowardly act that manifests itself as accusing others of doing something to you. This allows you to create a story that justifies your feelings, but it only hinders you from healing.

## Meeting life's challenges

Like a movie, you have a script. In your life, there are flawed, interesting characters with dynamic lives. There are events, lessons, and an audience. Through your words, thoughts, and behaviors, you've been writing, creating, and living your script. You didn't purposely script your life for failure; you were created for success, and you know it.

By not knowing your power and abilities, you may have drifted from the original storyline. That's why it's dangerous to be unaware of what you need to know to meet life's challenges daily.

You've learned by now that life doesn't always happen the way you expect it to. Your dreams can be crushed; you may have to breathe life back into them. Your trust and faith in family and friends can be violated; you may have to choose to rebuild or seek new relationships. Expectations for a great future with a loved one may take a nose-dive; you may have to learn to trust and love again.

Knowing that life can change in an instant — that some things are completely out of your control — is heart-wrenching. But that's what makes life fascinating. It's full of surprises because you don't know exactly what'll happen or when, but you most certainly know that it can happen. Accepting this is living in the real world of possibility.

Meeting life's challenges takes preparation. You need weapons of war to help you successfully transcend difficult moments. Expand your weaponry and sharpen the tools you already have by incorporating the following list of 21 must-haves to meet life's challenges:

- ✔ **Attitude:** Develop an attitude that sustains rather than destroys you. It's not what happens that matters, but how you see and handle it.

- ✔ **Awareness:** Pay attention to your life and the lessons it's teaching you. You're being prepared for what's next. Be present and connected to your internal power.

- ✔ **Compassion:** Being kind and understanding with yourself and others reaps a great return on your investment.

- ✔ **Confidence:** Know that what you're telling yourself is true despite what anyone else says.

- ✔ **Courage:** You're born with it. You can't do anything without it. Tap into it.

- ✔ **Creativity:** Add your unique twist to everything you do.

- ✔ **Faith:** Believe that what you desire will happen.

- ✔ **Focus:** Keep your eyes on your target, not the trivial issues that come up along the way to derail you.

✔ **Forgiveness:** People are going to get on your nerves. You'll even do things that will require you to forgive yourself. Forgive and move on.

✔ **Instinct:** Follow your gut; it'll never lead you wrong.

✔ **Integrity:** Live values that honor, respect, and celebrate you and others.

✔ **Listening:** Everyone doesn't think like you do. Listening helps you to understand and respond better in complex situations.

✔ **Love:** When everything else fails, love sticks around. Have plenty of it for yourself and others.

✔ **Message:** Be clear and consistent on the message you want to convey to the world.

✔ **Mission:** Understand what you're on the planet to do, and do it.

✔ **Openness:** Be open to discovering new things and be ready to take advantage of opportunities that come from unexpected places.

✔ **People:** Invite people into your life who flow with you, not against you. That doesn't mean they won't challenge you to be your best.

✔ **Persistence:** Keep working toward your goal until you achieve it.

✔ **Skills:** Keep sharpening yourself personally, professionally, and spiritually.

✔ **Vision:** Have an idea for a better world that others want to follow.

This list is not exhaustive. We encourage you to add to the list or create your own. Seeing what you have and what you need helps you best prepare for life's challenging moments.

## *Making important decisions*

Every day when you pick up the newspaper, watch a report on television, or read an update on social media, you become the witness to a good or not-so-good decision. Decision-making isn't new. You make thousands of decisions daily. You already have a model for decision-making. The question is this: Are your decisions leading you to the results you want?

If you're like most people, you weren't taught how to make decisions. As you matured, you were given permission to make decisions on your own.

Here's the problem with most decision-making: Decisions are often made based on short-term gratification rather than long-term success. Woven into short-term gratification are low self-esteem, pint-size expectations, past pain, and disappointment from unmet goals. Additionally, society, friends, and current circumstances influence the paths you choose to take.

Although you can't reverse a decision, you can change its direction. You do so by making another decision. Perhaps you never thought of it this way, but decisions should be strategic. The purpose of a strategy is to guide a project through a process to successful completion. Understanding that opposition can hinder the process, you consider various scenarios and solutions ahead of time to avoid failure or derailment.

Your decisions determine the satisfaction of your desires. Evaluate what's in your life that your fears and insecurities are holding onto.

Do you have a vision and mission for your life? Do you have goals you want to achieve before you depart from the planet? Read the following steps on how to make strategic decisions. Visit Chapters 13 and 18 to help you develop your mission, message, and goals.

Apply these steps to your strategic decision-making plan to help guide you as you move toward your goals:

1. **Have a vision and mission.**

   Your decisions are leading you somewhere. Your vision and mission should guide your decisions so that you can get there.

2. **Decide what you want in your life.**

   You get to decide what your life will look like today and 20-plus years from now. Here are some questions to help you become more attentive to what's important to you:

   - Who am I going to be in the world?

   - What kind of people do I want to be part of my life?

   - How do I want people to respond to me?

   - What will cause people to respond that way?

   - What impact will I make?

   - How will I make it?

   - Will I get married?

   - Will I have children?

   - What is an absolute "no" for me?

   - How will I handle the absolute "no's" when they're presented to me?

3. **Forecast distractions.**

   Some situations can distract you and get you off course. Think about what they may be and how you want to respond to them. Distractions can be your own thinking, people, situations, or opportunities.

**4. Evaluate partnerships.**

If you're in personal and professional partnerships, check to insure that your values and goals are in alignment with your partner's.

# Developing the Right Attitude

The contract read: "I agree to create and present a six-month program that will create paradigm shifts in 120 employees. It will be designed to improve self-images, attitudes, decision-making skills, and abilities to resolve conflict."

It was my (coauthor S. Renee's) first time standing before entry-level employees who had every reason to believe that life had dealt them a raw deal — and they knew it. A rah-rah speech about how 85 percent of success was attitude and 15 percent was skills and knowledge wasn't going to go over with this group — and I knew it.

Wanting them to see that attitude isn't just a thought but a state of ownership, I presented this perspective on attitude: "Your attitude is your preferences based on your likes and dislikes." Puzzled by this unexpected demonstration of attitude, the room began to buzz. "Let's assess this philosophy," I proclaimed.

If you like something, you form a positive perspective, right? If you dislike something, you form a neutral or negative perspective, correct? Your approach to people and situations is based on your experiences, and this is how your attitude is shaped. Your attitude is the conclusion of what you think something is or isn't.

If you want to change your attitude, you simply choose "yes" when you've always said "no," or vice-versa. Here are a few questions to help you to examine your attitude:

- ✔ Describe your attitude.

- ✔ What experiences make up your attitude?

- ✔ Would you rate your attitude as positive or negative?

- ✔ Do you have more likes or dislikes?

- ✔ Are your likes and dislikes valid?

- ✔ Do your likes help or hinder you from advancing in life?

- ✔ Do your dislikes help or hinder you from advancing in your life?

- ✔ If you were to say "yes" to what you're currently saying "no" to, how would your life change?

- ✔ If you were to say "no" to what you're currently saying "yes" to, how would your life change?

There will be times when maintaining a positive attitude isn't easy. In this section, we help you develop an attitude that will sustain you during good and challenging times.

## *Expanding your mindset*

Have you ever had "that" moment when you don't like your life? You don't know exactly what you want to do about it or what would make you happy, but you know you don't like your life as it is today.

It's easy to have a great attitude when things are going just the way you want them to. But maintaining passion, enthusiasm, and confidence when disruption, commotion, and misfortune come demands an expansion of your mindset.

Before developing plans to expand your mind through external avenues, start the development process from within. Follow these steps to assess your thinking:

1. **Observe what you're thinking.**

   Stop doing and start observing. By taking notice of your thoughts, you can determine whether a person, situation, or mood swing is creating the noise.

2. **Check-in with yourself.**

   Ask yourself, "What am I feeling?" Emotions are transient and thoughts can be relentless. They constantly scream for your attention. Are you suffering because of an unresolved hurt, problem, or current disappointment? Is it hormonal? Know what's going on with you.

3. **Identify the why.**

   Ask, "Why am I feeling what I feel?"

4. **Consider possibility.**

   You may not know that other options exist, but if you're open, one will show up.

5. **Make a decision.**

   Don't tuck your negative feelings away. Decide what you're going to do with your findings to resolve what's troubling you. The solution will create the expansion.

Here are some things that you can do externally to expand your mindset:

✔ **Read.** Reading introduces you to different experiences than your own. It helps you to see that there other possibilities. It uplifts and inspires you to do new things.

✔ **Be around positive people.** Being around people who have a positive view of life and are moving in the direction you want to go stretches you.

✔ **Choose your friends wisely.** Having diverse people in your life naturally opens your mind to a more expansive view of life.

✔ **Find ways to do what you love.** Doing what you love attracts more opportunities for you to grow.

✔ **Change how you respond to situations.** Challenge yourself to respond in a way that more accurately showcases who you are.

## Coming out of the box

Leaving your comfort zone isn't easy, but once you do, you find out that what you thought was your comfort zone was actually a holding cell. You were imprisoned by your own thoughts and perceptions of reality. Coming out of the box requires evaluating your current mindset.

I (coauthor S. Renee) have a presentation called "Come Out of the Box." I ask for a volunteer from the audience, who is asked to get into a cardboard box. While closing the box, I tell the audience, "This is how you exist in your mind; being alone in darkness with your perceived notions as to what life can be and what you can become." Once the box is closed, I continue, "How do you think she feels in that box?"

Imagine yourself in that box and follow the steps to identify what you need to get out of the box:

1. **Review the following list of adjectives and consider how well they relate to your own feelings.**

   Can you relate to any of them? If not, identify your own adjectives to describe the way you feel.

   - Lonely

   - Unappreciated

   - Invisible

   - Isolated

   - Silenced

   - Hopeless

   - Scared

   - Rejected

   - Depressed

- Angry

- Stifled

- Other

2. **State why you feel the way you do.**

3. **Identify what is keeping you in the box.**

   Consider which of the following factors apply. Feel free to add your own insights to the list.

   - False beliefs, perceptions

   - Negative emotions

   - Lack of information

   - Choice of friends

   - Lack of vision

   - Thoughts

   - Lack of understanding

   - Other

4. **What are you missing by being in the box?**

   The following list suggests some possibilities. Add your own thoughts as you see fit.

   - Personal balance

   - Professional advancement

   - Authentic freedom

   - Better relationships

   - Increased income opportunities

   - Other

5. **What will help you get and stay out of the box?**

   Consider the following suggestions and feel free to add your own thoughts as well.

   - Shift in beliefs

   - Goals

   - Different decisions

   - New relationships

   - New information

   - Other

## *Understanding that things may not be what you think they are*

Have you ever seen someone and thought that person was someone you knew? Maybe you called the person's name, he turned around, and once you looked at him again, it was clear that he wasn't who you thought he was. You apologized, and as you walked away you kept saying to yourself, "That looked just like. . . . "

That was an honest mistake, right? Isn't it easy to look at words, numbers, people, or situations and think you see certain things when, in fact, they're not what you think they are?

Is there any possibility that you may have mistaken your own identity? Could you be more powerful than you think you are? Are the obstacles you see really there?

Whatever is happening in your life right now that's annoying, confusing, or concerning you, it wants you to discover more of who you really are. You can't do that if you're having difficulty distinguishing the difference between what's real and what's perceived.

Start getting clear by answering the following questions:

- ✔ What is keeping you from you?
- ✔ Is what's blocking you from knowing the truth of who you are real or your perception?
- ✔ What's really stopping you?

## *Rewiring your thought patterns*

Like a computer, your mind stores files of information. Every experience is documented and stored in your mental file cabinet and emotional drive. When you see something similar to what you've experienced, you return to your mental file cabinet, search for the file, locate it, read it, and apply what you've previously learned to the current situation.

Prior experiences tell you how to think and determine what emotions will drive your reaction in a given situation. No file is ever deleted unless you choose to do so. Deleting files takes work and time. Sticking to your story of being the victim is easier and safer than seeking new answers and standing in your own power.

Understand this: You no longer need certain information because you have grown beyond its use. By letting go of the past and increasing your self-esteem, you build the capacity to handle and respond to situations differently — even if you don't realize it yet.

Rewire your thought patterns by creating thoughts that will support the new you. Believe all the good things you discover about yourself through this process. Trust what you're learning by using it. Continue to apply the information in your life daily. Chronicle your success and keep growing.

It's important to know whether you're living in your new truth or still hanging out with old habits. You may not be conscious of what you're doing, so observe yourself over the next week and use the following questions to help you determine where you are:

- ✔ Am I continuing to hold onto past experiences because they validate me, support the files I have stored in my mind, and give me permission to stick to the story of being the victim?

- ✔ Do the old and new messages cause confusion? If so, why? Which one needs to be deleted?

- ✔ Am I using new tools to help me operate differently? If not, why? What success am I seeing as a result of using these tools?

- ✔ Am I stretching myself by meeting people who are moving in the direction that I want to go? Am I making plans to pursue a dream opportunity or enroll in a class that will better prepare me for my future?

# Taking Charge of Your Life

I (coauthor S. Renee) had a client who wanted to get married. Her partner did not. Over a year, they talked about marriage over 20 times. Neither moved from their position. Exasperated by his steadfast position but not seeing her own, she began to search for answers. After I listened to her criticize and condemn his posture for 20 minutes, she declared, "I just don't know what to do."

Amidst the silence, I asked, "What do you want?"

She said, "I want to get married and have an honorable relationship."

I responded, "Is he willing to give that to you?"

She said, "No."

I replied, "You have two options. Accept what he's willing to give you or let him go so that he can get what he wants and you can get what you want."

How many times have you given your power away? You give your power away when you leave it up to another person to make a decision for you. Taking charge of your life is simple: Own your space. It's yours. You decide what comes in, what goes out, and what sticks around. Never let someone else decide for you how your life will look, feel, or be.

## Believing in your dreams

Can you recall ever hearing a person say, "She has it" or "He has it"? No one could tell you what the "it" was, but you knew it was something special. That person was marked for success. You may never have been told this, but we're saying it now: "You have it!" How do we know? Everyone has it.

Some people have it in different degrees, while others spend more time developing it, but that doesn't diminish the "it" that is within you. The "it" is the courage you have within that affirms "I am willing to fall knowing that I have the power within me to get back up."

Dream believers and creators know and live by the following:

✔ **Pursue what you want.** You can't sit on the sidelines and wait for it to happen.

✔ **Take one step at a time.** Dreams don't come true overnight. You have to be willing to be patient and watch them unfold.

✔ **Mistakes are inevitable.** You'll make mistakes that you'll later see were miracles. Don't go dim because of them.

✔ **You need help.** You can't do it alone. Embrace people and people will embrace you.

✔ **Stay focused.** You'll be presented with a lot of distractions that will cause you to question, get upset, and want to quit. Don't take your eyes off the target.

## Facing new changes

At the dawn of each day you don't know what you'll face. Instead of being a continuum of the day before, each day is packed with new, unexpected wonders. Life fluctuates, modifies itself, and transforms the lives of its participants.

Face it: Life gets turbulent sometimes and downright hard at other times. Don't let these uncertainties stop you from waking up, getting out of bed, and giving it your best shot every day.

Continue to courageously embrace your journey. Here are a few tips to support you:

- ✔ **Embrace change.** Whenever you resist what is, you create friction. Graciously and thankfully accepting what you can't change will help you get through it.

- ✔ **Have faith.** Life is a cycle of the good, the bad, and the ugly. You'll never stay in any phase forever.

- ✔ **Become aware.** By successfully navigating change, you'll see that you are more powerful than you ever imagined.

# Chapter 12

# Moving Beyond the Fear That's Zapping Your Faith

· · · · · · · · · · · · · · · · · · · · · · · · · · · · · · · · · · · · · · · · · · · · · · · · · ·

## In This Chapter

▶ Getting the facts about fear and figuring out how to face it

▶ Finding the faith to deal with your fears

▶ Coordinating your thoughts, words, and actions

· · · · · · · · · · · · · · · · · · · · · · · · · · · · · · · · · · · · · · · · · · · · · · · · · ·

*Y*ou may as well face it: Putting yourself out there can be scary. Just the thought of responding to your heart's tug to live your dreams can create anxiety and questions, whose unknown answers are enough to stop you dead in your tracks. Will I fail? Am I wasting my time? Will people like me? Am I ready?

You can't know the answers to these questions until you take a step into the unknown. Are you willing to do that? If you're not ready yet, don't fret. That's what this chapter is about — facing your fears and growing your faith.

In this chapter, you figure out how to stop dreadful worrying and take a leap of faith into possibility. You discover that you have more faith than you ever imagined and that it'll support you moving forward. You see that winning is within your grasp.

## Using Fear to Help You Grow

There's only one way to grow from fear: You have to step into it. Attempting to avoid fear is like trying to walk through the rain without getting wet. It's impossible.

Do you recall the first time you were fearful? Was it the first day of school? Or your first speaking engagement? Did it creep up on you during your first date? Fear is a frightening thought that you chase away by consciously acting on what's intimidating you.

Even though you've confronted the monstrous emotion before and proven its powerlessness, fear can still cause you to hesitate to act on something you desire because it makes you feel unsure of yourself. It can also come in the form of a message or an intuitive feeling that you shouldn't act on something.

In this section, we focus on this frightening thought that paralyzes you from moving your life's agenda forward. First, we help you to understand fear and where it comes from. Then, we show you how to use fear to your benefit.

Respond to the following questions to get better acquainted with how you deal with fear:

- When was the first time you felt fear?
- How did you deal with it?
- What did you learn from stepping into fear? Or not stepping into fear?
- What would you like to do today that you're not doing because of fear?
- What's stopping you from stepping into it?

## Understanding fear and where it comes from

You've likely heard that fear is an illusion, a deceptive tactic of an internal enemy trying to stop you from accomplishing your purpose. We don't want to insult you by telling you that what you believe isn't true, because whatever you believe is true for you.

Because fear appears at different times in your life and for different reasons, we want to help you develop the tools to identify where it comes from so you can gain an understanding of how to best deal with it.

You don't overcome fear by targeting fear. You feel fear because of what you believe will happen. Fear is a manifested emotion that consistently reappears to challenge you to overcome your internal issues, embrace yourself more fully, and move you closer to your life purpose. At times, you'll have to learn a quick strategy to outwit it until you have the time to go within and identify the core of what's making you feel fearful. In the meantime, through consciousness and practice, you can develop your own best tactics to use fear to your advantage.

This bombshell may puzzle you, but don't let it. It's simple; fear is the result of a deeper concern. It seems like fear is the problem because it's what bubbles to the top. Therefore, it's blamed for many false starts, abrupt stops, and unending delays.

## Fear of rejection

He was among my (coauthor S. Renee's) first clients. I'll call him Alvin. Alvin came to me in a state of confusion. He was living in two worlds and couldn't decide which world he wanted to commit to. He was bisexual — unbeknown to his girlfriend and lover, he was actively sleeping with both.

According to Alvin, he was entangled in a web of lies and deceit because he feared rejection from family and friends. If they discovered his secret passion for men, he thought they'd disown him. Alvin shared that his initial attraction to males had started while in elementary school, but he had never given in to his impulses. He had acted on his unspoken desires when his manager at his corporate job began flirting with him and expressed an interest in pursuing a relationship.

He came to me because he wanted to live his life as a gay man but didn't know how to tell his girlfriend and, most of all, feared being rejected by his mother whom he loved deeply. For months, Alvin and I met to discuss a plan to transition his life from deception to genuine truth and trust for the safety of himself and others.

Alvin reported that his girlfriend had suspected something wasn't right all along. Although hurt, she willingly accepted his apology and moved on. At the time his mother wasn't so gracious. But despite being shocked and disappointed, she eventually told him he had the right to be happy and that she loved him. As part of his transition plan, Alvin accepted a corporate position in a large city where he felt he could find acceptance, support, and peace with his decision to live his life as a gay man.

You never know how someone else will respond to your truth and you can't control that. When you find the courage to live life with integrity, you open up a safe place to trust yourself. As you grow into yourself and mature, you discover that your past truth isn't your current reality. At that point, grant yourself permission to choose another truth.

It's accused of destroying dreams, ruining well-practiced presentations, and terminating relationships. For example, suppose you fear public speaking. At the root of your fear is being accepted by the audience or fear of making a mistake. At the root of both of these concerns is confidence. Why aren't you confident? This book is being written to help you uncover the answer to that question.

Many concerns can drive fear — insecurities, past bad experiences, lack of information, undiscovered personal power, and imposed teachings. Many emotions can be found at the core of fear. But beneath every emotion that stops you from taking action is mistrust. *You don't trust yourself.*

Mistrust exists for many reasons, such as past letdowns, decisions that seem valueless, lack of experience, deception, and mistreatment from others. Also, you may never have been exposed to the importance of growing self-trust. These are just a few examples; you have your own reasons for not trusting yourself.

The bottom line is this: Fear wins when you feel incapable of creating a safe place to feel good about yourself after an attempt to live your desires, regardless of the outcome. It doesn't matter whether the attempt involves a love relationship, business idea, job promotion, or telling a friend you don't like how you're being treated. Fear is a self-inflicted wound that takes control of your life when you can't reassure yourself that — regardless of what's on the other side — you're going to be okay.

## Uncovering your core fears

The key to the mystery is the answers to questions that perhaps you have yet to ask:

- ✔ What do you fear?

- ✔ Why do you fear it?

- ✔ Do you trust yourself? Why or why not?

- ✔ What do you think you're incapable of doing or becoming?

- ✔ Do you want something to happen but fear the outcome? What is it?

- ✔ What's at the core of your fear? For example, is it past experience, lack of information, rejection, or uncertainty?

- ✔ Will you be okay if the outcome is different from what you expect? How can you reassure yourself of that?

Here's an exercise to help you face and move beyond your fears. You have a barometer that measures your truth. The truth is often funneled through your fears and emotional insecurities. Examine the following sample. Notice that the person wants to apply for a promotion at his job, but gives fear-based reasons for why he won't get the promotion. Beneath the fear are lies that he tells himself to justify his position. The result is self-stagnation.

| Accusations | Factors of Influence | Your Truths | The Truth |
|---|---|---|---|
| I'm good at what I do, but I won't get the promotion at my job. I'm not going to apply. | I don't have enough education.<br><br>Leadership doesn't like me.<br><br>It's about politics anyway.<br><br>I applied for another promotion and they gave it to someone less qualified. | You're making assumptions.<br><br>You're making excuses.<br><br>You're insecure. You lack confidence.<br><br>You're thinking negatively.<br><br>A past experience is influencing your current decision. | If you are objective and honest, you have no hard evidence to confirm that any of what you're saying to yourself is true. |

After careful review, consider your own accusations. Complete the exercise and use this table as a tool to start facing and moving beyond your fears.

## Developing a friendship with your fears

Developing friendship with friends, coworkers, neighbors, or pets requires establishing rapport. You have to take the time to compassionately and patiently understand who they are and what's important to them. Developing a friendship with your fears involves the same attention.

Remember, fear is an outcome. The goal is to establish a relationship with yourself and your deep emotional wounds that create the fear. The purpose of becoming friends is to learn how to compassionately love all of who you are. By doing so, your weaknesses become your strengths because you know what they are, and you learn how to flow with them and, when necessary, navigate around them.

It's nice to be able to say, "You can heal from every experience." That doesn't mean it won't leave any evidence of having been there. If a cut is severe, although it heals, a scar remains. The scar doesn't hurt. You can touch, hit, and press it. It responds like any other part of the body. The scar isn't a symbol of pain, but a sign of love. It says, "You can do it. You can make it through anything."

## Knowing your strength beyond what you see

You've done it before — over and over again. You've made it through the most difficult moments of your life. It's easy to forget how strong you are when you don't pause and take inventory of what you've been through. Evidence shows that you're amazingly powerful and strong.

We know at times you look in the mirror and see a vulnerable, confused individual you barely know. As you stare into your own eyes, you wonder: Where am I going? What am I doing? What am I going to do? These are key questions to ask yourself. They indicate that you're aware that you're again at a pivotal point in your life and that your life needs your attention.

Do people give you compliments that are difficult for you to own? Do they say things such as, "You're so talented" or "I admire you for how much you've accomplished against the odds"?

Seeing what others see in you is difficult. Your internal strength may have pulled you through the pain of a devastating divorce, an unexpected diagnosis, or an unforeseen death. Your personal power may have carried you through the loss of your job, betrayal from a friend, or gossip that nearly destroyed your career. Maybe you lived in a household where you were suffocated versus celebrated, and others often wonder how you made it.

Reflecting on your past can inspire you. The realization that you've made it through the rain and storms of life reflects back to you your inborn tenacity and fortitude.

Try this exercise for inspiration. Stop reading, close your eyes, and reflect on your life. Go back as far as you can remember. Think about what happened, how it made you feel, and what you did to overtake the situation. If you still have anger or any other negative emotion, take time to forgive.

Forgiveness comes easier when you realize that the person did the best she could at the time based on her experiences.

To help you organize your thoughts, divide your experiences into time frames based on age. Start with ages 0–5 and think about your experiences in five-year increments, for example, 0–5, 6–10, 11–15, and so on. If you haven't faced many major challenges, increase the increment to ten years.

Think about each incident and how you overcame it. For instance, say between ages 6–10 you were physically abused. You suppressed your pain until age 25. During ages 13–24, you self-medicated by abusing drugs and your body. At age 25, you forgave the perpetrator and took control of your life. At age 33, you have a healthy marriage and relationship with your children.

This is a huge accomplishment — a true display of courage, compassion, and faith. You're powerful far beyond what you imagined.

# Creating the Faith to Face Your Fears

We've established that you don't overcome your fears — you eradicate them by uncovering your core issues that are creating your fears. Your prime artillery is faith. Whatever you do takes faith. Faith is the belief that an unseen thought, feeling, idea, dream, or desire will manifest itself into visible reality. That's powerful.

To think that you have the ability to take a thought — something you can't see, hear, or touch — and turn it into something that you can see, hear, and touch declares that you're the most powerful creation on earth. Isn't it astounding to realize that you've done this your entire life? It's nearly overwhelming to know that you have that much power in your possession.

Consider this example: Before you landed the job you have, it was a thought, an idea. You acted on your thought, and Bam! — your thought became a reality. Who you think you are and everything that you have began as a thought. Your faith in yourself moved you to action. But you have bigger dreams, don't you? These dreams are so incredible that you secretly hold them within yourself, wondering whether you can achieve them.

Are you unaware of what you possess? Are you unaware that you have something incredibly enormous within you? Or are you oblivious about the degree to which you have it?

Are you saying to yourself, "Yeah, right. How do I tap into and use my 'supernatural power'?" We aren't talking about a cartoon character that kisses a ring or spins around three times to gain greater strength. This is authentic, natural power that you've always had and have always used. Perhaps you just didn't know it.

Fear has had the upper hand and won many battles in the past because you were uninformed. But the war isn't over. Now is your chance to turn the tables. Follow these steps to consciously tap into and use your power to create your dreams by exercising your faith:

1. **Ask for what you want.**

   Sometimes the hardest part of the process is deciding what you really want. Get clear on exactly what you want and ask for it. Who are you asking? God, the universe, yourself — whatever you believe in.

2. **Believe that what you ask for will happen.**

   Your beliefs guide your decisions daily. If your behaviors don't line up with what you believe, then you don't believe it. Move in the direction of what you believe and you'll see opportunities along the way that will take you step by step to where you want to go.

3. **Watch it unfold.**

   Although you believe it, you'll still be surprised when your victory shows up. The reason: There'll be times when you'll feel it'll never come or you'll think you're off track. If you were leaving New York and heading to California, you wouldn't turn around because you ran into a traffic accident. You'd wait until the road was clear and then keep driving. Don't lose faith when obstacles come.

This exercise is designed to help you replace thoughts of fear with words of faith. Statistics show that 90 percent of what you worry about will never happen. Your thoughts become your beliefs, and your beliefs enter into your heart and eventually come out of your mouth. If you change how you think, you'll change what you speak, which means you'll hear something different. What you hear will create a change in what you see and do.

Here are the steps to make it happen:

1. **Police your thoughts.**

   Think of your mind as a busy highway, with your thoughts being the constant flow of traffic. You have to monitor your thoughts by stopping them and finding out where they're coming from and where they're going.

2. **Make a decision if your thoughts are too dangerous to be on the highway.**

   Is your mental traffic going in the same direction as your physical body? If your thoughts are causing you to take dead ends, get you involved with people and situations that lead you nowhere, or cause you to have accidents, they're too dangerous to be in your mind. Tell them to get off the highway. You can use quips, quotes, or scriptures to make negative thoughts disappear instantly.

3. **Your body, mind, and words must be in alignment.**

   Once you establish a vision for your life, your thoughts and words must line up to produce your desired results. As you practice Steps 1 and 2, you begin to see your body turning in the direction of your vision and your feet taking steps toward it.

## Realizing the value of increasing your faith

What is faith worth to you? Everything. The life you desire depends on your faith in creating it. Without sureness in what you believe is possible, you're doomed. Therefore, knowing what it takes to sustain and increase your faith is critical.

Take a look at the nearby sidebar, "Faking you out." You can apply the wrestling tactics mentioned there and the ones that follow to your arsenal when you have to wrestle fear and other opponents in your life.

- **Respect your opponent.** When wrestling, you have to respect your opponent. You never know what he's thinking or what new moves he'll make next. Never assume you're not in for a real fight.

- **Have razor-sharp focus.** During a wrestling match, each participant has successes. If one opponent celebrates too soon, taking his eyes off the prize of winning, his opponent can exploit this and create more obstacles and frustration. Enjoy small successes, but stay focused on the target.

✓ **Use a flexible strategy.** Wrestling requires a flexible strategy. You can go into the match expecting to use one technique, but because of the opponent's move, it may not work. Knowing yourself and your capabilities helps you to make the necessary adjustments.

✓ **Prepare to have undying endurance.** Once the match begins, it doesn't end until someone is pinned to the mat or says, "I give up." This takes a mindset of relentless persistence and commitment. Don't forget, if you get tired, you can pause for the moment; just don't give up.

✓ **Plan for superior discipline.** Wrestlers have to stay within a certain weight range to wrestle in their class. If they go up in weight, they're forced to wrestle a heavier opponent. Self-development and the success that comes from it take discipline. Make a commitment and stick to it.

For every match you win, you'll increase your faith in yourself and your capability. Because of what you learn about yourself, the next face-off will be less challenging. The challenge is only as difficult as your lack of confidence to conquer it.

## Faking you out

I (coauthor S. Renee) have three brothers. All were athletes in high school. Mark, my youngest brother, played football and tennis, and wrestled. Although nerve-wracking, my mother and I used to love to watch him wrestle.

Mark wasn't a fancy, flashy wrestler. Unlike many of his competitors, who appeared anxious, energetic, and ready to take him out, he was calm, composed, and unexciting. This caused my mother and me to scream continually, "Come on, Mark! Get him! Come on, Mark! Get him!" I don't know whether he could hear us, but if he did, it didn't change his demeanor.

Instead of going in for the tackle, behind his protective head and face mask, Mark would seemingly taunt his opponent. Bent over, looking his contender in the eyes, he would swing at him for what seemed like minutes at a time. Once the attack began, the loud thump on the mat would cause me to cringe, but my mother wouldn't flinch. She'd keep screaming, "Get him, Mark! Get him!"

While in the heat of a move, with his legs locked behind his opponent's head and his shoulder nearly on the mat, Mark would just stop moving. With my brother and his opponent interlocked like a smashed pretzel, the onlookers on the opponents' side would explode in excitement. Some would think it was over, and others, like my mother and me, would be hoping something exciting was about to happen. The way Mark wrestled, you never knew what to expect.

Suddenly, he'd make his move. Before your eyes could see what happened, the opponent would be on the bottom and Mark on top pinning him to the mat. Every year this strategy landed him among the state's top-three wrestlers in his weight class.

## Increasing your self-esteem by increasing your faith

Faith is what produces the result. Whether you believe in yourself or something greater than yourself, or you just believe, the principle works for whomever chooses to use it. When you create the intended results, your self-esteem increases. Interestingly, when your self-esteem increases, your faith increases. Faith and self-esteem are traveling buddies.

You can assert that you have faith, but your behavior has to back it up. And your life will confirm that fact. If you're struggling, here are a few pointers to help you:

- **How strong is your faith?** Hoping and believing are often used synonymously. We don't advise this. Hoping has doubt. Believing has possibility. Knowing is claiming completion even before something is completed. You sit in one of the three categories in the various areas of your life. Identifying where you are helps you to see where you need to increase your faith and confidence.

  Use the following matrix as a sample. Notice Lisa's strengths and weaknesses. Create your own matrix like this one to gauge where you are and what areas need your attention.

| Lisa | Hope | Believe | Know |
|---|---|---|---|
| Self-confidence | | | X |
| Attractiveness | | | X |
| Intelligence | | | X |
| Capabilities | | | X |
| Respect | | | X |
| Mental stamina | | X | |
| Relationships | X | | |
| Physical strength | X | | |
| Emotional awareness | | X | |
| Education | X | | |
| Public perception | | X | |

- **What's nagging you?** Is something calling you? A new job, relationship, or business? Is there a reason you're not responding? What is it?

- **Do you believe you have what you need?** Taking on a new challenge is difficult when you don't know whether you have what you need. If you're questioning yourself, respond to the questions in the earlier section "Uncovering your core fears," if you haven't already.

If you continue to lack faith, consider trying the following:

- ✔ Read the scriptures, an autobiography, or another inspirational work.
- ✔ Watch an inspirational movie.
- ✔ Join a positive support group that focuses on self- or spiritual development.
- ✔ Volunteer for an inspiring organization.
- ✔ Write your life story and be inspired by the times that you doubted yourself but moved forward anyway.

## *Dealing with big challenges*

Sometimes life delivers to your doorstep challenges that appear too complex for your mind to process and too problematic for you to decode their meaning. The range of these moments can be as complicated as trying to understand the passing of a child, the abandonment of a 50-year marriage, or the slaying of a family member.

As you look within your own world and the world around you, tragedy strikes — falling planes, school massacres, and death by war. These are big challenges without apparent answers. Humbled by their magnitude of destruction and internal terror, it's in these moments that even experts are brought to silence.

We can only extend to you our encouragement to stand in the strength of your faith, in the belief that truth will deliver justice, and in the power of knowing that love always wins.

# *Getting Your Mind, Mouth, and Motions in Alignment*

Every thought you think, every word you speak, and every step you take plant the seeds that blossom into your reality. Throughout this chapter you are presented with the tools to form the thoughts, words, and behaviors that will shake your fears and give you the confidence to walk in faith.

Inconsistency in your thoughts, words, and behaviors creates instability and keeps you off balance and out of alignment with the truth. When you choose this path, you create your own suffering.

With proper arrangement of your thoughts, words, and actions, you can survive disappointment, use the power you possess, and overcome life's challenges by outmaneuvering your fears. When you choose this path, you zap your fears and walk in faith.

# Chapter 13

# Creating and Reaching Your Goals

· · · · · · · · · · · · · · · · · · · · · · · · · · · · · · · · · · · ·

*In This Chapter*

Deciding what you want

Turning your goals into reality

· · · · · · · · · · · · · · · · · · · · · · · · · · · · · · · · · · · ·

**A**nd the winner is . . .

Have you ever wondered what determines who takes home the trophy? Who gets the promotion? Who lands the contract?

Is there something that losers fail to do that gives their opposition an advantage? Or is it something winners do that gives them an edge?

When it comes to reaching a goal, all things may appear equal, but they never are. People who experience success believe in themselves, develop the right attitude, and refuse to take no for an answer. People who experience the success they want and beyond do those things and more.

In this chapter we give you the "more." Intentional success comes through the clarity of your mind, the understanding of your heart, and knowing the endurance of your body. If you want to be like a well-trained athlete who listens, learns, and follows the instructions of his coach to get the results he wants, continue reading — we take you to the edge.

This chapter is interconnected. It helps you build from the bottom up. We highly recommend that you read each section in order and complete all the exercises as presented.

# Measuring Success through Goal-Setting

If you could measure your success, would you say it's a teaspoon, tablespoon, cup, quart, or gallon? Are you thinking that's a weird way to measure success? We do, too, but try it anyway. Close your eyes, ask yourself the question again, and feel for the answer. What was the first thought that came to mind? Did you think about your personal growth, professional progress, or spiritual development? How successful were you?

Now, think about your long-term goal — the goal you've set for yourself in the same category. Have you accomplished the goal? Are you moving in the right direction? Are you almost there, or not even close?

The first exercise causes most people to think about a specific area of their lives and then measure it. The first area of your life that comes to your mind is your priority. Use the following table as an example, taking your own measurements.

|  | Personal Growth | Professional Progress | Spiritual Development |
| --- | --- | --- | --- |
| **Teaspoon** |  |  |  |
| **Tablespoon** |  |  |  |
| **Cup** | X |  |  |
| **Quart** |  |  | X |
| **Gallon** |  | X |  |

The second exercise, which requires a yes or no, measures what you've accomplished against what you said you wanted to accomplish. It's easier to measure, but a more difficult pill to swallow if you're not where you expected to be in life. Again, use the example and fill in your own goals and answers.

| My Goals | Yes | No |
| --- | --- | --- |
| **Personal Growth Goal:**<br>*To work on myself daily to become a kind, loving human being by showing patience toward others and myself* | X |  |
| **Professional Progress Goal:**<br>*To become a senior vice president by age 40* |  | X |
| **Spiritual Development Goal:**<br>*To increase my compassion toward others by volunteering for three events per year that provide direct contact with people in need of food, clothing, or shelter* | X |  |

As you can see in these examples, the individual thought about her professional success, first measuring it at a gallon, only to realize that her professional goal had not been met. Interestingly, she measured her personal and spiritual life at a cup and a quart, respectively, but then found that she was actively satisfying those goals.

What you're likely to notice is that you've excelled in different areas of your life. This may have caused you to miss a target in one area, but we hope it has resulted in a more delightfully balanced life.

# Checking in with yourself and deciding what's important to you

Are you off track with the goals you established for yourself? Like when you take the wrong turn on a busy highway, the sooner you know that you're going in the wrong direction the better off you are. We hope the previous exercise opened up the following for you:

✔ Your mind's wishes and heart's desires can work against one another if they aren't deliberately required to work together.

✔ What you thought would bring you joy 10, 20, or 30 years ago might not be the same thing that will bring you joy today.

Either way, we have to get you on track. Answer the following questions in the order in which they are presented. This is paramount because before you can decide which direction you need to go, you have to know who you want to be. What you spend your time doing, the final question, answers how you get there. The questions in the middle take you step by step in helping you to get clear on the significance of your existence.

1. **Who do I want to be?**

2. **What do I want to do?**

3. **What do I want to have?**

4. **Who do I want to help?**

5. **How will I help them?**

6. **Who do I want to spend time with?**

7. **What do I want to spend my time doing?**

# Naming your goals

The purpose of setting a goal is to keep you focused and to determine whether you're creating what you say you want. Because goals only take into account raw data called *outcomes,* we as self-development experts don't believe the achievement or lack of achievement of a goal is the complete picture of success.

The journey to achieving your goal can significantly enrich your life — increasing your confidence and introducing you to phenomenal things about yourself. This philosophy doesn't negate the importance of goals; it only seeks to ensure that you don't believe your self-worth is contingent on a projected outcome, because it isn't.

Success means different things to different people. But what's constant is that you won't know whether you're moving toward or away from success unless you do the following:

- ✔ Clearly define what success means to you
- ✔ Set goals that are in alignment with what you believe success is
- ✔ Create the network to support your goals
- ✔ Develop a strategy to reach your goals

Answer the following questions to further clarify your goals:

- ✔ What will I feel when I am a success?
- ✔ What will I be doing when I am a success?
- ✔ Who will be part of my life when I am a success?
- ✔ How will people treat me when I am a success?

Based on what success means to you, list what you want to accomplish in your personal, professional, and spiritual lives. As you name your goals be sure they have the following qualities:

- ✔ **Purposeful:** Your goals must have meaning for you and your life's mission.
- ✔ **Service driven:** What you do must serve others, while getting you what you want.
- ✔ **Truthful:** Your goals must be in alignment with your beliefs.
- ✔ **Authentic:** Your goals should give you the opportunity to use your gifts, talents, and skills.
- ✔ **Encourage growth:** Your goals should force you to look for ways to engage in new experiences that challenge you and help you to grow.

## Dealing with missed targets

Many factors influence the achievement of a goal. For the most part, achieving your goals depends on you. But *when* and *how* you achieve your goals can be influenced by external factors.

For example, most Olympians train from the time they're 5 or 6 years old. Each athlete is well trained by a top coach. Each has pushed himself beyond his limits. Each has prepared himself to win. Each has set the goal to take home the gold — but only one will.

## Before they die

For over 20 years I (coauthor S. Renee) had an index card with one goal written on it. I wanted to honor my parents before they passed by starting a scholarship fund in their name. In my mind, I had it all planned out. I would work as a television talk show host. The audience would absolutely love me. I'd make millions of dollars before age 40, and with my earnings I'd launch the scholarship. It seemed simple to me.

It was what's called a "SMART" goal: It was specific, measureable, attainable, realistic, and timely. The only problem was that it didn't happen. Although I didn't look at the index card often, year after year the goal nagged at me as it occupied space in my subconscious. So I continued to look for the million-dollar jackpot, which is yet to be found.

In 2010, my parents celebrated their 50th wedding anniversary. I had no idea what to get them. I saw the goal again handwritten on a pink index card placed in the corner of a picture frame in my guest room. If only I had those million dollars, I thought.

It dawned on me. I didn't have a million dollars, but I did have an opportunity.

I was sitting on an advisory board that helped people who wanted to help others through giving. I didn't have to start a nonprofit, and I didn't have to have a lot of money. I'd found my alternative.

My siblings, their children, and I had an anniversary church service to launch the scholarship fund. The community came together and we raised the first $10,000. As of this writing, the William J. & Rev. Shirley M. Smith, Sr. Scholarship Fund has awarded $15,000 in college scholarships and over $54,000 remains in the account. Most importantly, my parents are alive to witness and be part of it.

The reality of setting goals is that you will face defeat. The purpose of defeat is not to hurt or stop you or cause you to give up. It's simply to offer you the lessons you need to sustain you when you reach your goal. There are several ways to deal with failed attempts at goals:

- ✔ **Try again.** Believing in something when there isn't any evidence that it's likely to happen can be difficult, but your willingness to persevere and keep trying is the force that manifests it into reality.

- ✔ **Find an alternative.** There's more than one way to reach any goal — be creative. See the nearby sidebar, "Before they die," for an example.

- ✔ **Improve your abilities.** Some goals aren't reached because you're not ready. Keep practicing, improving, and building your skills.

- ✔ **Evaluate your focus, desires, and drive.** Some goals require more than you expect. Make sure you're giving it all you have and that you have the fortitude to go the distance.

✔ **Accept that it's not meant to be.** Positive thinking, affirmations, and practice won't help you become a brain surgeon unless you are gifted in math and science and have an educational foundation that will support you. Although anything is possible, everything isn't always practical.

When external factors force you to adjust your goal, you haven't failed; you're being guided to the exact place where you're meant to be.

# Accomplishing Your Goals

Goals are established to generate opportunities, spawn personal achievement, and increase confidence. Setting goals stimulates interest, inspires hope, and sparks enthusiasm.

While setting goals, you're given the opportunity to bask in the dream world of possibility. But, if you don't understand the amount of work, time, and talent you'll need to achieve your goals, you can become delusional and quickly fall into a world of despair — and choose to exchange your wish for a ticket to withdraw.

At the beginning of this chapter we promised to give you the "more" that you need to achieve your goals. Before we do, here's a list of basic artillery you need in your personal arsenal to achieve your goals:

✔ **Faith:** Never lose hope in the possibility; doubled-mindedness creates internal chaos and instability.

✔ **Attitude:** Be passionate about what you're doing, or don't do it.

✔ **Perseverance:** No matter how tough it gets, remember that you're tougher.

✔ **Flexibility:** Be willing to make necessary adjustments.

✔ **Commitment:** No matter what, commit to seeing your goals through until the end.

✔ **Focus.** Don't get discouraged or become confused about where you want to go and what you want to do when others give negative opinions.

Failing to reach a goal can be disheartening to any person who dares to set one. It's important to reiterate that the lack of achievement of a goal isn't the measure of success. But if you find yourself writing goals but not achieving them, and you think people who achieve their goals must be doing something differently, it's likely that they are. That's the "more" that we've been talking about.

Here are the secret weapons goal achievers use to give them the edge to hit their targets:

- **Intention:** Your intention drives the direction of the goal, not the goal itself.

- **Trust and respect of the unknown:** From start to finish, each goal has an evolutionary process. You're not always going to be able to see where you're going; you just have to trust that you'll get there.

- **Gratitude:** The unexpected will happen. Instead of being consumed with what doesn't happen, focus on what does.

- **Decision-making:** Recognize that every decision is crucial to your success. Each decision must be made deliberately and strategically with the target in mind.

- **Resources:** Identify and assemble the people, knowledge, and financial resources you need to hit the target.

- **The gumption to get started:** Don't wait for everything to be perfect — start today.

- **Acknowledgement:** You co-create the experiences you have with your mental and emotional thought processes. Accept responsibility for what's happening and change when you need to.

- **Preparation:** Be open to opportunities that come along the way. They may look like distracters, but they're opportunities that will better prepare and position you to get where you're trying to go.

- **Release:** The journey to your goal never looks exactly the way you expected it to. Most often it's bigger and better than you can imagine. Release the final outcome to whatever or whomever you trust that is greater than yourself.

## Inspecting your internal driving forces

Have you set a great goal for yourself? Have you thought about what it will take to reach that goal? By now you realize that setting goals can increase your confidence or burst your bubble. After you decide what your goal is, pause, look at it, and ask yourself the following questions:

- Is this goal so specific that can I see myself achieving it?

- Is it so meaningful that when I have to work extraordinarily long hours and everything still seems to be falling apart I will stay on course?

✔ Can I manage a process that will require me to act prudently to move forward?

✔ Do I have the stamina, and have I given myself enough time to develop all the relationships and skills I need to make it to my goal?

There will be times when you experience little or no return on your investment. During those times you may find it difficult to keep doing what seems senseless and unproductive. Reaching your goals requires consistency. Understanding what drives you will help you remain loyal to your expected outcome.

Ask yourself the following questions to understand why your goal is important to you:

✔ Why do I want to do this?

✔ Whose lives do I want to change?

✔ Why do I want to help them?

## Setting long-term goals

As you continue the goal-setting process, you'll discover that the toughest part of setting goals is having the courage to believe and own what your heart is telling you is possible for your life.

Your words, thoughts, and actions create your reality, so be sure that once you decide on what you want, you don't deceive yourself by saying or doing things that are out of alignment with your decision.

You have many facets to you that make you the amazing, brilliant person you are. We believe in the holistic approach, which looks at your total well-being and seeks to bring you into alignment in every area of your life. Therefore, you need to set goals that keep every aspect of your life growing. These include the following aspects of your life:

✔ **Mental:** This is your mindset. How do you see the world and your role in it? What do you need to do to improve your self-development?

✔ **Emotional:** This is how your feel. What do you believe about yourself and others? What is the value of these relationships to you?

✔ **Spiritual or moral:** This is your relationship with the universe, the higher power, God, or whatever name works for you. The key is this: You have an internal regulatory compass that keeps you in alignment with your integrity. What does it mean to you to do the right thing? What are your core beliefs?

✔ **Physical:** This is your understanding that your health makes it possible to reach your goals. How are you going to preserve it?

✔ **Family:** This aspect answers the questions: Do you want to get married? Do you want children? What do you want your family culture to feel like?

✔ **Educational:** This is your decision to be a lifelong learner. What information engages you? What topics keep you hungry or quench your thirst?

✔ **Career:** This is what you want to do with your life that will help others and generate income.

✔ **Social:** This includes your friends and networks, and the activities you'll participate in to strengthen your social life. What types of people would you enjoy being around? What do you want to get from and give to these relationships?

✔ **Financial:** This is how much money you want to make to take care of your family and save for retirement. How much will you need to live well today and through retirement?

## Setting short-term goals

In recent years, the term *quantum leap* has become popular. It means a huge and sudden increase or change in something. The association of this word with the rise to speedy success along with an unprecedented increase in millionaires in their 20s has created a false impression that those who are financially successful are skipping steps.

Read their stories, and you'll discover that they started in their teens or earlier with visions and passions, and some had plans for providing a service that satisfied problems. Taking one step at a time, they achieved their goals.

The only things that will help you to make a quantum leap — saving time and money — are good information and decisions that move you toward your goal, one step at a time.

Can you eat an 8-inch pie in one bite? If you can't perform that miracle, then don't try to tackle your goal all at once. Giving yourself time removes the intensity, stress, and feelings of being overwhelmed by your goal, which can eventually make you sick. In the same way that you would eat a pie a slice at a time, create short-term goals to help you do the work and digest the challenges in a mentally and emotionally healthy manner.

By using this system, you'll be able to see and celebrate short-term successes, which will keep you motivated and inspired to stay the course. Consider the following physical goal as an example: I will go from 150 pounds to 130 pounds in three months.

You can develop the short-term goals by answering the following questions: What will you eat? What time will you eat? How many times a week will you work out? How long? What types of exercises will you do? How often will you weigh yourself?

Take note that goals should be positive if you want to mentally and emotionally support yourself and build your confidence. Affirm what you will do, and leave all the "don'ts" at the curb.

Use all the information and answers to the questions throughout this chapter to help you get clear on your goals. Then write down your goals and create short-term aims. Check out the following sample to get an idea of how this works.

| Career | Goals |
|---|---|
| Long-term goal | Write a 12-chapter, 12-pages-per-chapter book in 12 weeks, based on a table of contents. |
| Short-term goal | Write one chapter per week. |
| Short-term goal | Write two or more pages per day. Review on the seventh day. |
| Short-term goal | Write from 8 a.m. to 12 p.m., Monday through Saturday. |

## Watching out for people and resources to help you

You can't achieve any goal without turning to resources outside of yourself. Every goal requires the use of a person, place, or thing that already exists. That's why it's important to recognize your relationship with everything and everyone else on the planet.

After you decide what goals you want to achieve, you need to identify what you need to learn, the people you need to ask for help, and any resources you need to help you advance toward your goal.

If you are consistent and persistent, this method of goal-setting will take you where you want to go.

ANECDOTE

## Confession of a coach

I (coauthor S. Renee) have a confession to make. I often share this in workshops, and in the spirit of being fully transparent, I know sharing it with you is the right thing to do.

After trying traditional goal-setting in my early 20s and experiencing many setbacks early on, I developed an alternative to goal-setting that continues to work for me. I write down goals, affirmations, and "I am" statements that are meaningful and very much from my heart. I don't look at them every day, week, month, or year. In fact, many of them are written down in journals between the pages of a day of gratitude and a moment of wonder.

Perhaps if I had some elaborate, well-laid-out plan, I would have "made it big" and be independently wealthy by now. The truth is this: My goal every day is to wake up with an open heart and be used by God. Interestingly, this approach has taken me to every place and created nearly every experience and "more" that I've scribbled down over the years as important to me.

For example, in January 1999 I wrote this: "I will write three books." This book is the fourth, and I suspect there will be more. I've worked hard, had super-sized faith, and dug deep within myself when I've needed to. I've made good and bad decisions that have taken me on detours, yet I've never gone down a dead-end road. I've worked harder at being a quality human being — a person whom I and others can trust, depend on, and believe in.

My confession isn't to negate the value of every written word in this chapter; in fact, it confirms the power of it. What it offers is an alternative for some people who may not have the courage to write a goal according to the standard laid out in the preceding sections or the strength to look uncertainty in the eyes every day.

I offer this to you as a lifeline to give you hope — something that will get you started. All you need is an open heart and the willingness to scribble down your desires, put them in a secret place, and then quietly ask: "What do I do next?"

# Part V

# Dissolving Internal Barriers to Success in Love and Work

| Inquiry | Assessment |
|---|---|
| Situation | Accepting criticism |
| Body response | Body stiffens |
| Feeling response | Put down, attacked, demeaned |
| Core response | I didn't do it right. This person is disappointed in me. |
| Pain spot | Growing up often criticized. Told I should get it right the first time. |
| Action response | Defensive, combative, guarded |
| Truth of the situation | Being helped. Being encouraged to do a better job. |
| Awareness and solution | Was criticized in the past; hence, it's difficult to see that someone is simply offering me help. I have the right to accept or reject the advice, so there isn't a need for me to cause conflict by defending my position. Simply thank the person and move on. |

Would you like to find out how to create a buzz about yourself? Check out an article that tells you how at www.dummies.com/extras/selfesteem.

# In this part . . .

- ✔ Discover how to identify internal barriers and the triggers that bring them up. Also, find out how to nurture yourself while self-correcting and use some self-development tips to keep external conflict down and your confidence up.

- ✔ Find out how to write a new love story and where to find real love. Discover how to own your power.

- ✔ Gain a deeper understanding of what love is and why love seems to create pleasure and cause pain. Also, find out how to best prepare for love and where you can find love that lasts forever.

- ✔ Discover strategies to successfully navigate difficult moments with loved ones and to make a distinction between your issues and those of the people you love.

- ✔ Get proven strategies to package, present, and position yourself for a promotion in the workplace.

- ✔ Understand the core causes of confusion in the workplace and find out whether it's possible to have people from different backgrounds, experiences, and skill sets effectively work together and genuinely like and value one another. Find out how to develop into a leader who knows how to break through barriers and build effective relationships and confidence in others.

- ✔ Discover the secrets to presenting with presence, passion, and power. Find out about attention-grabbing techniques and specific things to do to keep your audiences engaged.

# Chapter 14

# Examining Your Role in Creating Conflicts in Your Relationships

*I*magine for a moment that the approximately 7 billion people on the planet disappeared — except you. The thought may excite or scare you. Either way, it's not going to happen. That means you need to strengthen your innate abilities to get along with others, while maintaining your self-esteem.

Although they're not always easy, self-examination and correction build your self-esteem and the respect you get from others. People who learn to monitor and correct their own behaviors create healthier homes, workplaces, and communities. They feel good about themselves and make better spouses, friends, leaders, and employees.

In this chapter, you discover how to identify internal barriers — those feelings that unnecessarily cause you to protect and defend yourself — and the triggers that bring them up. You also find out how to nurture yourself while self-correcting and use some self-development tips to keep external conflict down and your confidence up.

## Becoming Aware of Internal Barriers

Becoming aware of yourself, your internal barriers, and what triggers them changes your view of the world and the world's view of you. The reason is this: If an external event bothers you, it's caused by your internal interpretation of the event.

When you look to and within yourself first for understanding of what's driving you to think and feel the way you do, you grow in your understanding of yourself and become more likable because you feel freer to be yourself and others feel free to be themselves around you.

Have you ever been around a person who wants to control everything? What does it feel like? Suffocating? Uncomfortable? Unless you've become highly skilled at dealing with people and their issues and situations, you can feel that person's emotions and they can impact your emotional state.

We take a look at your internal barriers, which keep you from being your authentic self, and your perception of the people whose emotions you take on as a result of being around them.

Have you ever been around a person who is miserable? Did you start your day feeling great, but feel miserable after spending time with that person? Have you ever wondered, "How did I go from feeling happy to feeling awful?"

Consider the following possibilities:

- ✔ I hold the person in high regard, and this is my way of respecting him.
- ✔ I want to be liked by this person, and this is my way of getting him to accept me.
- ✔ The person is in a position of authority, and I think this is the response he expects from me.

Taking on negative emotions isn't the best way to show your loyalty and respect toward a person. When you learn to stand in your own power, you understand the importance of setting and living according to your own emotional state.

## *Looking at the impact of internal barriers*

Allowing your pain to create internal barriers controls your life and leaves you feeling disconnected from friends and family. Often these secret feelings have enormous effects on your relationships with others and, more importantly, yourself. According to an article published in *Psychology Today,* studies show that unhealthy personal relationships create "a toxic internal environment that can lead to stress, depression, anxiety, and even medical problems."

The Whitehall II Study followed more than 10,000 participants for an average of 12.2 years. Researchers discovered that people "in negative relationships were at a greater risk for developing heart problems, including a fatal cardiac event, than their counterparts whose close relationships were not negative."

It's time for a checkup. Answer the following questions:

- ✔ Do you feel disconnected from others?
- ✔ Do you want to disconnect from others?
- ✔ Do you experience anxiety or any form of discomfort when you're around family or close personal friends?
- ✔ Do you experience anxiety or any form of discomfort when you're around business associates?
- ✔ Have you recently been diagnosed with a condition that is related to stress?
- ✔ Do you dread attending certain events?
- ✔ Do you feel safe around the person or people you're spending time with?
- ✔ Do your energy levels go up or down when you're around others?
- ✔ Do you feel like you have to defend yourself or be careful when interacting with others?
- ✔ Do you give a lot of thought to the prospect of spending time with others before doing so?

## Listening to your body

You may be asking, "How do I know my triggers?" You can become aware of them by paying close attention to your body. Every time you see, hear, or feel an experience that is unpleasant, your body responds. Instantly, your animal instincts kick in and you go into survival mode. This changes your communication style, which signals to the recipient, "I don't like what you just said or did."

A message is instantly sent to your brain to alert you to beware; a pain spot has been hit. You feel discomfort that may show up as anxiety, embarrassment, or annoyance. A pain spot is a past experience that you've labeled as unpleasant. The trigger is anything that looks, sounds, or acts like the unpleasant experience.

When a pain spot is hit, it instantly sends an alarm to your internal defense system. The internal barriers go up, triggering an unconscious response. Your unconscious response can appear as fiery, touchy, or even angry.

# Using your awareness to move yourself forward

The purpose of observing yourself is to identify your pain spots so that you can recognize your internal barriers and heal yourself. This observation helps you see the role you play in creating situations in your life that hinder you from advancing in your career and personal relationships. By keeping an eye on yourself, you can discover what causes you to mentally and emotionally get upset and lose opportunities.

Here's an example: During a workshop on branding, I (coauthor S. Renee) asked a participant to list three adjectives to describe herself. After stating the three adjectives, I asked her why she chose those adjectives. She began to cry. Although I had no idea at the time, the question hit a pain spot and triggered her internal barrier to go up. I then said, "I notice you are crying; what's coming up for you?" She revealed, "I was always told that you should never talk about yourself." Deeper conversation uncovered that this beautiful, bright, highly educated woman who needed to communicate her value to advance in her career was struggling in the boardroom because her parents had told her that talking about herself was arrogant and inappropriate.

Messages from your parents and situations from the past taught you what you should believe. Whether true or false, you own these beliefs as your own, like this client, who carried her childhood beliefs for years only to discover that there's a difference between sharing information about yourself with others and boasting. You have to ask yourself: "Is what I believe the truth?"

After you identify the internal barrier that causes you pain, the goal is to move yourself from the passenger seat to the driver's seat. Here's how:

1. **Get to your core.**

   There's always another level of self-discovery. If you aren't producing the outcomes you desire, that's a sign that it's time to stop, look, and listen to yourself. Ask yourself: What do I want that I'm not getting?

2. **Identify what you're unintentionally communicating to others.**

   Although you may not be talking, you're communicating nonverbally — all the time. You're sending messages to people about who you are and how to treat you. For each challenge you are facing, ask yourself: "What message am I sending?"

3. **Identify why you're blocking.**

   When relationships are out of balance, one or both parties are blocking. *Blocking* is defending, protecting, or resisting. Ask yourself: "Why am I resisting? What am I resisting?" (See the nearby sidebar, "Blocking equals burdens" for an example of the detrimental effects of blocking on your personal and professional lives.)

## Blocking equals burdens

A client I'll call Amber hired me (coauthor S. Renee) to coach her on negotiating contracts. Early in the session, I discovered that for ten years Amber consistently underpriced her products and services — even giving them away — to avoid talking about money. Deep in debt, she came to me to help her shake her bad luck by learning strategies to increase her income.

For nearly an hour, she gave me answers before I could even complete my questions. Defending herself, protecting her image, and blaming others, she claimed that all she needed was a way to charge more for her services. But this is what I knew: She needed a mental and emotional breakthrough.

At first, I couldn't understand why an attractive, talented, highly educated, confident client would block me, the person she'd hired to help her, from her inner world. As a life and branding coach, I help people overcome their inner barriers to ensure the long-term effectiveness of the strategies I teach.

Finally, exhausted from her internal fighting, she surrendered. "I never had anything. My family was poor. My parents, grandparents, cousins, friends — everyone was poor. They're still poor. I'm the only one who made it out." The weight of her words fell on her. Silence filled the gap as I waited for her to continue.

I gently asked, "Did you really make it out?"

She remained quiet.

I added, "What are you fearful of?"

"Failing. That I'll always be poor. I just don't feel worthy of what I know I'm worth."

Her internal barriers were blocking her success. Despite her prosperous image, she was standing behind the walls of poverty and people sensed it. Although she'd left the neighborhood, the penetrating images and experiences of the neighborhood hadn't left her. She was depleted financially, mentally, and emotionally.

By the end of the session, she was able to hear and see herself. She learned how to observe herself during negotiations. She discovered how to listen to, feel, and mentally watch herself as her body shrank, which was caused by the burden of poverty.

Today, if a potential client tries to dismiss the value of her work, instead of backing down during discussions about money, Amber sits up in her chair, leans in, and repositions the conversation to demonstrate her value and the problem she can help the organization solve.

**4. Observe yourself in action.**

You may be surprised, shocked, and maybe even mortified by what you witness yourself doing and saying. Don't take yourself too seriously. Have fun! Here are some of our comical responses to our moments of insanity: "Girl, what were you thinking?" "What possessed you to say that?" "Now, that was hilarious!" Keep in mind that the objective isn't to judge. It's to become aware and identify the inner perpetrator that is blocking you from having what you want out of life.

5. **Practice the strategies you learn.**

   If you want to build and maintain a healthy self-esteem and enjoy your life, you have to work at it. The stages of the self-development process are as follows: learn, practice, and improve — and they repeat.

Once you learn what is blocking you, you become aware of your pain spot. Unless you choose to ignore your feelings and awareness, you'll notice that every time your pain shows up you get a clear message. At that point, you get to choose to either continue on the same path of defending yourself or open yourself up to a new behavior.

If you choose to continue your habit, nothing changes and your life remains stagnant. By practicing a different, intentional response to your pain, it loses its power over you and you improve your relationship with yourself and others.

# Tracking Your Behavior in Relationships

Becoming familiar with yourself and your behaviors is extremely helpful in developing healthier interpersonal relations — with yourself and others.

Although tracking your behavior may appear to be for others — your family, friends, or coworkers — *you* get the most benefit. You're learning to better understand and love yourself while standing in the truth of who you really are.

## How to track your behavior

Follow these steps and refer to the sample worksheet in Table 14-1 to start tracking your behavior:

1. **Decide on what emotion or situation you want to work on.**

   You may be tempted to work on more than one at a time. We suggest that you choose only one. As you get in the habit of observing and tracking your behaviors, you'll naturally begin to pick up on when you're out of alignment with who you want to be.

2. **Notice your responses to specific people and situations.**

   Look out for your typical response to certain people and what they say or do. Pay special attention to how it makes you feel and how you address the person or situation. Also, take note of who and what triggers the emotion. If a particular person activates an unbecoming response, that's invaluable information. It means that, although you may not be aware of it, trust has been broken with this person or someone who reminds you of the person. You need to watch for deeper, unacknowledged connections.

For example: You have strong, unjustified opinions about a beautiful woman you work with, but you don't know why or you've made up a reason. When you track your experiences, you recall that the guy you liked in high school chose a beautiful teen who looked like or had mannerisms like this person over you. As a result, you unconsciously developed strong negative opinions about women who present like the teen you perceived to be your competition.

This assumption just isn't true. However, your unresolved pain from high school still impacts how you see and interact with certain people because of your interpretation of a past experience.

3. **Feel your body's response.**

When your body responds to a particular behavior or statement, allow yourself to feel it. At first, you may want to resist because you don't want to feel like a bad person. Remember, no judgment. In case you're wondering whether your body will respond, be assured that it absolutely will!

4. **Listen to and feel your emotions**.

While the conflict is in process, you will experience what I call *first responders*. Most often they show up in your thoughts. Have you ever been in a meeting with a person who says something that you don't like? From that moment, you miss the next five minutes of the conversation, right? Pay attention and catch your thoughts. Instead of holding onto them, let them pass through so you can get back to the conversation. Typically, these thoughts communicate your present-moment feelings about the person or situation.

5. **Listen to what core responses are coming up for you**.

When something happens, if you pay attention, you'll notice that you have a gut reaction. That's your core talking. Give yourself a voice and listen intently to what that voice is telling you. This is your current truth. This voice speaks to and about you. This is who you are targeting in this exercise.

6. **Watch how you respond to the person who triggers the emotion.**

At this point, it's game on. You're ready for battle. And that's okay because you're growing and you need to witness your habitual action response. This is the point where the adrenaline rush comes and it's off to the races. All that's brewing inside of you is now being released. It's what's calling you to change and why you want to modify your behavior.

**7. Do the reflective work.**

Now that the incident is over, it's time to assess, reflect, and implement. Use the developmental behavioral tracking sample in Table 14-1 to record your experience. Then ponder the questions in the next section.

| Table 14-1 | Developmental Behavioral Tracking Sample |
|---|---|
| *Inquiry* | *Assessment* |
| Situation | Accepting criticism. |
| Body response | Body stiffens. |
| Feeling response | Put down, attacked, demeaned. |
| Core response | I didn't do it right. This person is disappointed in me. |
| Pain spot | Often criticized while growing up. Told I should get it right the first time. |
| Action response | Defensive, combative, guarded. |
| Truth of the situation | Being helped. Being encouraged to do a better job. |
| Awareness and solution | Was criticized in the past, hence, it's difficult to see that others are simply offering me help. I have the right to accept or reject their advice, so I don't need to cause conflict by defending my position. I can simply thank them and move on. |

By taking these steps to track your behavior you are taking your life back. This gives you power over *you!*

## *Reflecting on what you've learned from your tracking*

Whenever you learn something new, it's important to reflect on what you learned. The self-reflection process helps you to get clear on what you learned, the value of what you learned, and how to best apply what you learned to your life. The following questions can help you focus:

✔ What type of relationship do I have with the person?

✔ How long have I known him or her?

✔ Does this happen often?

✔ Is my response getting more intense?

✔ What did the person do or say that caused a change in my mood?

✔ Was it the person's tone of voice, body language, choice of words?

✔ What emotion was I feeling? For example: controlled, unsafe, or ignored.

✔ Why was I feeling that way?

✔ What comparable past event causes a similar internal rumble?

✔ Do I always feel this way around this person?

 When doing reflective work, it's important to be open. Sit in a quiet place and listen for the answer. The possibilities are limitless. The answer could be connected to a past encounter, strong opinions, or unconscious feelings toward the person you're dealing with, a childhood experience, or a mood swing caused by another situation. A commitment you made to yourself years ago and determined never to break could also be at the core. For example, "I'll never love like that again." You may have long forgotten the commitment, but these hard decisions become a part of your sub-conscious — creating your behaviors.

# The blame game

I (coauthor S. Renee) have a client I'll call Sue. She's one of the funniest people I know. She loves to laugh — at herself. She's open to learning and has a relentless determination to change the direction of her life. She arrived on my doorstep with shame, guilt, and low self-esteem.

In a dire state, Sue worked very hard every week. She lingered between two worlds — life with her husband and life without him. All indications pointed to a deep desire to save her third marriage. With little time left, I decided during our fourth session that she could handle and would immediately see the value of behavioral tracking.

For one week, she couldn't hold her husband accountable for anything. She had to track only her own responses to him and his behavior.

What she discovered changed her life, and to date, she is still with her husband.

Behavioral tracking introduced Sue to her manipulative tactics, unscrupulous motives, tendency to be dishonest, and craving to be loved and accepted by any means necessary. While watching herself, she saw the abandoned, scared little girl who had been in foster care and always felt unsafe and unloved.

This 40-plus-year-old has earned her title of overcomer. Today, she is earning a college degree, running a start-up business, and raising her beautiful children.

# Appreciating the results

Okay, so you've spent some time tracking your behaviors, and you can recognize your typical responses. Now what? Here are things to keep in mind as you use the results to help you better understand and love yourself:

- **Don't judge yourself.** Make a decision that you will not judge whether your behavior is right or wrong.

- **Be mindful and clear of the purpose.** This isn't an opportunity for you to go on a guilt trip, nor should you validate or take responsibility for someone else's behavior. The purpose is to connect you with your feelings so that you can better understand your triggers, tone, and presentation in difficult moments.

- **Decide what you want to do.** You're not required to do anything with the information. Don't feel pressured to jump into making promises to yourself that you aren't ready to commit to. If changing will add value to your life, decide what adjustments you want and need to make. The solution may require healing work. You may need to work on communication — tone, body language, and presentation. Or it may be time to have open communication with the person with whom you have issues. Openly and honestly share how you feel.

# Using the information wisely

By acknowledging, accepting, and properly using the information you discover about yourself, you destroy the home of your pain — forcing it out of your personal space. Instead of being an emotional, reactive person, you learn to confidently stand in your own power.

Here's how to use the information to increase your confidence:

- **Increase your compassion — for yourself.** You've had experiences that have altered who you really are. These experiences have caused you to suffer. Deal with yourself as two people — the altered you and the real you. Keep calling the real you forward by affirming who you really are. Thank the person you unwillingly became due to negative experiences. Be thankful for everything that she taught you. Then, release her.

- **Identify your lovable qualities.** You've helped many people over the years. It doesn't matter whether they said thank you or not; that doesn't diminish the value of the act. Giving to and of yourself is what makes you important in the world. Think about and write down the times that you unselfishly gave of yourself and knew in that moment that you made a difference.

> ✔ **Identify your lessons.** Have you ever taken stock of how much you know — about you? If you're having difficulty coming up with something, think about moments that caused you to pause. Go as far back as necessary. Discover at least three amazing lessons you've learned over the years that have made you a better person.

When you conquer one internal barrier, another one will surface. Don't be discouraged; living your highest self is a lifelong journey.

VISUALIZE

# Forgiving and loving another

Sit or lie down in a comfortable position. Uncross your hands and feet and close your eyes. Now breathe in deeply and exhale. Breathe in deeply again and exhale. Completely relax.

See yourself outside, walking along a road. The birds are singing. The road is lined with magnificent trees that blend with one another. You can see streams of sunlight coming through their branches and shining on the road before you.

On the right side of the road is a flowing river. You can hear the river splashing and running, creating a peaceful and serene feeling within you. The road takes a right turn, and you walk over a bridge.

You see a large building before you. It is a beautiful building and you want to go in. You go up the steps and walk under an archway. Before you is a large room, in the middle of which is a circle of deep pink.

Now identify a person you are having a difficult time with now or have had a difficult situation with in the past. See that person in front of you. Consider the lesson you have to learn from this person. Thank this person for helping you learn the lesson that is important for you.

You softly step into the circle, and you are immediately surrounded by the pink color. The person you have had difficulty with also walks into the pink circle. You join hands with this person within the circle. You see the pink color pass from your heart to the heart of the person who is in the circle with you. Feel the forgiveness and love that you have for this person and yourself.

The pink color again enters into your heart, and you pass this pink color to the heart of the other person. Feel love and kindness toward this person.

One more time the pink color passes into your heart and now to the heart of the other person. You feel calm and serene. Let tenderness toward this person emerge like a stream from your heart to this person's heart.

It's time to come back now. Thank the other person for helping you to be more loving. Step out of the pink circle, walk out of the building, under the archway, over the bridge, and onto the road.

Feel yourself coming back into your body. Breathe deeply and exhale. Breathe deeply again and exhale. Continue to carry the vibration of forgiveness and love with you in every situation. Bring tenderness and strength into all your relationships. Feel the feeling of love shining through you into the world. Become aware of your hands and feet. And when you are ready, you may open your eyes.

# Creating Positive Behaviors That Build Lasting Relationships

I (coauthor S. Renee) was having a difficult time with a close friend. This friendship was over ten years old. Out of seemingly nowhere, the person began to say things when we spent time together that sounded like underhanded attempts to degrade me. The comments were suffocating and annoying.

At first, I would have a snap reaction to the condescending comments. This made me unhappy. To bring myself back into alignment with who I am, I briefly stepped back and out of the relationship. Limiting the person's access to me gave both of us space. But the friendship needed communication to survive. I had to confidently stand in my truth and say exactly how the comments troubled me. But I couldn't just rush in and blurt out what I wanted to say.

When situations like this occur, if you don't want to damage an already fragile relationship, you need to be intentional about how you approach the person. By doing so, you grow and honor the relationship and, if the person is open, the relationship is given what it needs to breathe again.

## Building and saving long-time relationships

If you don't develop the skills to respect, accept, and get along with others, you'll spend a lifetime looking for the perfect friend and he won't be found. Here are the steps to creating positive behaviors that build and maintain lasting relationships:

1. **Check in with yourself first.**

   Carefully check your pain spots and triggers to ensure that what you're seeing and experiencing is being driven by the other person's internal issues and not your own.

2. **Observe the other person's behavior over time.**

   Anyone can have what I call a crazy moment. Observe the person's behavior over time to see whether there's a real issue. Depending on how often you interact with the person, seven to 14 days is fair.

3. **Inquire about the person's well-being.**

   People don't always share their personal problems. At the right moment say, "Are you okay? It seems like something is bothering you." Do not ask that question during an argument because it'll seem like you're trying to be patronizing.

**4. Prepare for the meeting.**

Before asking the person to engage in conversation, make a list of a few incidents that made you feel uncomfortable. They should have occurred within seven to 14 days of the meeting. This step is crucial because most people who are called on the carpet for intolerable behavior will either deny that it ever happened, say they can't remember, or ask for proof.

**5. Have the conversation.**

Without accusing the person of what you believe is happening, tell him the exact behavior that makes you feel uncomfortable. Don't analyze, diagnose, or give an ultimatum.

**6. Stand in your truth.**

If the person isn't open to hearing and respecting your feelings, don't fight to be heard. If you do, it will become the model and a condition of survival for you within the relationship. A selfish, closed-minded, insensitive individual will eventually consume your energy and demolish your self-esteem.

*REMEMBER*

Not all relationships, personal and professional, last until death do you part. They're not meant to. When you have given your best and it's not benefitting you or the other person, politely excuse yourself from the relationship.

*WARNING!*

Don't allow anyone to mistreat you. Regardless of what he's going through, his problems are not your problems and no one deserves to be verbally or physically abused for any reason. You need to create an exit strategy for when this occurs (see the next section to find out how to go about this).

## Backing out of bad relationships with good behavior

Your goal should be to leave a person in a better place than she was in when you met her. When you're honest and live with integrity, at the very least, the dignity and respect she had when you met her should still be in tact when you depart.

This can only happen when you're a clear thinker and genuinely feel good about yourself. Good relationships gone bad get ugly when you allow your ego and pride to take center stage. A well-thought-out exit plan will support you and help you stay in a peaceful place.

Here's how to prepare your exit plan:

✔ **Accept responsibility.** I (coauthor S. Renee) have never met a person or coached a client who didn't see warning signs in the beginning of a now-dying relationship. As the chief operating officer of you, take responsibility for who you interview and invite into your space.

✔ **Support yourself.** When you peel back the layers of emotions, you'll find a disappointed little boy or girl who is heartbroken because things didn't go as planned. Comfort, love, and remind yourself that you're okay. Tell yourself that you'll find a new boss, lover, or friend. Look yourself in the mirror and hear yourself say, "I love you!"

✔ **Don't take bad behavior that has impacted you personally.** People aren't perfect. Understand that layers of experiences form beliefs and determine behaviors. Readily forgiving yourself and others and moving forward are vital to maintaining your self-esteem.

✔ **Know what outcome you want to create.** Setting your intention ahead of time is a powerful weapon for any conversation, especially when you want to be on your best behavior in a bad situation.

✔ **Don't go until you're ready.** If you meet the person before you've resolved your internal concerns and haven't made a firm decision for yourself, you could find yourself revisiting the terms of the relationship. This could put you and your self-esteem at risk.

✔ **When you feel it coming, acknowledge the feeling and leave.** Some people just don't get it! You can't help them. Stay aware. When you see that the conversation is going nowhere — and you will — thank the person for showing up in your life and helping you to grow. Leave the person's presence on that high note. It's not for them, but for you!

*Internal conflicting messages* are communications that disagree with one another. They originate when a trusted source sends you inconsistent messages. This self-coaching exercise will help you get to know your internal conflicting messaging and show you how to tell yourself the truth.

1. **Think about a pivotal event in your life.**

2. **Recall how it made you feel.**

3. **State how you interpreted the meaning of the moment.**

4. **Ask yourself: How is this moment influencing how I feel about myself today?**

5. **Based on what you know today, what is the truth about the person who violated the safe space that was created?**

6. **What really happened in that moment?**

7. **What is the truth about who you are?**

8. **Flush out your old messaging by repeating this process.**

By definition, a habit is a practiced behavior that becomes involuntary over time. Change requires awareness and reprogramming. This exercise guides and supports you as you break through habits that hinder your self-esteem. We recommend that you work to develop two or fewer new behaviors at a time unless they're in different areas of your life.

1. Decide what behavior you want to change.

2. Choose what you want to change your behavior to.

   For example, if you don't receive compliments well, you may decide you want to learn to respond to them confidently by looking the person in the eyes and saying thank you.

3. Write down your choice response and put it in a place where you can see it each morning when you wake up and before you go to bed at night.

4. When you experience the event, such as when you find yourself being given an unexpected compliment, become fully present in that moment.

5. Feel the habitual response rise in your body and pass through.

6. Happily respond as planned.

7. Repeat for 21 days.

# Chapter 15

# Rewriting Your Love Story

. . . . . . . . . . . . . . . . . . . . . . . . . . . . . . . . . . . . . . . . . . .

### In This Chapter

▶ Getting on the right path to finding love

▶ Becoming your own best friend

▶ Looking within yourself to discover who you are and what you want

▶ Living authentically and identifying your core traits

▶ Accepting and loving yourself

. . . . . . . . . . . . . . . . . . . . . . . . . . . . . . . . . . . . . . . . . . .

Advertisers sell products by enticing you with one of the four strongest forces on the planet: money, sex, power, or love. Interestingly, love is also the driving force behind the other three. Marketing experts know that you're looking for the path that leads to love.

Despite advance warning signs, your yearning for the intangible desire to be loved has led you down destructive roads. The lessons you've learned while trusting the deceptive tactics of impersonators of love — sex, money, and the fantasy of your wedding day — have forced you to return to the question: "Where might I find real love?"

Examining where you've been, where you're going, and the shape you want to be in when you get there points you in the right direction. Writing a new love story and redefining the main character shines light on the truth of where to find real love. You discover that giving yourself permission to own your power is the right lane to travel in.

If you're ready to follow that path, continue reading.

## Pinpointing Your Location

Pinpointing your location is a crucial step to moving your life in the right direction. By pinpointing your location, you can get the help you need to get back on the right path. The following analogy explains why this is important and what you need to do next.

You're traveling to a friend's house. You get lost. You call your friend for directions. What's the first question your friend asks you? "Where are you?" Your inability to pinpoint your location makes it impossible for your friend to help you.

Sometimes you may feel the same way while navigating your life — like you don't know where you are. Although it may feel that way, there are signposts that can help you determine your location:

- ✔ **Look around you.** Does anything close to you look familiar? Do you see family, friends, coworkers, neighbors, or your pastor? As people are talking, do you hear any helpful clues? If you don't see any familiar faces, who is around you? How do they act? What do they believe?

- ✔ **Determine how you got there.** Retrace your steps. Something was enormously appealing to you. Your unmet need created an opening for something to seduce you. Focused on satisfying your appetite, you followed the impersonator to an unspecified location. What was appealing to you? What were you looking for?

- ✔ **Ask for help.** Someone is familiar with your location. They've been there before. They know exactly where you are, how you feel, and what you need. Most importantly, they're willing to help. Ask for assistance. For tips on how to go about asking, check out the sidebar "Requesting help."

---

# Requesting help

"Fake it until you make it." "Act like you know." "Never let them see you sweat." These ego-centered catchphrases advise you to protect yourself from being embarrassed, judged, or viewed as incompetent. They also convey the message that people are judgmental and merciless. Is this the truth? Is it wise to sit in the dark, suppress your feelings, and refuse to ask for help?

If you ask for help, you'll be surprised at the number of compassionate people who will assist you. Here's how we suggest you prepare before you ask:

- ✔ **Get clear on what you need.** I (coauthor S. Renee) received a call from a young leader. She asked, "Will you be my mentor?" I asked, "What does that mean?" She said, "I don't know." Relationships, resources, and time

are invaluable commodities. Knowing what you want before you ask is essential.

- ✔ **Summarize your story.** Prepare by knowing what you want to say in a concise manner. The person doesn't need to know every detail. Give a high-level view, then give her an opportunity to ask questions. Remember, brevity rules.

- ✔ **Be yourself.** A sincere request is endearing and doesn't go unanswered. Be yourself. Be honest, transparent, and grateful.

The first person you approach may not be able or willing to help you. Don't take it personally. You don't know what's going on in her life that may be preventing her from helping you. Simply keep asking until you get the help you need.

# Making Friends with Yourself

How do you think you'll feel if at the end of your life you come to the realization that you made a big mistake? That you failed to see what you were capable of achieving, miscalculated your value, or rejected your incredibly brilliant self?

Have you ever thought about the person living inside you? Have you ever asked: What's important to me? What do I like to do? What impression would I like to leave on the world? Getting to know yourself requires the same desire and interest that you invest in getting to know someone else.

You don't always act the way you expect that you should. There are moments when your performance isn't up to par. You may even succumb to peer pressure or make a decision that takes you outside your belief system.

Instead of beating yourself up, gently ask yourself, "Why?" The purpose is to understand "why" you did something, which lies beneath "what" you did. This is how you get to know and make friends with yourself.

Practice these ten principles to build and maintain a friendship with yourself:

- ✔ **Decide what you believe about yourself.** Whatever you believe is true — for you. At any time you can decide to change what you believe. Deciding what you want to believe about yourself and owning that belief are paramount.

- ✔ **Speak positively about yourself.** Everyone makes mistakes. Because of perceived mistakes, you may mentally and verbally abuse yourself sometimes. Notice when you do, and remember to be patient, loving, and gentle with yourself. Building self-esteem is a never-ending growth process, so be good to yourself along the way.

- ✔ **Be honorable in your relationship with yourself.** Have you ever been cheated on or lied to? How did it feel? You're worthy of being treated fairly. Don't lie to, cheat, or dishonor yourself. Put simply, do the right thing for yourself.

- ✔ **Trust yourself.** Trust is earned over time. You have to prove that you can be good to yourself before you can trust yourself.

- ✔ **Be proud of who you are.** Be open to making changes. You can be satisfied with yourself and still seek to improve yourself — and you should. Building self-esteem is an improvement process that requires your ongoing attention in all areas of your life: mental, emotional, physical, and spiritual.

- ✔ **Make choices that celebrate who you are.** You're offered choices daily. What you do and who you choose to spend time with either celebrate and uphold you in a good light or diminish you. Choose wisely.

✔ **Make decisions that are in alignment with what you believe.** You make decisions every moment. With every decision you make, you're creating the life you believe you are worthy of.

✔ **Treat yourself in a special manner.** Nothing feels as good as knowing that you're special to someone. But nothing keeps your life on track as well as knowing why you're a special person who deserves to be treated in a special manner. Treat yourself by doing things that make you feel good about being you.

✔ **Check in with yourself daily.** Moment by moment, situations arise that can shake you and cause you to question yourself: a bad review from your supervisor, a missed contract opportunity, or a date that goes wrong. Check in with yourself to stay abreast of what's happening on a subconscious level.

✔ **Nurture your relationship.** Your needs change as you grow and encounter new experiences. As you evolve, cultivate a relationship with yourself by being aware of and responding to your needs.

---

# Deceiving yourself

I (coauthor S. Renee) received an email with "Need Your Help" in the subject line. Although the single, professional woman who sent the note was a stranger at the time, as I read her email, I was moved by her transparency, ambition, and heartfelt desire to understand why she wasn't married at 40 years old. After our initial get-to-know-you session, I discovered that she was most disturbed by the engagement of her long-time boyfriend to another woman a few months after the breakup of their five-year relationship.

During coaching sessions, she elaborated on her perception of his ruthlessness. She dwelled on the complicated, unwanted outcome of their relationship. My goal was to evaluate her level of self-knowledge and understanding so we could get to the core of her challenges.

After listening to her accuse him of countless evil acts, I asked, "Are you spending your money to continue to fight with a person who doesn't know or care about your tantrums, or do you want to heal and rebuild a relationship with yourself?"

Although she was reluctant to let him off the hook, we ventured into questions that exposed her anger and self-hate. She confessed to being disgusted by her looks. She admitted, "Every time I look in the mirror I become depressed." Although she was verbally blaming her ex-boyfriend for his possible infidelity and unwillingness to commit to her after five years, she was secretly blaming herself — her look — for his abrupt exit.

Despite intense coaching, she wouldn't take responsibility for any part in the downfall of the relationship. She also couldn't see any link between her self-hate and how she presented herself in relationships. Therefore, I thought it was important for her to test her hypothesis.

As a part of her releasing him and herself through forgiveness, her assignment was to sincerely congratulate her ex on his engagement. The face-to-face meeting was an eye-opener. He expressed his love for her, but told her that he despised her way of communicating with him. He described her as a beautiful but angry woman with unpredictable, cruel outbursts.

During our follow-up session, she admitted to the outbursts, but thought her apologies following her periods of emasculating him solved the problem. I had to help her understand that every time she looked in the mirror and denounced her beauty, she separated herself from herself. The disconnection over the years had led to self-hate. Self-hate is a poisonous venom that kills everything around it.

I offered her this: "Love is the expression of your acknowledgment, appreciation, and embrace of your inner beauty, yet because you can't see your beauty, the verbal abuse isn't against him — it's really against yourself."

# Assessing What You Like About Yourself

You're multidimensional. Your personality has many characteristics that make you exclusively you. At times, the fact that your life is in movement and constantly changing makes knowing yourself and what you want complex. We encourage you to grant yourself permission to make mistakes, change your mind as often as you want, and have fun as you become an active participant in your own unveiling.

Complete the following statements to assess what you know and like about yourself. Revisit this list often. By doing so, you'll observe changes in your perception of yourself and the world — great measurements of your growth.

- ✔ I enjoy . . .
- ✔ I need . . .
- ✔ I cry when . . .
- ✔ I'm good at . . .
- ✔ I believe I am . . .
- ✔ I feel safe when . . .
- ✔ I'm happy when . . .
- ✔ I need to develop . . .
- ✔ I'm motivated by . . .
- ✔ I need to know that . . .
- ✔ I make people feel . . .
- ✔ I'm disturbed when . . .
- ✔ My purpose in life is to . . .

    ✔ I like learning most about . . .

    ✔ I'm most comfortable when . . .

    ✔ I feel uncomfortable when . . .

    ✔ When I'm alone I think most about . . .

    ✔ What I like most about myself is . . .

    ✔ The people whom I'm most comfortable being around are . . .

    ✔ The type of people I'm most comfortable being around are . . .

    ✔ The most important lessons that I've learned over the years are . . .

# Setting Your Own Standards for Your Happiness

The reason that self-doubt is one of the leading battles in your life is not a mystery — and you're not alone. Feeling insecure and uncertain is linked to many different outcomes, such as alcohol and drug abuse, bullying, depression, and missed goals. As a consequence, it's difficult to measure with assurance the number of people who sit in this place of emotional dis-ease.

## Answering the call

I (coauthor S. Renee) was having a conversation with a communications executive. He shared with me that he was concerned about the security of his job. Confessing his fears, he admitted that for a long time, he felt he was being called to a higher place of service. He believed his life had greater purpose.

"Without a doubt, I know I have a message that will change the course of a massive number of people," he declared. "I have five books in me." I listened as he looked me in the eyes and explained that by setting and living by his own standards of success, he would lose money and influence.

Sitting straight up in the chair and interrupting him, I asked: "Could you be wrong? Could your calling be the gateway to greater financial success and influence? Are you failing to become open to the voice within you because you've been duped into believing that the power others give you is greater than the power that lies within you?"

I left the meeting saddened that he had been deceived by the veil of false security. Perhaps one day it will be lifted.

The reasons are plentiful: the emotions you absorbed in your mother's womb, while growing in divine creation; the messages you received after you were born; the images that captivated your psyche; the continuous stream of information that screams at you telling you who you are and defining for you who you should be and what you should look like.

Setting standards of intelligence, beauty, and behaviors, scandalous societies create for their inhabitants an artificial expectancy full of hoopla and foolishness that can only serve to disgrace you.

Believing that you can find solace in one of the many subcultures — family, school, college, workplace, church, and community — you're again faced with political warfare and unwarranted pressures to conform. Fighting for your remaining ounce of self-respect, you confront the attempts to crush your remaining dignity.

The truth is that everything you need lies within you. It's up to you to find it.

Freedom is setting your own standards and being authentic as you live them. The following are tips to help you get started:

✔ Decide what makes you happy.

✔ Give yourself permission to follow your heart.

✔ Release yourself from societal and cultural expectations.

✔ Look within for answers.

# Knowing the Difference between Being Authentic and Inappropriate

It's important to understand that authenticity comes from a place of love. When you're authentic, you're being yourself — a trustworthy resource who has set good intentions for what you do and those whose lives you affect.

Inappropriate behaviors are actions that are unbecoming of you and unsuitable for a particular environment. I (coauthor S. Renee) have spoken to and coached women in prison, disgruntled employees across numerous industries, and troubled teens. I've noticed this common thread: As they're nudged to awaken to the truth of who they are, they realize they've been acting out of pain. Their demand for attention and attempts to prove their point in self-defeating ways are due to their need to be seen, heard, and valued.

Here's the point: You wouldn't wear your swimsuit to the office, would you? As outlandish as that sounds, knowingly behaving in the wrong way, at the wrong time, and in the wrong place can appear that outrageous.

It's important to know which characteristics of your personality are most appropriate at which times and places. Behaving in such a way doesn't make you inauthentic: You're simply being wise.

Authenticity comes from a place of love, not pain. You need to know the difference between authenticity and acting out.

When in doubt, check in with yourself by responding to the following questions:

- ✔ **Are my perceptions of the people I work and interact with positive or negative?** Your overall perception of others is a reflection of the perception you have of yourself. If you pay close attention to what irks you about others, you'll most often see that quality in yourself. This is an easy way to see how you act out your pain.

- ✔ **Are my feelings toward the people I work and interact with positive or negative?** You interact with yourself first. How you feel about yourself creates your behavior. When you have ill feelings toward others, check your met and unmet expectations of yourself. Feelings of disgust and anger return to you.

- ✔ **Are my values in alignment with the values of the culture I work and live in?** If you don't agree with the corporate culture you work in, you are likely in the wrong place.

- ✔ **Do I enjoy my work?** You are on earth to do what you were born to do. Passionately making a difference in the lives of others through your work is true authenticity.

- ✔ **Do I feel I'm treated fairly?** When you feel you are mistreated, do you speak up or shut down? Feeling oppressed and not standing up for yourself is self-abuse and living inauthentically. This causes you to act out when you least expect it.

- ✔ **Do I often regret what I do or say?** Regret is a sign that you know that you weren't being your authentic self.

- ✔ **Are my actions contrary to what I believe about myself?** When your behaviors are contrary to what you believe, you are operating out of your pain.

# Embracing Different Aspects of Your Personality

"Keep it real" became a well-known expression that communicated: Be yourself; don't be phony. But what does that mean? Who are you — really? Are there situations in which you're shy and others in which you're outgoing?

Are there times when you're feeling ambitious and others when you're feeling laid back? Do you behave the same way around family as you do around coworkers?

Each day you enter into different environments and encounter a variety of situations. Some may say your ability to turn certain aspects of your personality on and off at will is being phony. But most often, to sustain your own well-being and support others in theirs, these encounters demand diverse levels of emotional intelligence. This level of personal and professional competency exhibits your skillfulness in managing yourself and the relationships in which you participate.

You have core traits in your personality that are expressed through your behaviors. Regardless of where you are or what you do, they're directly linked to your values and how you decide to show up in the world. These traits are what make you exceptional and distinctive.

Embracing the different aspects of your personality requires full acceptance of who you are and how you conduct yourself in each moment. Have you ever noticed yourself questioning yourself? In most cases, the reason you question yourself is because you're basing the success of your performance on someone else's expectation of you.

To help support yourself, pick up your notebook and do this exercise to help you connect with yourself and embrace your brilliance. Make a list of your core personality traits. These are the traits that most influence your motivations, behaviors, and thought processes. Some examples include passionate, adventurous, inspiring, or even-tempered.

Here are some questions to help you process your ideas:

✔ What wakes you up each morning?

✔ What are your most common behaviors regardless of where you are or what you're doing?

✔ How do you process what you're going to do in specific situations?

✔ In order of priority, list the top five important things in your life that you can't live without.

✔ What makes you joyful and what makes you miserable?

Whenever you begin looking around and questioning who you need to be, become aware of your internal dialogue and ask yourself, "Who am I trying to impress, avoid, or protect?" Once you've identified what's causing you to question yourself, it no longer has power over you.

# Accepting Who You Are and Living in Great Anticipation of Who You Can Be

When you decide to establish a standard for yourself that includes not comparing yourself to others and receiving all of who you are without judgment, you have advanced to self-acceptance.

Answer the following questions to help you determine whether you fully accept yourself:

- ✔ Do you like yourself?
- ✔ Do you like the way you look?
- ✔ Do you like how you handle conflict?
- ✔ Do you accept your shortcomings?
- ✔ Do you like the way you walk?
- ✔ Do you like the way you talk?
- ✔ Do you like what you do?
- ✔ Do you like your life?
- ✔ Do you like the shape of your body?
- ✔ Do you like what you think about?
- ✔ Do you like how you respond to people and situations?
- ✔ Do you like how you express negative emotions?
- ✔ Do you like the way you converse with others?
- ✔ Do you like how you own your personal space?

If you answered "yes" to each question, then more than likely you have accepted yourself, and overall, you have a positive perception of who you are. If you struggled, don't feel bad about it — continue the process until you can say, "Yes!" without hesitation to each question.

When you're able to answer "yes" to the preceding questions, you're able to release who you think you are and embrace the fullness of who you can be. Becoming a witness to the unfolding of your greatness helps you to understand the evolutionary journey you're on. You now know that as much as you love who you are, there is more to be discovered.

If you're committed to your development and understand you have an ever-evolving personality, it's of utmost importance that you get this: You're constantly changing. As a part of this course in human development and maturing, how you see yourself and the world today will more than likely look different six months from now. As a consequence, accepting who you are and what you think right now is important. Of even greater importance is that you shake dogmatic views and vows to yourself because they close your mind and impede your growth.

# Opening Up To New Opportunities in Life

So what does rewriting your love story mean? What are we asking you to do? Are we telling you to erase all the amazing experiences you've had over the years? Are we suggesting that what has occurred in your life has been a waste of time? Absolutely not!

Rewriting your love story is rewording how it's told. We want you to rework the meaning of those awful moments when you couldn't stand to look yourself in the mirror. We want you to revise what you thought those oops! moments meant for your future. We want you to modify how you see yourself and who you believe you're entitled to be in the world.

Rewriting your love story means standing within yourself for yourself. Without regret, you're authorized to give it your best shot again — and again. It means you're open to possibility and that no matter what happens or doesn't happen, you're enough. You have permission at all times to love, forgive, and fully embrace yourself — just as you are.

## Understanding your life lessons

There were probably moments in your life from which you remember the feeling but missed the lesson. When you hold onto the feeling without learning the lesson, the feeling sticks with you, causing you to unconsciously create more situations to validate the beliefs that remain inside you.

To help my clients become more aware of the lessons they are meant to learn, I (coauthor S. Renee) give them this exercise, which is a critical step in understanding why they wrote the love story they did and what lessons they need to acknowledge to write a more accurate version.

In Chapter 4, you're encouraged to complete an exercise where you write the significant events of your life from birth until the present. Choose pivotal moments in your life that you discovered. Draw a table like the example in Table 15-1 and use the same prompts to arrive at the lessons learned from these events.

| Table 15-1 | Reflecting on Lessons Learned from Life Events |
|---|---|
| **Prompt** | **Example** |
| Significant life event (What pivotal moment occurred?) | I was teased and bullied by my classmates while growing up. |
| My thoughts (What thoughts about myself did this event prompt?) | I thought I was different from everyone else, and, as a result, no one liked me. |
| My feelings (How did I feel about this event?) | I felt alone, scared, and helpless. |
| My action (What action did I take in response to the event?) | To be diplomatic versus honest. The reward was popularity. This made me feel safe. |
| The actual lesson (What was the lesson I was actually meant to learn?) | To learn to confidently speak up for myself without fear of being rejected. |
| The lesson returned (What subsequent event reflected the same life lesson that I had yet to learn?) | The lesson returned many times, but the consequence of not speaking up on my job more assertively led to my being fired unnecessarily. |
| Outcome (What were the results of my actions this time?) | As a result of not speaking up, I would blame others for not meeting my needs; therefore, I experienced a lot of unfulfilling relationships. |
| Lesson learned (What lesson have I since learned?) | I've learned that by speaking up for myself, I give people a choice of whether or not to acknowledge and meet my needs. If they choose not to meet my needs, it doesn't mean they don't like me; it simply means their attention is elsewhere and that's okay. It doesn't diminish who I am or the value I bring. We all have choices. |

# Writing yourself a love letter

Do you remember receiving your first love letter when you were growing up? It may have been brief: "Do you love me? Yes or No (circle one)." At the time, whether you liked the sender or not, it was flattering to know that someone cared about you.

Take the time to remind yourself that you love yourself. Write a love letter to yourself. Don't focus on what you didn't do. As you write, think about what it would be like to fall in love with you. Consider telling yourself the following:

- How much you miss and want to be with you
- What you love about you
- Why you love you
- What you want most to happen for you
- What you want from you
- Why you can't live without you
- Why you make you happy
- What you want to do for you
- How you will protect and show love for yourself
- What you see when you look at yourself in the mirror
- Your needs and how you will fulfill them

# Chapter 16

# Getting Beyond Loving Love

**W**e bet you've had that tingling sensation. The feeling that something magical is happening between you and another person. You look in his eyes and you see yourself — a part of you that you've never seen before. You want to capture that person, that feeling, again and again.

Falling in love makes you feel amazing. The intensity of your happiness and excitement changes how you walk, talk, and think. One thought chases another as you become consumed with the idea that your future is lining up just the way you thought it would.

But wait. Is it true? Is it real? Will it last?

In this chapter, we explore the possibilities of love. What is love? Why does love seem to create pleasure and cause pain? How can you best prepare for love? Where can you find love that lasts forever?

## Breaking Through the Fantasy of Love

You've seen love come and go. Bitter endings, harsh realities of forsaken truths, and scattered dreams of an ideal future. Nothing comes easier than falling in love, but nothing hurts more than facing the heartbreak of its unexpected disappearance.

Is it love that is causing you to suffer? Or has the fantasy of staged love stories and melodramatic songs carried you away on a cloud of despair?

Are you causing love to flow through you, instead of remaining with you? Love doesn't hurt, but the truth does when you're not ready to receive it.

# Understanding what love is

What do you mean when you say to a person, "I love you"? Are you expressing your intense desire for that person? Are you telling him you want the best for him? Are you expressing an indescribable feeling that is flowing through you? Does it depend on who you are talking to?

While writing this chapter, I (coauthor S. Renee) decided to take a mini poll on the question: What is love? The answers were as varied as the 50-plus people who responded via social media and telephone interviews. Is love so simple that it's hard to explain?

From my mini research and lengthy meditation on love, I got this: There is only one form of love. Love is a deep, intimate closeness that gives tender care and respect.

Love expresses itself based on the level of intimacy created between two people. Intimacy is created over time by communicating and sharing secrets and aspects of yourself according to the level of trust between you and the other person. The foundation of trust is the integrity of each person's word and the care with which the two handle each other's thoughts, feelings, ideas, emotions, and secrets.

# Appreciating what love should look and feel like

The latest lingo used to describe a love relationship in limbo is "complicated." Any and every type of relationship — romantic, parent to child, friend to friend — gets off course when respect, safety, and unconditional acceptance are nonexistent or have faded as a result of violated trust.

Because love is a deep, intimate closeness that gives tender care and respect, it creates a safe place for you and your loved one to live in unconditional acceptance. This is what we call *love space.*

What kind of love space do you create for those you love? What kind of love space do the people you love create for you?

Answer these questions to help you determine whether your love space is healthy:

- ✔ Are you affirmed, encouraged, and treated kindly? Do you offer the same care?

- ✔ When you communicate, are your words and emotions heard patiently? Do you fully hear what the other person is saying?

✔ Are anger and disappointment expressed without name-calling and degrading comments? Do you provide the same level of respect?

✔ Are you ever hit, punched, or pushed for any reason? Do you refrain from doing the same?

✔ Without comparisons or bringing up past issues, are you gently and lovingly told the truth? Do you offer the same?

✔ Do you feel free and totally relaxed being around the person? Do you provide the same level of comfort?

✔ Are you a better person because the other person is in your life?

## Preparing yourself for love

You may have heard the saying: "You attract to you what's in you." To test this truth, take a moment to think about your past and present relationships objectively. If you're honest, you'll see the behavior of those you've allowed to get closest to you mirroring your behavior toward others and the secret messages you tell yourself about yourself. Your secret messages are what we call *personal truths*. These truths tell you how you should see the world and yourself in it.

What others say — good or bad — doesn't matter. The only truths are the conscious and unconscious truths you tell yourself.

Your struggle with love is a struggle with yourself. To best prepare yourself to experience authentic love, you have to change the relationship you have with yourself first. Taking great care of yourself by protecting yourself from unnecessary hurt teaches you that you can trust yourself with your own life.

Here are five steps to help you prepare for love:

1. **Examine your view of love.**

   If it's rooted in fantasy, paint a different picture.

2. **Assess whether you react or respond to people.**

   If you react often, there's a good chance you haven't forgiven yourself or someone else for a past hurt. Forgiveness is an absolute requirement for you to express love to others.

   Here's a suggestion for how to forgive. Think about the person who hurt you and where she was in her life at the time of the offense. Consider all that she's been through in her life. Try putting yourself in her position. Ask yourself: "If I went through what she went through, might I possibly do the same thing?"

   Sometimes people's pain rules their heart — forgive them.

3. **Give yourself and others permission to make mistakes and grow.**

   You're going to make mistakes — sometimes disappointing yourself. People you love are going to make mistakes — sometimes hurting you. Holding yourself and them to an impossible standard of exactness is going to drive you and them crazy. Give yourself and those you love the opportunity to grow and discover a new truth.

4. **Care enough not to want to hurt yourself and others.**

   There will be moments when you'll feel like you've done all you can, and you'll shrug your shoulders and say, "I don't care anymore." Those who love authentically never stop caring and never want to see the one they love in pain.

5. **Understand that love doesn't stop when the relationship does.**

   Love builds; hate destroys. Love and hate cannot reside in the same place. Preparing for love demands your understanding that whether it comes, goes, or stays around, it's still love.

## Identifying what you want in a romantic love relationship

What you need from a love relationship is different from that of anyone else on the planet. Your unique needs are directly connected to what you did or didn't get in relationships over the course of your life. And although you can learn to fulfill many of your own needs through increased self-esteem, love calls for you no matter how confident you are. You were meant to love and be loved.

Before you answer the call, know what's important to you in a romantic relationship. Here are ten questions to get you started:

- ✔ What is your most favorable physique?

- ✔ What facial features are most important to you?

- ✔ What lifestyle choices are essential for you?

- ✔ What personality traits are extremely appealing to you?

- ✔ What past choices are you comfortable with accepting? For example, are divorce, children, same-sex relationships, or sexual lifestyle choices okay with you?

- ✔ What age or age range best suits you?

✔ Is race significant?

✔ Is religious background critical?

✔ Does educational achievement matter?

✔ Is financial success relevant?

## Defining the terms of your ideal love relationship

If you're willing to do the work to heal your life and be patient with the process, you can have the love relationship you want. The challenge is this: being certain that what you proclaim you want really is your heart's desire and your core need.

All things in the universe are in constant motion. As a result, you're continuously changing. At times you make leaps and at other times you barely notice a change. As you age, your physical, mental, and emotional states become different through the maturation process.

Although you change, your core needs remain the same. Your core emotional needs are safety, love, acceptance, appreciation, and intimacy. As you mature, your needs in terms of how these emotions are expressed toward you and how you express them toward others changes, but these core needs never leave you.

You have other needs that are unique to you. For instance, you may have the need for affirmation. Words may comfort you and make you feel supported. On the other hand, your friend may need your presence because seeing your face may provide the positive reinforcement that he needs to feel grounded and connected.

It's important to stay connected with yourself enough to know what your needs are and how you desire to express them and have them expressed to you.

What and who can meet your needs before you heal your life are different from what and who can meet your needs after you heal — unless you and the other person grow together. A healthy connection requires you to be what you're looking for.

## Core requirements

I (coauthor S. Renee) had a client I'll call Brandon. Brandon called my office eight years ago while going through a divorce. After I helped him successfully navigate that delicate time of his life, he started dating again. He met a woman, and over the course of three years of dating, he grew to love her. She also loved him. Before getting married, she wanted to make sure they were right for one another. She requested to take a break from the relationship, and he willingly obliged.

Brandon returned to me for coaching while he tried to understand the breakup. During the time of our coaching sessions, she decided to return to the relationship. Brandon hesitated; he needed to know that she was all in. He requested that she express her feelings about him and her commitment to the relationship in writing.

To ensure that Brandon understood his own core needs and current behaviors, I had him state what he liked most about his past relationships and why. He said, "I liked the security I felt from knowing my ex-wife had everything under control when I wasn't home."

Then I asked, "What was missing in your past relationships that you need today?"

"Nothing," he said hurriedly.

"Nothing?" I probed further. "Then why aren't you still together?" There was a long pause.

I continued, "What do you want in your current relationship?"

"Ease and comfort," he responded with a sigh.

I then asked, "What did the letter you requested represent?"

Realizing where I was taking him, he laughed and gently said, "Security."

Here's an exercise that can help you define your ideal love relationship by getting in touch with your core yearnings, which are encoded in your personality. Past relationships can help identify clues and decode the mystery of your unique core needs. Relationships dissolve when needs aren't mutually met. These experiences can help you create your best love space yet.

1. **Reflect on your past relationships.**

   List what you liked most about each person you dated. If someone comes to mind and you ask yourself, "What was I thinking?" don't give it another thought. Go to the next person. Choose the top ten qualities that made the love space satisfying. Narrow down your list to the top three to five qualities.

2. **Think about your unmet needs in each relationship.**

   Make a list of the top five unmet needs that were essential to your well-being in the relationship.

You now have an accurate list of your core needs and desires for a love relationship.

# Discovering How to Date Successfully

When you apply for a job, you're interviewed by the prospective employer before you're hired. This process is set up to help the organization understand who you are, how you think, and the value you bring to the relationship. Hiring, training, and developing a new employee only to discontinue the relationship before the new hire's work performance can yield a profit is costly.

During the interview, you're asked a series of questions to see whether your responses are genuine and warrant introducing you to the leadership team — and ultimately hiring you. The organization is contemplating its needs and your skills. The interviewer is considering the company's culture and your personality. He's examining the company's values and your attitude.

Once you're hired, there's a probationary period. If you don't perform according to the anticipated results, depending on your strengths the company will either cut its losses or seek to develop your weaknesses.

If you don't want to waste your time and become frustrated by the dating process, you need to have a "job description." It should answer the question: "What does it take to love me?" Do not show it to potential candidates.

Before jumping into the dating pool, consider the following questions to help you put together a "job description" for your ideal candidate. When you've completed this exercise you'll have a profile of your mate, which will help guide your thinking as you meet people.

- ✔ What do I expect a companion to do for me?
- ✔ What activities do I enjoy that I want my companion to enjoy with me?
- ✔ What skills are needed to love me?
- ✔ What type of person would best fit the cultures that I live and work in?
- ✔ What values best align with my values?
- ✔ What personality type best fits my personality?
- ✔ What is my companion's general attitude toward life and love?
- ✔ How will I be able to tell if a person is not for me?
- ✔ How will I be able to tell if a person is for me?

## Dating with confidence

To date with confidence you have to know what you're doing, why you're doing it, and what results you expect. If you're beyond "hanging out" and are looking instead for a serious commitment, you have to be thoughtful and purposeful as you meet people.

Before going on a date, establish your intention. State what you want to get out of the date. You may be looking for information, a deeper connection, a fun time, or all three. Whatever you decide, be clear.

You're getting to know the person; stay alert. Don't be taken in by the excitement and newness of the relationship. If something feels uncomfortable, don't ignore it. We advise you to stay away from trying to change a person. You're looking for the right mate. You're not trying to create one.

Depending on how and whom you decide to date, you can meet people from around the world. They'll be from different backgrounds and have different beliefs and associations. Their agendas will be varied. You may even be invited to participate in activities that violate your values. This level of exposure needs to be handled with care and confidence.

At times you'll think you and the person you're with have chemistry. You may date for a while and think everything is going in the right direction. Then, seemingly out of nowhere, *bam*! — the person tells you he wants out. This scenario can be emotionally painful and devastating to your self-esteem.

You question yourself. You ask, "Where did I go wrong? Why aren't I loveable? Did I talk too much? Did I not talk enough? Am I attractive enough? Am I successful enough? Am I too fat? Am I too skinny? The questions don't stop. And neither do the play-by-play run-throughs of your time together.

Before long, you're criticizing and blaming yourself for everything you did during the course of the relationship. This mode of resolving hurt feelings is guaranteed to strip you of your confidence.

Attract the love you are worthy of. Complete the following exercise to get off the injury list and back into the game.

Follow these steps to understand and reconnect with yourself, so that you can regain your confidence while dating:

1. **Close your eyes and take a deep breath. Offer yourself love.**

   If you begin to cry, support yourself. Say, "You're okay. I've got you." Allow yourself to feel what you need to feel and respond accordingly. You can wrap your arms around yourself. You can talk to yourself as though you are another person. This time is for you to love yourself in all your hurt, missteps, missed messages, and whatever else you may be feeling.

2. **Think about the relationship from your perspective only.**

   You have no idea what the other person is thinking. Who cares, anyway? He's gone. Ask, "What did I see that I didn't pay attention to?" Write it down. It'll be easy to say, "I didn't notice anything," and get agreement from your friends, but that won't do you any good. There's always a sign, and there's always an excuse to ignore the sign.

3. **After you've identified the sign, state what you wanted from the relationship that superseded your willingness to acknowledge the truth.**

   Once you recognize it, you'll be able to deal with the pain spot.

4. **Ask yourself, "What's driving my pain?"**

5. **Identify ways to heal your pain.**

   For example, if your pain is a lack of faith that you'll one day find someone to love you, the issue is misplaced beliefs and a lack of clarity about the penalty of settling for less than what you want. Write down what you believe. Next, write the truth about what you believe. Finally, list how you'll feel if you choose someone who doesn't meet your needs.

   Now that you've accepted responsibility and learned the lesson that showed up for you, you're ready to get back into the game.

## Enjoying the process of dating

Earlier in this section we talk a lot about the business aspect of dating. We encourage you to have your game face on and be ready to interview potential candidates. What's principal is that you enjoy the thrill of meeting diverse people. Have fun learning about who they are and what they want out of life. Be open to being inspired as you listen to them share their accomplishments with you.

You'll have moments that'll make you laugh. You'll have times that will shock, surprise, and even frustrate you. Either way, enjoy the journey. You'll discover far more about yourself than you will about others.

## Discovering your best dating system

There are numerous ways to meet the person whose eyes you want to spend countless hours gazing into under the stars in the moonlight. You can use all or a combination of any of the systems outlined in the following sections.

Here are a few quick tips to use regardless of the dating system you choose:

- Trust your intuition.

- Interview potential companions thoroughly.

- Seek the opinions of those closest to you.

- Build the relationship slowly and steadily.

- Let the person's behavior confirm all the wonderful things she says about herself; don't take words at face value.

The following sections discuss some useable dating systems and note some challenges each method may entail.

### Getting a referral from a friend or family member

This is a great way to meet someone. You and the person come highly recommended, and most often the mutual friend will introduce you. Although you can be a bit more relaxed, the interviewing process should always remain intact, regardless of how you meet.

*Possible challenges:* You may willingly offer your trust to a person you know nothing about. You may fail to be fully objective and in touch with your own needs because you've been told the other person is great, and you don't want to miss out. Both parties may make the assumption that it's "meant to be" because of the role the mutual friend plays and how they've been introduced.

### Encountering someone in a public place

People are everywhere. You can meet them at the post office, church, the grocery store, the shopping mall, events — the list goes on. If you have time, talk to the person you meet to get a sense of who he is. Ask questions and listen attentively for his answer. The more you get the person talking about himself, the more you'll discover about who he really is. If you exchange names and numbers, give your cellphone number, because it's harder to track than a home telephone number. Avoid sharing your last name until you find out more about the person.

*Possible challenges:* The way people present themselves in public may not be how they present themselves in private. To get a quick feel for their mannerisms instead of rushing to pick up the phone when they call, let them leave a message. You may be surprised by how quickly they become comfortable. Listen for what they say and how they say it. If they begin a conversation with you via text, you'll have to decide whether that's acceptable.

### Dating via the Internet

This is the fastest-growing platform for meeting people and developing love relationships. Despite all the sensational love stories touted by the industry, don't be anxious when interacting with people online. Use the system properly to protect yourself.

Avoid sharing your name or any other personal contact information until you establish a history with the person. If someone insists, end communication. Respecting you and your wishes is the first order of business. Once you share your name, it's easy for a person to find you, especially if you're on social media.

*Possible challenges:* Photos may not reflect the person you're speaking to. It takes longer to uncover whether the people you meet are who they say they are.

## Breaking through feelings of being judged

You may feel nervous when you go on a date because you know the person you're with is judging you. He's looking at your appearance, mannerisms, body language, facial expressions, and verbal communication. It's natural to want to impress your date. But we want to impress upon you to be yourself. Nothing is more stunning and sexier than an authentic, confident person — a person who can stand in his own truth and power without being full of himself.

If the person decides you're not the one, don't take it personally. In most cases, it has more to do with him than the brilliance he sees or can't see in you.

# Building a Lasting Relationship

Relationships are built on trust and destroyed by lies: lies that you tell yourself and others and, of course, the lies that others tell you. It is paramount that you know and live your truth as you know it. And as your truth changes, you have to be willing to courageously embrace it.

Before you jump in with both feet, give the relationship the time it needs to grow. A lasting relationship needs clear expectations, met needs, and consistency. These qualities create the safety and confidence you and your partner will need for longevity.

We encourage you to be yourself, enjoy the journey, and listen closely as your heart speaks to you.

## Liberating yourself from the need to please

When two people come together and sense a genuine connection, each person is attempting to embrace and understand what is being or can be created between them. At the beginning of a relationship, you can easily fall into the trap of trying to please the other person instead of showing her your unique interests and sharing your desires. This approach has no permanency.

Healthy relationships require your full participation. It's essential that you give your opinion when you have one. Others can't read your mind nor should you expect them to. Give yourself a voice in the beginning, and it won't be hard to find it later in the relationship.

If you need further development in this area, read Chapter 8 to learn how to use "I" statements to more assertively express yourself.

## Celebrating differences

The world is often viewed in absolutes — black or white, right or wrong, good or bad, left or right. But when you're open to possibilities, you realize that the answer isn't always found on one side or another — sometimes you have to dig around in the middle. By doing so, you expand your thinking and invite others to do the same.

The world has become as diverse as it has ever been. Learning to walk away from judgment and toward the celebration of all people and their uniqueness serves you well in and outside your relationship.

As you and your new romantic interest build the foundation of your relationship — trust, safety, and integrity provide the entrance for intimacy and love to develop. If you don't know how to hear, acknowledge, and celebrate your mate, feelings of uncertainty can arise, causing him to feel unappreciated.

Celebration of your differences is simply acknowledging that both of you are necessary ingredients to creating love.

## Protecting yourself

Just as you can't put a roof on a house before it has a foundation, you can't put love ahead of trust — don't be too eager. While you're exploring similar interests, childhoods, and past experiences and "hanging out," guard your heart. Your heart is the shelter for all your emotions. It's your sacred place of well-being. Before you invite someone into your safe haven, that person must prove to be credible, honorable, fair, and pure in intentions.

Here are some suggestions on how to guard your heart:

- ✔ Don't share information you don't want repeated until you know the person you're considering sharing that info with is honorable.
- ✔ Build intimacy through communication before having a sexual encounter.
- ✔ Before committing, watch the person's behavior toward you closely for an extended period of time. We recommend a minimum of 60 to 90 days.
- ✔ Observe how that person interacts with family and friends.
- ✔ Listen closely for excuses or explanations for unbecoming behavior. Don't tell the other person how he should behave. It's up to you to decide whether the offensive behavior is acceptable under the circumstances. If not, move on. Don't continue in the relationship with hopes of changing the behavior.

✔ Compare the person's actions to what you're seeking in a love partner. Don't linger if those actions don't meet the minimum criteria.

✔ Don't lower your standards to accommodate an unqualified candidate.

## Choosing a mate

There are as many paths to choosing a mate as there are people who will read this book. Building your self-esteem is learning to trust yourself with your life. You have to decide for yourself the criteria you'll use to select a mate.

This is what we know for sure: If you're silently thinking about all the things you'd like to change about the person, you have the wrong individual.

We suggest you identify your core needs, decide on your desires, and get clear on what you want from a relationship and mate. In addition, we recommend that you look for commonality — someone you respect and who keeps you intellectually stimulated. Consider someone you can believe in, perhaps a close friend. Our best advice is to choose someone who loves you and who you love so deeply that you never want to see him hurt.

Here are some questions for you and your potential mate to discuss:

✔ How often should we visit in-laws?

✔ How should we divide house and yard chores?

✔ Do we want to have children (or more children)?

✔ How should children be raised and disciplined?

✔ How will we handle finances?

✔ How will we interact with our friends?

✔ Where will we live?

✔ Is staying at home rather than being employed an option for either person?

✔ What are our standards for organization?

✔ Do we share the same spiritual practice?

## Sharing your life

Deciding to share your life with another person is a pivotal decision for both of you. We believe you've given great thought to this decision. You may even have a list of what you believe you're saying yes to.

Here's our list of what it means to say, "Yes, I love you. I want to share my life with you":

- I will honestly share with you what's on my mind.
- I will directly ask for what I want and need from you.
- I will gladly believe that you have my best interest at heart.
- I will dismiss anyone who intrudes in our relationship.
- I will carefully choose my battles and let the insignificant ones go.
- I will be a partner who supports you in your life pursuits.
- I will quickly forgive you.
- I will openly share with you all that I have and all of who I am.
- I will eagerly celebrate your strengths and carefully help you develop your weaknesses.

Finding love that lasts forever begins with loving and understanding yourself. It may sound like a cliché to say that you have to love yourself before you can love someone else, but it's true. If a friend asks you for a nickel and you don't have it, you can't give it to her. When you enter into a relationship, you're not the only one asking to be loved; the other person is too.

Give yourself deep, intimate closeness that provides tender care and respect and you'll attract to you someone who'll give you the same. When you meet at that intersection, it'll really be two people coming together as one.

# Chapter 17

# Improving Personal Relationships

*Y*our family and friends are likely most important to you. Yet there are times when your relationships with these individuals can be painfully difficult to understand and navigate. In fact, due to the hurt and difficulties that these relationships cause you, it may seem easier to walk away — but you don't. With 20, 30, or 40-plus years invested, you probably feel like you can't. But, can you? Should you?

A popular saying points out, "You can pick your friends, but you can't pick your family." With new-age thinking, if the law of attraction, which states that "like attracts like," is true, even that's debatable. So what can you do?

We want to help you gain a deeper understanding of relationship dynamics. In this chapter, we share with you strategies on how to successfully navigate difficult moments. We also share how to make a distinction between your issues and those of the people you love.

## Understanding Relationship Dynamics

You and every person on the planet have layers of conscious and unconscious experiences. These experiences shape values, attitudes, and idiosyncrasies. The notion that we're more alike than different proves to be erroneous when we look at this concept more closely.

You're different. No other person on the planet thinks and responds to stimuli exactly like you do. Neither does anyone else respond to specific stimuli for the same reasons. Even if you and another person share the same interests, it's for different reasons. The understanding that every person has been uniquely shaped by his experiences and how he interprets those experiences is the foundation for accepting and appreciating relationship dynamics.

## Danger zone

I (coauthor S. Renee) had a client I'll call Chris. Chris became my client while experiencing severe challenges in her marriage. According to Chris, extreme debt was overwhelming her 20-year marriage. I wasn't expecting to discover that at the core was a history of lies, infidelity, and mistrust that had invaded the once-happy couple's relationship.

The phone rang. After my usual "Good afternoon, S. Renee," a traumatized voice said, "I need to talk now."

Surprised by the unscheduled call and the insistence in her voice, I responded, "Chris?"

Without acknowledgement of my question, she blurted, "John (her husband) beat up my Mike (her lover) and he (her husband) was arrested."

Today they're divorced. They have limited contact and a relatively mutually respectful relationship — for their children's sake. Mike didn't last a week after the bout.

The danger zone wasn't the altercation. The danger zone is the place where spoken and unspoken tensions and tempers are at their peak. It doesn't always have to be both people who feel this way. One person can be angry with another while the other person is unaware. The key is to know and respond to your feelings and be aware of unspoken emotions between you and the other person. It's dangerous to pretend that everything is okay for the sake of being polite instead of standing in your truth and saying, "I can't be in your presence right now." In many cases, the truth comes out, and the results are tragic.

---

Here's what's true: At the core, everyone wants to be loved, accepted, and appreciated for who he is and what he does. That's the strand of commonality that humans share. Hence the reason we work tirelessly to earn the accolades that'll lead to the euphoria that the fulfillment of these needs creates. Interestingly, we're so different that love, acceptance, and appreciation even need to be expressed toward us in ways that feed our unique hunger pains for these things. Without them, we can potentially starve.

The realization of our differences is the foundation for understanding relationship dynamics.

## Putting your feelings in perspective

Your feelings are important. They drive, inspire, and support you. They alert you to danger and give you a different signal when it's safe to proceed. They help you express what's happening inside you, and provide direction when your mind can't figure out what matters.

With that being said, you may be wondering, "If my feelings are so valuable, why do I have to put them in perspective?" The reason you have to learn how to put your feelings in perspective is that feelings are transient.

Feelings come and go based on your understanding of what's happening in the moment. In unpleasant situations, most often your first response is reactionary. If you listen and respond to your feelings, you may create a disastrous outcome. For example, imagine your spouse says something about you that makes you angry. You lash back. Before long, the back-and-forth exchange turns into a full-blown argument loaded with hurtful comments.

Having pierced the heart of your loved one, your words can never be extracted from the deep place where they land within him. Your loving relationship becomes a land mine — nearly impossible to navigate without resistance every step of the way.

Put your feelings in perspective to avoid creating unnecessary distress. Here's a checklist:

✔ Be accountable for your behavior.

✔ Don't look for someone to blame; seek to solve the problem.

✔ Give yourself time to process your feelings.

✔ Be honest with yourself about how you feel.

✔ Step back from your emotions and totally release your pride before forging ahead with a response.

✔ Seek an unbiased opinion.

✔ If you have ill feelings about a person, don't unnecessarily put yourself in a situation where you have to interact with her until you can resolve your feelings.

✔ Set an intention for your meeting.

✔ Have the courage to speak your truth.

✔ Be compassionate and open to hearing someone else's truth.

## Separating your issues from others'

To help workshop participants better understand the causes of low self-esteem, I (coauthor S. Renee) developed a presentation called "That's Not My Stuff." I've done several variations to meet the needs of different audiences, but here's the point of the visual illustration.

Every person who is or has been a part of your life has issues. Those issues manifest themselves in different forms — for example, harsh words that crush you from within, physical abuse that leaves emotional and visual scars, or an inability to be responsible that leads to abandonment. The list is inexhaustible.

You must get this: Mom, Dad, Grandmother, whomever, did the best they could with what was projected onto them. Unfortunately, because they didn't know what to do with the negative experiences that were given to them, they gave them to you.

Because you were young and vulnerable, and lacked the understanding of what was happening, you accepted their stuff and possessed it as your own.

Now that you are older and wiser and have come to understand that others have given you their stuff, you have to identify what you're still carrying that doesn't belong to you. When you separate your stuff from other people's stuff you'll discover that, in many instances, you're acting out the pain of others.

It's difficult to remain cool in heated situations when you're carrying the pain of the past. That's why it's important to identify and release other people's stuff that, for years, you've claimed as your own. When you do so, a more authentic you will come forward. The following six steps help you identify whose stuff you're carrying and how it's impacting your life:

1. **Ask yourself these questions and write down the answers:**

   What do I love about me? What behaviors don't fit who I really am and want to be?

2. **Look at your list of behaviors that aren't in alignment with who you are. Ask yourself:**

   What discomfort are they causing me? Am I making others feel uneasy? What is it costing me? What could it cost me?

3. **Identify the people you've seen behave like that. Ask:**

   The first time I saw them act that way, what did I think of them? What did I say about them?

4. **Think about your life and what you do, intentionally or unintentionally, that counters the love you have or would like to have for yourself.**

   Make a list of these learned behaviors and negative emotions.

5. **Compare the lists you created in Steps 3 and 4, and give back what doesn't belong to you.**

   Put each item on the list you created in Step 4 under the name of the person to whom it belongs on the list you made in Step 3.

   Now that you've given them back their stuff, you can shred this exercise, knowing that you can move forward without carrying the issues of others.

# Improving Your Relationships With Your Family

If you want to successfully navigate family relationship dynamics, you'll need to sharpen your interpersonal relationship skills. You may often see family as people who will love you unconditionally, but when you hurt or get hurt by a family member, it cuts deeply. The unintentional pain imposed on you or your loved one can take a lifetime to understand and to heal.

To minimize misunderstandings and to prevent broken relationships, we want to help you develop the skills necessary to keep your family relationships intact.

## Building relationships with blended and extended family members

The world is rapidly changing. Although this change is being met with resistance by some who want to maintain traditional values, the exposure to an unprecedented amount of information has created new freedoms, which are reshaping how people see themselves, their roles, and their opportunities to participate in a global society.

For many people, this change has opened up a smorgasbord of choices about how to live, love, and experience joy. A big part of the change is a shift in family beliefs and what a family should look like in order to be called a family.

Despite the ongoing increase in divorce rates, multiple marriages, and same-sex marriages or the continuous fight for the same, there remains a perplexity of how to seamlessly integrate one's exes, children, their children, in-laws, ex-in-laws, and grandparents. If there was only one way to do this well, we'd get rich sharing it with the world.

From coaching clients going through divorces or starting to date, I (coauthor S. Renee) have learned that broken commitments often come with anger, revenge, and conflict. Decisions have to be made that impact many people, including children. When you're experiencing those emotions, it's difficult to see yourself and everyone who is being impacted by your behavior.

Here's a list of suggestions that can help you as you and your loved ones work together to create the best environment for yourselves and your families. They apply to dealing with exes and new companions or partners. We call them the "ten B's".

Keep the following tips in mind when dealing with exes:

✔ **Be respectful.** When deep hurt and unresolved pain have flooded your relationship, you can become vindictive and tempers can flair over irrelevant issues. These reactions can cause innocent people and your relationships with them irrevocable harm. Regardless of whether you agree or disagree with your ex's choices, unless they're harmful to your child or you, respect them.

✔ **Be considerate.** Show common courtesy when interacting with your ex and her new family. For example, speak to everyone when you walk into the room, call if you're going to be late picking up your child, and don't invite yourself into her home when you know you're not welcome.

✔ **Be rational.** Your ex's parents and family will want to spend time with your child, so let them. You and your child need that experience for their healthy development.

✔ **Be supportive.** There's no way around it: If you have a child together, you'll have to support your ex to help support your child. To ensure that your child maintains a healthy outlook, this means you'll have to care even when you don't want to.

To minimize conflict with a new companion and maximize your efforts with your ex, have open, honest communication with your companion. Come to an agreement on how you'll handle situations. If you take it upon yourself to do whatever you want, your companion will feel you're sharing secrets with your ex, which is not a good thing.

✔ **Be loving.** This is probably the farthest thing from your mind right now. As you let go of resentment and heal past pains, you'll discover how to love your ex despite her past transgressions and shortcomings — and she'll do the same for you.

As time goes by, you'll learn to do what you couldn't do in your marriage — understand who the person is and how to work with her. While you're trying to keep peace with your ex and work for the good of that relationship, make sure you're satisfying the needs of your new companion. Feelings of insecurity come into a relationship when someone is saying, "My needs aren't being met."

Consider these tips for relating to a new companion:

✔ **Be fair.** The scales are unbalanced when you've spent ten years with your child and two years with your stepchild. The feelings you have for someone you've just met and know little about can't compete with your feelings for people you've known for years. Don't try to feel something that isn't there: You'll only frustrate yourself. Simply be fair to the child. Treat him the way you want your child to be treated when he's with your ex's new companion. Most importantly, let the relationship evolve naturally.

✔ **Be open.** Your mate comes as a package that includes her ex, children, parents, siblings, and so on. You and your mate can't live in an isolated world: Family members need one another. Be open to all the people in your companion's life.

✔ **Be participatory.** Every family has a culture. You're not going to change that. Pay attention and understand the makeup and how your mate's family culture is structured and run. Don't resist; join in and enjoy. Teach your child to do the same.

✔ **Be cooperative.** There are times when families have to come together to share a special day, such as confirmations in the church, graduations, college visits, or weddings. These situations don't have to be chaotic. As the newcomer, you may feel like an outsider, but be cooperative and flexible. When you decided to love your mate, this was one of the countless experiences you signed up for.

If you decide on a mate with a child and you don't have any children of your own, there may be times when a special event for you and a special event for your mate's child will fall on the same day. Your loved one will be torn. Your decision to become a member of a blended family included these types of conflicts. Find the place in your heart to have compassion and understanding — no one should have to choose between you and her child.

✔ **Be patient.** It may sometimes feel like the ex has the upper hand as she mingles with family and friends while you're trying to establish your relationship with the family. Change is a process and building relationships takes time. You can't wipe away 10, 20, or 30-plus years of joy, pain, and growing together, so don't try. Be patient and just flow with it: Your time will come.

## Dealing with difficult family members

Some people have a way of bringing out the best in you — or the worst. Some people would recommend that you run as fast as you can to get away from the latter, but what happens when they're family? Is the gate locked with no way of escape?

Some family members' behaviors seem intolerable. There are others whose behaviors really are out of control. Either way, it can wreak havoc on your life and emotional well-being. At what point is it okay to cut these people off and never have to deal with them ever again?

Unfortunately, we can't tell you if and when you should walk away from a family member because only you know your level of understanding, patience, and tolerance for a particular behavior. Additionally, there are so many layers to family relationship dynamics that if anyone tells you what to do, we advise you to run from that person because it's your life and your decision.

VISUALIZE

# Speaking and acting confidently with your family

Sit or lie down in a comfortable position. Uncross your hands and feet and close your eyes. Now breathe in deeply and exhale. Breathe in deeply again and exhale. Completely relax.

Imagine you are in your favorite room in your house. You know that soon you will be talking to a family member who you need to be honest and firm with. You walk to the window, and on the windowsill, you see a box. You open it up, and inside is a piece of paper with writing about the best way to say what you need to say. Look at it and hear the words in your mind.

You are going to be talking to this relative soon. See the words "bold," "strong," and "confident" written on the bottom of the piece of paper from the box. Feel your strength. Feel your confidence.

Now see yourself with this family member. You are either in your home or your family member's home. Look around the room at the colors of the walls and furniture. Listen to the sounds you would hear.

See yourself talking confidently, telling this person exactly what your thoughts are, exactly how you feel, and what you'd like to see happen in the future. Be calm and kind but firm, explaining your point of view.

Imagine what this person's response would be. If this family member doesn't appreciate what you have said, listen to this person's point of view and then state what you'd like to see. Listen to the conversation back and forth and work with this person for a win-win situation where everyone's needs and wants are satisfied. Keep explaining yourself so the other person understands you.

See your family member agreeing with you. The two of you smile at each other because you both know that this is the turning point; this is the time that your relationship begins to be better.

Now it's time to come back. Know that you can communicate with people with strength and ease. Begin to come back gently. Become aware of your physical body. Breathe in deeply and exhale. Breathe in deeply again and exhale. Become aware of your hands and feet. And when you are ready, you may open your eyes.

---

What we would like to offer you here is a three-step strategy to help preserve your sanity while you interact with difficult family members:

1. **Live according to how you want people to respect you.**

   Your family knows you beyond your image; they treat and respect you according to how you live daily. Nothing will make your family respect you more than you establishing your expectations by living your values. By doing so, you let them know in advance what you like and don't like and how far to go with you. The majority of your family members will follow your lead.

2. **Immediately address any transgression.**

   If others don't see the line of respect, show it to them. Don't let them even put their longest toe at the tip of the line. If you do, they'll start pushing buttons just to see which ones work. Draw a line in the sand, and firmly and unapologetically let these people know that their behavior will not be tolerated under any circumstances.

3. **Show repeat offenders the door.**

   If you don't set the standard in the beginning, you'll have to fight to get your power back because some people inevitably say, "You can't tell me what to do." This typically happens when they suffer minor consequences, if any, for past infractions. In this situation, you have to put your foot down and let them know that this is the last time you'll tolerate that behavior. If it happens again, they'll no longer be invited to share time with you until they can respect you and your space.

We don't advise that you say, "I don't ever want to see you again" or "I can't stand you." These types of words and behaviors negatively impact you and the other person while destroying the relationship. You'll maintain respect and order if you address the behavior instead of criticizing the person.

# Detecting Where You Fit within Your Friendships

In this age of social media and text messaging, acronyms are the latest craze. BFF is used to express the status of a special friend in your life. It means "best friend forever." Is it just cute and sexy, or does BFF have real meaning?

Perhaps adding BFF to a status update means nothing, but when it comes to interacting with your so-called best friend forever, grandstanding may not be as easy as you expect. To determine whether "#BFF" is more than a way to spread a message about how important you are in a variety of platforms, ask yourself the following:

✔ Does your friend accept you for who you are?

✔ Is your friend actively supportive of what you want to do?

✔ Does your friend encourage you when you're down?

✔ Does your friend share equally in maintaining the relationship?

✔ Can you depend on your friend?

If you answered yes to those five questions, then you have more than a social cyber friend.

## Creating deeper connections

Over time you've come to trust your friend. If you spend a lot of time with your friend, more than likely there have been moments that have made you wonder whether this person is truly your friend. That's the nature of relationships — having moments of doubt and concern about behaviors that make you secretly call them crazy.

The fact that you're still in the relationship indicates that you're getting satisfaction from the friendship and, overall, the good outweighs the bad. You also understand that perfect friendships don't exist, and you believe that regardless of what happens, your friend has your best interests at heart.

If you want to develop deeper connections with your friend, you have to invest time to build trust and a greater appreciation for who your friend is and who she's evolving into.

Consider the following to develop the richness of the relationship:

- ✔ Take a mutually enjoyable trip together.
- ✔ Have transparent conversations about your hopes, dreams, and fears.
- ✔ Commit to communicating regularly.
- ✔ Ask, "How can I best support you?"
- ✔ Give unselfishly and keep secrets loyally.

## Overcoming disagreements and hurt feelings

Friendship should be a place of safety, refuge, laughter, and complete authentic freedom. You may have some friends that you never disagree with, whereas moments with others may cause you to pause and ask yourself, "Why are we friends?" More than likely they passed the BFF test we talk about earlier in this section.

Their presence in your life is evidence that you're willing to accept them as they are — or at least work with them. To do so, you need to build the skills necessary to understand and work through difficult moments that cause hurt feelings.

When people express themselves in a wrongful manner, it's due to a level of disrespect and a lack of appreciation. This issue must be addressed.

The information that follows should be viewed holistically to best help you work through disappointing moments and hurt feelings:

- **Be aware of what's happening in your friend's life.** There are times when a situation in a person's life can cause him to be more temperamental than usual. If you're aware of this, give your friend the opportunity to talk about it without being interrupted or hearing your opinion. If you're not aware of any concerns say, "You don't seem like yourself. Is something bothering you?"

- **Understand your friend's personality and internal issues.** You likely have a lot of information about your friend that can help you understand what drives him and why he thinks and acts the way he does. Take this into account when disagreements come. Most often, what was said or done comes from a place where your friend is experiencing pain, and it has nothing to do with you.

- **Share your concerns.** Understanding your friend doesn't resolve your hurt feelings. You should never feel that you have to choose between your feelings and any relationship — both are important and should be satisfied. Be transparent and tell your friend what hurt you and why. Be clear so that she understands the lines that were crossed and how it made you feel. If she values you and your friendship, she'll apologize. When she does, forgive her and move on.

Most often you'll know when you've done something wrong. When you do, go to the person and apologize. Friendship isn't about competition or who's right; friendship is knowing that regardless of what state you find yourself in, there's someone in the world who has your back.

## Assessing the value of personal friendships

You probably have many people in your life. Out of literally thousands, you may have a handful of personal friends and perhaps a smaller inner circle of genuine friends. Who are your friends? Do you categorize them? If not, should you?

You can't tell everyone everything. People can't handle it, nor do they want to. Others will teach you what they can handle and what is of interest to them. Therefore, it's important that you listen and know with whom you can safely share specific information, without risking inaccurate conclusions being drawn about you or ill feelings developing between you and the other person. Wrong conclusions and bad feelings can cost you valuable relationships.

The following criteria characterize different levels of friendship — inner-circle friends, outer-circle friends, and acquaintances — to help you put your friendships in perspective.

✔ **Inner-circle friends:**

- There's an even exchange of sharing confidential information.

- There's a proven record of reliability, and you depend on one another for support in different areas of your lives.

- You have mutual interests and enjoy sharing in activities.

✔ **Outer-circle friends:**

- Talking comes easily when you connect. It can be days, months, or years since you last spoke, but the invisible, inexplicable connection is there. This connection can make someone appear to be an inner-circle friend. However, the lack of consistency, reliability, and other failed appearances puts the person outside your inner circle.

- The interaction and caring between you and your friend is genuine, but core differences keep you from aligning as inner-circle friends.

- They're in and out of your life based on what's happening in their life and yours.

✔ **Acquaintances:**

- They really aren't your "friends," but because you've shared some experiences together, you call one another friends; "acquaintance" seems too unfriendly.

- You see one another on a regular basis because you participate in a program, serve on a board, attend classes together, or live next door to one another. These consistent touch-points give you the feeling that you "know" each other, but, if asked, you would know very little about each other.

- It's an unspoken understanding that you have very little in common. Warm pleasantries are exchanged, and personal questions are avoided or asked out of curiosity rather than concern. Detailed conversations are topic-specific.

- There's a mutual understanding that asking for something is considered a favor, and at some point the favor must be returned.

Use the preceding criteria to place the names of your friends where they belong. If you have your own standard of categorizing your friends, feel free to use it, or add your personal touch to the guidelines offered here.

## Knowing when a friendship isn't right for you

Maybe you're struggling with a friend and trying to figure out whether you should excuse yourself from the relationship. The struggle is likely coming from the feeling that either you're not being treated in a way that you believe you deserve, something is intentionally being done to you that you don't like, or you're giving more than what you're receiving. At the core, your needs aren't being met in a way that satisfies you.

Take a look at this from two perspectives:

- ✔ **Is your friend your teacher?** Every person and situation shows up in your life to teach you something about you. Could you be focused on what your friend is or isn't doing and failing to see what lessons you're to learn?

  I (coauthor S. Renee) have many clients whose friends' behavior mirrors their own, yet they hate what they see. Step back for a moment and ask yourself, "What do I dislike the most about my friend? Do I ever do the things that he does? What is this experience meant to teach me?" If this is the case, find ways to increase your confidence and skill set in dealing with your friend. By doing so, you'll grow as a person and your friendship will take a different turn.

- ✔ **Are there compatibility issues?** Some people aren't meant to be in your circle. Although this may be difficult for you to own, you invited them into your life because of your need at the time. Now that your need has been satisfied or the problems the person causes offset the value she brings, you want her out. You don't have to trigger hard feelings by telling her all the things you don't like about her; simply scale back the amount of access she has to you and move on with your life. She'll get the message.

## Balancing your old friends with your new future

Your career is forging ahead, but your friend's life is humdrum. Or, you decide to get married and your friend is still single. Changes in your lifestyle can change your relationship's dynamics, the quality of your conversation, and common activities that once interested both of you. Can your relationship survive the changes?

Career success doesn't necessarily denote that you're outgrowing your friend. And marriage doesn't mean that you'll no longer have time for your friend. If your friend becomes jealous, demanding, or insensitive to your new opportunities and the necessary changes to your friendship, then he didn't prepare for the inevitable.

Career success is a barometer for your hard work, and taking on family responsibilities is a life transition. Friendship is a measurement of acceptance, genuine concern, and consistent support, even if it looks different in the future.

# Chapter 18

# Re-Creating Your Image for Professional Success

"**A**ny questions?" I (coauthor S. Renee) asked. I had just concluded a 90-minute workshop on personal branding. The questions started pouring in when suddenly, everyone fell silent as we heard these words:

"Why can't I get the promotion? I'm a great worker. I arrive early and stay late. I ace special projects, and I'm often praised for my work performance." Pausing, he continued, "I shut my mouth, do my job, and go home."

Do you ever feel that way — devalued?

In this chapter, we coach you through a brand-building process. Expect a shift in your perception of your value and the opportunities available to you in the workplace. Providing proven strategies of how to package, present, and position yourself, we give you the information you need to give your career the boost you've been looking for.

# Building an Effective Personal Brand

Have you ever thought of yourself as a product?

Personal branding, in theory, is very similar to product branding. Products have a purpose. They have specific characteristics that make them appealing. They solve problems for targeted markets, which are also called audiences. When they bring the anticipated value, a buzz is created and demand increases.

How would you like to create a buzz about you? A few misconceptions often confuse people during the brand development process. We want to share them with you along with the foundations of effective brand building.

- ✔ **Your brand is not identical to your reputation.** When a group of people is asked the question: "Do you have a brand?" typically, the majority respond, "No." The next question is, "Is your brand your reputation?" Most say, "Yes." That's partially correct. Reputation emphasizes your character. Your brand is your reputation and what people expect to get from what you do.

  Here's the difference. "He's a good, honest businessman" is an example of reputation. "He's a good, honest businessman who sells quality, well-priced used cars to middle-class families" exemplifies a brand.

- ✔ **Image and branding are different.** Many people are also under the impression that their image is their brand. Your image is the perception that people have of you as a result of seeing and/or having minor interactions with you. Your image is an opinion without any real understanding of who you are or what you do. Your brand is a result of others having direct contact with you or a testimony from a reputable resource who has had an experience with you. Your brand has an image component that we address in this chapter.

- ✔ **People are clear about your brand, even if you aren't.** As mentioned, most people don't believe they have a brand. Nor have they given much thought to personal branding. Although you may not know the value you bring to your business and personal relationships, that doesn't mean the people you interact with haven't calculated the value you bring to their lives. What they know about you is the barometer they use to determine which promotions, assignments, and invitations are extended to you.

- ✔ **You can revamp your brand.** Committing a faux pas can shake your confidence and cause you to question whether you should begin writing your letter of resignation. Despite what you may be thinking or feeling, you're not stuck in past mistakes or failed attempts to make a positive impression and to have your work seen as valuable. At any time you can find out what is being said about you. If you don't like it, you can change your message.

# *Letting Go of Failed Performances*

People understand making mistakes. When you require yourself to hit the bull's-eye every time, you create a false expectation of yourself and others. Subsequently, you probably find it difficult to accept your mistakes and forgive others for theirs. The greater shame is that you miss the good fortune of the mistake — the lesson. Plus, you set the conditions for yourself to have to repeat it again.

Letting go requires three steps:

1. **Acknowledge responsibility.**

   Without shame or guilt, take responsibility for the mistake.

2. **Look for and learn the lesson.**

   You subconsciously created the lesson. Understand what you were to learn.

3. **Share what you learned with someone else.**

   By sharing the lesson with someone else, you replace your feelings of disappointment with feeling of gratitude for the opportunity to help someone else. This is how you mature. Additionally, when you share the lesson, it works as therapy for you in that it releases its power over you.

Recovering from past mistakes requires letting go, but making a comeback from past mistakes requires an understanding of the following:

✔ **You have to know your purpose.** What does purpose have to do with it? Everything. Branding isn't just for celebrities. And it's not about making a lot of money, although it can increase your income. At the foundation of genuine brand development is authenticity. The process encourages you to identify your passions and live out your purpose.

✔ **You have to develop a message.** Have you ever said, "I'm multi-talented; I can't decide what I want to do?" Talent doesn't equal passion. Like a famous product jingle, you have to have a message. It's the message that alerts the market to what you have to offer.

✔ **You can determine your value.** I'm worth millions. I'm priceless. Of course you are. But, how much is your knowledge worth? You can select a contractual amount or salary of your choice. However, your client or employer decides whether he'll pay it. Learning how to substantiate your value increases your chances of getting what you want.

Here's an exercise to assess your current personal brand: Write three adjectives to describe you. Now ask three to five people to write down and give you three adjectives that they think describe you. You should ask people who interact with you for different reasons and on different levels. Here are a few suggestions: family member, coworker, supervisor, pastor, teacher, or friend. Don't influence the person's response by giving your opinion. The adjectives that appear consistently are your current personal brand. Process the data and lay it aside for now. You are trying to determine whether how you see yourself is in alignment with how others see you and whether those opinions are consistent.

Like a lawyer shaping a story in the minds of a judge and jury, building a brand requires a story. Your story should pique a person's interest because of its human elements and value to the organization. Your answers to the following questions will help shape your story:

- ✔ Who do you help?
- ✔ Why do you help them?
- ✔ How do you help them?
- ✔ What results do you create when you help them?

## Feeling invisible

I (coauthor S. Renee) received an urgent call from a former workshop participant. I'll call her Dr. Dee. Recently, due to new leadership, Dr. Dee had been released from her responsibilities in academia. She called me after months of applying for jobs she was well qualified for but failing to get even an acknowledgment of her interest. After earning a terminal degree, accumulating years of experience, and having a published book under her belt, she expressed to me that she felt invisible.

We decided that a reasonable goal would be for her to get interviews. I requested that she email me the current materials she was sending to potential employers along with a few job descriptions.

After careful review, I could clearly see why she wasn't landing any job interviews. Her materials were well written. Like most people, they communicated her experience, but they didn't reflect the results she created. I decided that the most time-effective strategy would be to interview her.

After I had gathered the data, she was astounded by how much she had contributed to increasing profits through student retention, negotiation, and leadership. She had implemented student development programs that increased student retention. She had increased productivity by bridging the communication gap between the administration and faculty. Her motivational style and reward system created healthy competition and focus within her department.

After we packaged and positioned her value, I was confident that she had a competitive advantage. Within a week, she had her first interview. Before the 14th day, she sent me an email saying she was a finalist for a vice president position. She didn't get that position, but within 30 days, she was named the vice president of student affairs at a university.

Keep in mind that the "why" component is enormously important. How many times during an interview have you been asked, "What motivates you?" On the surface, it appears to be a simple get-to-know-you question — a question that's seeking to determine whether you'll show up every day for work. But for the person who has to make a ruling about being around you for conceivably years to come, the question really being asked is "Why did you wake up today?"

# Identifying Your Life Purpose, Message, and Value

Like the products you use every day, you were created for a reason. You solve a problem. Whatever it is that you are meant to do, it will bring you gratification while satisfying the needs of others. People need to know who you are and what you do; therefore, you have to develop a message that resonates with them. When you do, a value is assessed that justifies paying for your services.

## Your purpose

We know you've heard this before: You have a purpose in life. If you have yet to uncover yours, hearing this statement again may only increase your uncertainty about who you are and your value.

Knowing your purpose doesn't add to your value. Knowing and living your purpose is an expression of the value you already possess.

Since the day you were born, you've been in possession of your purpose and all your real value. You just have to remember what and where it is. For example, if you find a quarter in your pocket that you forgot you had, is it now worth a dollar? Of course not. It's still worth a quarter. The value in finding the quarter is this: You can now choose to do whatever you want with it. You can spend it, save it, give it away, or invest it.

There are different paths to discovering your purpose. The process I (coauthor S. Renee) often use is what I call "Pain Meets Purpose." I developed this process because numerous clients were requesting greater success — but on a subconscious level, they were seeking to increase their confidence by discovering their life's purpose.

Here's a high-level view of a series of questions I ask. It's different for each client because it's a natural question-and-response process, but this list will give you an idea of how it works. You can walk through it yourself. If you have difficulty getting to your core, which can be the case when people try to do the process for themselves, here's the main point behind the strategy: For every question, keep asking, "Why?" until you get to your core. Or talk with someone who has the skill set to help you, or hire a coach.

1. **From as early as you can remember, what interested you when you were young? What was your favorite subject?**

2. **Was there anything in particular about that subject that interested you?**

3. **Why was this important to you?**

4. **Starting from where you left off, share more.**

5. **What caused you to like or dislike that experience?**

6. **How did that make you feel?**

7. **Why is that important? You've reached the core!**

When you get to your core, you'll understand why you've been so profoundly impacted by a situation. You'll get clarity on why certain things make you cry and why others bring you joy. There's most often a link between how you were impacted and what you are meant to do in the world. This information will also tell you why you are moved to do it. If the preceding questions didn't get you there, here are some additional questions that will give you clues:

- What do you enjoy learning about?
- What television programming do you enjoy? Why?
- What do you like to see happen? To whom? Why?
- What do you hate to see happen? To whom? Why?
- What moves you to action? What is the action you often take?
- What are you doing when you feel at home?
- What is the earliest event of your life that most shaped your thinking?

An important clue to solving the mystery of your life purpose is this: Your purpose is what makes you likable. It's what you enjoy giving and what people love receiving from you most!

## *Your message*

In deciding to purchase a product, you create a profile or mental sketch of what the product will do for you. You don't do this alone. Using real-life scenarios — sometimes exaggerated — television commercials and radio advertisements tell you a story about the product or service in 15 to

60 seconds. Magazine ads use pictures and words to do the same. Unless the product comes highly recommended from a reliable source, the story you're told must be convincing enough for you to buy the product.

Unless you're a business owner, you more than likely don't use these traditional platforms to tell your story. The platforms you use are live interactions — telephone, texting, email, and social media such as Facebook, LinkedIn, Twitter, and Google+. You use these mediums daily to communicate your story through your words and actions.

Creating a message that speaks to others requires thoughtful consideration and some research. By doing the work, you can develop a message that can help distinguish you from your competition!

Ascertain what your message is. Determine whether it's what you want to communicate. Decide whether it clearly states what you can do for your audience. The following steps will help you:

1. **Create forms with tables that look like the ones that follow.**

   Complete and place them in a folder. Don't share your opinion of yourself with others.

| Current Message | At Work | At Home | On Social Media | Other |
|---|---|---|---|---|
| What do I do? | | | | |
| How do I make others feel? | | | | |
| What do others get from me that adds value to their life? | | | | |

| Suggested Message | At Work | At Home | On Social Media | Other |
|---|---|---|---|---|
| What should people know about what I do that they don't know already? | | | | |
| How should they feel after interacting with me? | | | | |
| What should I deliberately do to add value to their life? | | | | |

**2. Recruit three to five people to be your market research team.**

Your team doesn't have to be marketing experts. You need people who are willing to be honest with you and help you evaluate your message. Identify a person in your family, on your job, and in your social network. Enlist someone who knows little about you. The diverse group should provide a well-rounded, precise view.

Send a blank copy of the table that follows to your marketing team via email, or make copies and distribute. Ask them to fill it out and return it to you. It's okay if they solicit others' opinions.

| Value to Others | At Work | At Home | On Social Media | Other |
|---|---|---|---|---|
| What do you know about me that you think everyone should know? | | | | |
| How do I make you feel? | | | | |
| What do you get from me that adds value to your life? | | | | |

**3. Process the data.**

Using the information gathered from the first and second exercises, complete the following table. As you think about what others see in you, ask yourself the following questions. Do you present in the same way across all platforms? Does your current message effectively communicate the message you want people to receive? Are people's perceptions of you in alignment with the message you want to convey? Do you need to make adjustments? What do these adjustments need to be?

| Necessary Challenge | At Work | At Home | On Social Media | Other |
|---|---|---|---|---|
| How can I better communicate my message? | | | | |
| What do I need to improve to intentionally leave people feeling the way I want them to feel after seeing or interacting with me? | | | | |
| What do I need to do to add greater value to others' lives? | | | | |

4. **Watch television commercials, listen to radio ads, and look at ads in magazines.**

   Pay close attention to how they position their product, problem, and solution.

5. **Create a 30- to 60-second commercial about yourself using the product, problem, and solution formula.**

   You can write it, record it, or videotape yourself. Be creative and have fun. The purpose is to get comfortable with your message until it rolls off your tongue like your name.

6. **Practice your commercial until you're comfortable with it.**

## *Your value*

You calculate your financial value to an organization by computing the cost of the problem to the organization.

Here's a hypothetical situation: You teach stress-relief techniques to employees. You're pitching your services to a business with 120 employees. Ten percent, 12 employees, are sick 10 days a year due to health complications that are caused by stress. Collectively, the 12 employees miss a total of 120 days. Say each employee earns $60,000 per year. That's approximately $239.00 per day ($29.88 per hour) based on 251 working days per year. Consider the financial loss when employees are sick. Multiply $239.00 by 120 days. That equals $28,680 per year for sick pay. The organization makes 25 times the employee's per-hour costs, which is $747 per person per day ($29.88 multiplied by 25). That's $89,640 ($747 times 120 days) in non-productive-employee costs. Add $89,640 and $28,680 to calculate the total financial cost to the organization, $118,320. To continue to showcase the value of your services, consider other costs — taxes, impact on morale, customer service, and turnover. You can see from your ability to reduce absenteeism and increase productivity that you could easily demonstrate a value of more than $75,000 for three training sessions.

This confidence booster for brand building is applicable when you're interviewing for a promotion or a new position or when you're trying to land a client. Most often the customer won't see your value upfront. You'll have to ask the right questions to best position yourself. The preceding model is how others in the same position that you are maintain their confidence and relevance in the marketplace. They stay current on industry changes, and they know what they know and make sure their audiences know what they know.

By following this model, you can do it too!

# Packaging Your Image

Have you ever walked into a room, looked at someone for the first time, and asked yourself, "Who is that?" Something told you the person was important. You wondered, "What does he do for a living? Which department does he work in?"

How you look and present yourself at a distance stimulates people's interest in knowing more about you. Their curiosity is inspired by how you walk, talk, stand, sit, and dress. Your smile, nonverbal communication, and personality play a vital role in this mysterious attraction.

You can create a presence that draws people to you. They'll want to talk to you — making you feel important, valuable, and necessary. If you desire, you can create this inquisitiveness everywhere you go. With practice and precision, it can become part of your being.

Here's how to rework five vital areas of your presentation skills to help you shift your presence and increase the probability of someone looking at you and asking, "Who is that?"

✔ **Your personality:** Character isn't something people see right away, but they can sense it. It's the energy or vibe you give off. It tells people what you believe about yourself and others, how you think, and what they can expect from you. Lack of confidence and other internal issues can unintentionally cause your behavior to be inconsistent with how you want to present or think you're presenting yourself. For instance, a shy person may present as standoffish. To work on your personality, make adjustments to your attitude.

✔ **Your dress:** You have to look the part you claim to play. For ten years, I (coauthor S. Renee) worked in the entertainment industry. When my agent would call me for an audition, she'd give me a brief description of the role. She would also advise me on what to wear that would best fit the look of the character. If movies reflect real life, then real life should reflect the movies, right? From your hairstyle down to your shoes, how you look should complement your body type, your size, and the job you want. Besides, the better you look, the more confident you are.

After you get dressed, look in the mirror and honestly ask yourself, "Would I take a second look at me?"

✔ **Your walk:** Walking is an art. It's an expression of your unique style. Your posture can say, "I'm confident and classy" or "I'm clumsy and self-conscious." Most people's postures fall somewhere in the middle. You can improve your posture by taking the good old advice of walking with a book on your head. Using this technique can help you train yourself to keep your head up, shoulders back, and legs straight.

The pace of your walk can indicate purpose, importance, urgency, complacency, or contentment. Regardless of where you fall (no pun intended), you can improve or change the message of your walk. Just as what you wear determines how you feel, it also influences how you walk. Women don't walk the same in sneakers as they do in heels. Men don't walk the same way in jeans as they do in a suit.

✔ **Your talk:** For years research has suggested you have a minute to a minute and a half to make a good impression. You can use your facial expression (55 percent), tone (38 percent), and words (7 percent) to influence the receiver of your message. New research shows people make judgment calls on your trustworthiness within a few seconds of meeting you. Television talk shows, reality television, and other imaging through the media and social engagement have claimed more space in our mental and social DNA. Whether accurate or not, people feel more gifted and qualified in making quick conclusions on how likable and trustworthy you are. This means you have to work on developing your communication skills, particularly the tone in which you present your words.

To increase your approval rating, consider doing the following exercise: Record yourself talking. Use your cellphone's voice or video feature. During playback, listen for tone, diction, and warmth. Ask yourself, "If I heard this voice, how would it make me feel? Is it convincing? Is it trustworthy?" Share this exercise with your friends. Have fun giving opinions about each other's communication style.

However you sound, your nonverbal communication and tone should line up with your desired personal brand.

✔ **Your smile:** A warm, engaging smile sets most hearts afire. To maintain your confidence and ensure that your smile is effective, the condition of your teeth plays a vital role. Brushing and flossing twice a day is recommended. Go to the dentist twice a year for maintenance. Nothing says, "Nice meeting you" better than a beautiful smile.

# Nailing the Job You Want

Every person who is doing what she was born to do has a story to tell that outlines how she arrived at the doorstep of her dream job. There's no one path to paradise. However, there are some things you can do to help yourself get there:

✔ **Be confident in yourself.** People are drawn to confident people. Present with confidence your problem-solving package: mission (purpose), message, value (your skills, knowledge, and experiences).

- ✔ **Make yourself known.** Be in the eye of the public. People don't know you exist unless you introduce yourself and your services. Attend conferences and networking events.

- ✔ **Connect with your network.** People will only know what you want if you ask. Tell everyone you know what you're looking for.

- ✔ **Access your network's network.** When you tell people what you are looking for, they may not be able to help. But they may know of someone who can. Ask them for a recommendation of someone they may know who may know someone.

- ✔ **Be a volunteer.** People who help people volunteer. When you volunteer to serve, you set yourself up for success.

- ✔ **Get impressive endorsements.** Getting respected people to endorse your work is added credibility.

- ✔ **Do the work and be open.** When you earnestly believe in something, it will happen, most often in a way and at a time that you least expect. If you are transitioning from one career to another, you may have to take a reduction in income or surrender your title for a less glamorous one. Enjoy the journey of pursuing your passion. Follow up with people occasionally; keep learning new things and building your brand — trust us, it works.

## Stepping into success

I (coauthor S. Renee) spoke at a national bank. I had an hour to give a high-level, impactful view of personal branding and its importance to the bank associates' lives and careers. Unbeknownst to me, in 60 minutes the information shared would change the course of an employee's life. I'll call him Jack.

According to an email communication from Jack, he was frustrated because he had no idea what he wanted to do in the workplace. He declared the greatness within him but didn't know how to use it.

He said, "Literally the day after your presentation, I decided to get off the sidelines and into the game." Public speaking interested him. He joined the company's Toastmasters Club. Before long, he was taking on leadership roles. Then he was earning first place in area competitions. Because of the internal newsletter that provides updates on employees' successes, Jack is making a name for himself.

He has become a better communicator with leadership, managers from various departments know who he is, and most importantly, he reports that his wife really likes his new style and confidence.

# Preparing Yourself for Success

It can appear that out of nowhere, suddenly a person is successful. We assure you, that's not true. For years that person has been refining his skills, sharpening his image, and strengthening his relationships.

Most successful people plan their journeys to success. You may have heard people say, "I wasn't expecting this." It may have been an unconscious effort or they may not have been able to predict with precise accuracy the results they created, but more than likely, somewhere within themselves, they knew they were headed for success. Who works hard to get nothing or go nowhere?

Success does increase confidence. It says, "I have something to offer. I'm valuable." Do you want to feel that way? The following sections show you how.

## Gearing up

Here's how to prepare for your success:

- **Have a vision.** Everyone has a dream. Isn't there something you've always wanted to do? If you're unsure, don't be afraid to try different things to see what speaks to you. Not having a vision is like walking through life wearing a blindfold. Your vision doesn't have to be big. Start with something small if necessary. We just want you to start imagining yourself doing something that will make you feel alive.

- **Have a plan.** Nothing fancy is necessary. Some people are systematic and need a well-crafted plan. Some people can flow with life and see and seize opportunities as they come. You have to know what works best with your personality and level of faith and confidence.

  I (coauthor S. Renee) confess; I have never had a long-term plan — for anything. I have desires. I learn what I need to do to satisfy those desires. I work hard to achieve those desires. That's what I call my plan. For example, despite my height (5'3") and being told I wasn't model material, my vision was to be a model. My plan was to get training, approach department stores to build experience, and get an agent. I was a model for ten years working with some of the biggest names in the business — nothing fancy was needed.

- **Know what you need.** Industries are looking for their next star performer. Today, innovation and intellectual property rule. Are you prepared? Do you know what the industry you work in is looking for?

- **Develop resistance to rejection.** Be prepared to hear "Not interested" or "I don't see how this would work." If people offer good advice on how to improve your pitch, accept it with gratitude. Ask them whether you can stay in touch. Offer to work on a project with them. If the response is something like, "I'm sorry I wasted my time with you," be respectful, thank them, and after you're out of their presence, affirm yourself rather than letting it shake you.

✔ **Develop your attitude.** For years it has been said that 85 percent of success is attitude. Fifteen percent is skills and knowledge. A positive outlook on life is contagious, uplifting, and inspiring. People hire people they like. Your attitude will take you to, through, and beyond the doors of success.

✔ **Develop a support network.** You can't do it alone. No one can. Seek support from family, friends, a mentor — or people you haven't met. Find people who share your values and dreams. Look for people who say things that let you know they believe in you. The words from your network should enrich, encourage, and challenge you to pursue your dreams.

✔ **Be strategic with your time and priorities.** Everyone on the planet is seeking to get her needs and desires met — including you. Your time should be spent on things and people that help move your agenda forward. And you should help them move their agenda forward. That's not selfish; it's smart.

✔ **Be confident, but humble.** After you've built self-esteem in yourself and gained success as a result, be willing and open to help others do the same. Remain in gratitude and always remember your story, even if you never have to live or tell it again.

## Structuring your day for greater productivity

Emails, text messages, follow-up calls, meetings, reports, and project deadlines can be mentally taxing. Family responsibilities, personal growth, special quiet time, and maintaining friendships can make living in a hurried society seem nearly impossible. Staying hip by posting updates on Facebook, LinkedIn, Twitter, Google+, and Instagram can cause you to ask, "How can I do it all without losing my mind?" You can't. Having priorities is vital to your mental health, physical well-being, and professional success.

Increase your productivity and decrease the stress in your life by developing the following habits:

✔ **Start your day with the most important tasks first.** That's not always easy when you have management and colleagues dictating your time — calling you into unscheduled meetings, assigning you to last-minute projects, and "needing your help." To jump-start your day and feel a sense of accomplishment, arrive early and close your office door to have uninterrupted work time. If you work in an area without a door, get a personalized clock sign that reads: "Uninterrupted Work Time; I'd be happy to help you at . . ."

✔ **Detox from your mobile device.** If your mobile device can be found in your hand (and in your bed) the majority of your day, unless your job calls for it, there's a possibility you're under its spell. Emails, text messages, social media, and casual unimportant conversations are time thieves. Pinpoint specific times in your day when you'll download and respond to emails and other messages. Place your mobile device in a concealed place until you complete important tasks. This will eliminate its ability to constantly draw you in, swallowing up your time.

✔ **Take mental breaks to be proactive about greater sustainable health.** Studies show closing your eyes for 10 to 15 minutes after four to six hours of work yields a high return of greater productivity.

✔ **Eat and drink healthily, take vitamins, exercise, and get your rest.** This combination keeps your body in balance and your energy up.

✔ **Be flexible; make quick decisions.** Situations and challenges come up throughout the day. Don't complicate life by fussing over everyday challenges and situations. Make quick adjustments and keep your day moving forward.

# Positioning Yourself for Success

You can and should position yourself for success without being shrewd, underhanded, or inauthentic. Positioning your product — you — in the busy workplace requires deliberate strategic planning. Regardless of the size of the organization, four important elements help to successfully navigate this difficult terrain:

✔ **Understand the culture you're working in.** This is where employees get tripped up. They fail to know and understand the landscape of the organization before making a move — committing faux pas. Like your family, every company has a culture. To get what you want, you realize over time how to interact with all the personalities in your family — and still be authentically you. Workplace cultures are the same. Determine their systems and processes. Get to know the people, the internal networks, and who is connected to whom.

✔ **Know what you want and where you want to go.** You have to know where you want to go within the organization. This knowledge helps you to properly position yourself. Begin researching what you need to know to be selected for the position:

- Who does the hiring?

- What are their expectations?

- What do you have in common with them?

- What's their management style?

- What's important to them?

- Would it be pleasant to work for them?

- Who's on their team?

If you can contribute to the team, consider volunteering to work on a special project. This interaction will give you a sense of what it's like to work with the person you think you want to work for. Don't forget to ask your current supervisor for permission.

✔ **Know who the players are and how much power they have.**

✔ **Respect all people, regardless of position.** That's the most important lesson about getting ahead. As you think about positioning yourself, never under- or overestimate a person. If she take ideas to the board-room and those ideas get passed, she's an influencer.

✔ **Understand the vision of the CEO.** Read the CEO's vision for the organization and align your vision with hers.

Every industry has standards. Sometimes you have to introduce the industry to a new standard. Companies are looking for innovative ways to maximize their profits.

Leadership works within budgets, and they take calculated risks. Don't present ideas alone; include facts and figures that help leadership understand how and why the market will respond to your idea.

## Nurturing yourself and your relationships for greater professional satisfaction

Developing relationships with others can be complicated, but most relationships are multifaceted. Your natural and first instinct is to do what you think will help you survive in a culture or situation.

Building relationships with others requires intentional awareness when your survival instincts kick in. You have to pause and give thoughtful consideration to the impact your behavior will have on the big picture of your life, the lives of others, and the organization.

This doesn't mean you allow your time and talents to be overtaxed and underpaid. Neither does it give people permission to disrespect you. We want to keep it simple and encourage you to follow the rule you were taught when you were young: "Treat others as you want to be treated."

Here are 12 specific things you can do to help nurture relationships with the people you want to get to know:

- ✔ Seek those people's advice about something that's important to you and will make them shine.

- ✔ Extend an invitation to lunch.

- ✔ Volunteer to work on a department initiative.

- ✔ If you can add credibility, offer to provide an endorsement.

- ✔ Serve on community boards that are important to both of you.

- ✔ Send short email communications inquiring about the progress of a project they are working on. Offer to help.

- ✔ Provide some information — a news article, blog, or resource to help them move their career or a project forward.

- ✔ Congratulate them on a recent success.

- ✔ Connect with them on the company's internal social networking system.

- ✔ Record a short, unique voice message and send it via email.

- ✔ Ask if you can interview them. Tell them you appreciate the work they do and that you want to write an article about them and submit it for publication in the company or division newsletter. Extend to them the opportunity to review the article before submission.

- ✔ At the appropriate time, find out what is most frustrating to them. Then meet the unmet need.

## Moving up and building your self-esteem to support yourself

As you advance in your career, you need to continue to build your self-esteem. The dynamic, challenging assignments you face and the countless conditions you have to operate in require a mature confidence and ease in peculiar situations.

High-level, highly visible positions put more at stake for the organization — and you. This means mistakes are magnified and sometimes public. You have an extremely limited number of people you can talk to but, in most cases, the advice you seek is from people who have years of experience.

The system you use to build your self-esteem is reusable at every level. Acknowledge what you feel, learn the lesson, affirm who you really are, and say, "Next!"

Being intentional about defining who you are, what you want to do, and how you want to show up in the world is crucial for your success. Review all the data you have gathered about yourself throughout this chapter. Identify what feels right for you and move in it. The following exercise gives you some ideas on how you can position yourself within the organization you work for.

Use the following system to guide your thinking in crafting a 90-day plan to begin to distinguish yourself as the go-to person in your area of expertise.

Consider the promises the organization makes to its customers, the community, and its employees. Write down your solution for meeting these promises in each of these three categories.

Identify your audience within the organization. Your audience is the people whose attention you're trying to get. In which of the previously named areas do you see yourself being an expert?

After identifying your area of expertise, draw three columns and label them "Audiences," "Their Desired Outcomes," and "Your Solution," respectively. Then fill in the columns with your thoughts.

Now set a specific goal for yourself. For example, "Within the next 90 days, I will grow the awareness of who I am and my expertise by increasing my exposure within the organization. I'll do this by engaging three people in leadership and two up-and-coming influencers who would be interested in what I have to offer."

With your goal in mind, create three more columns, this time labeled "Person's Name," "Leadership Role," and "How I Can Help," respectively. Enter the relevant information in each column.

In the following list are activities that you can engage in that will help create buzz about you. You can employ more than one, but focus on one area of expertise. You don't want to confuse your audience. If possible, over the course of 90 days, have at least six touch-points with each person you want to engage. To help you keep track of your progress, write your chosen area of expertise and your goal across the top of a piece of paper. Beneath these statements, draw three columns headed "Person's Name," "Strategy," and "Date of Engagement," respectively. Fill them in with the relevant data.

- ✔ Share ideas in public forums.
- ✔ Preplan for meetings with leadership feedback.
- ✔ Listen for complaints; present solutions.
- ✔ Anticipate change; develop a plan.

- ✔ Identify unmet needs.

- ✔ Attend company events.

- ✔ Attend department meetings.

- ✔ Develop missing skill sets.

- ✔ Manage the relationships you want to develop.

- ✔ Seek advice.

- ✔ Work on department initiatives.

- ✔ Launch a newsletter.

- ✔ Join and be active in internal social networking forums.

- ✔ Give and get an endorsement.

- ✔ Schedule a lunch meeting.

- ✔ Help someone achieve success.

- ✔ Agree to serve on a community board.

- ✔ Create video or audio updates.

- ✔ Volunteer for special projects.

- ✔ Create partnerships.

- ✔ Recognize special occasions.

Becoming the go-to person means you know your stuff in a specific area. If you're an amateur, use this system to continue to grow your skills before putting yourself in the spotlight. When you step out, you'll be challenged. If you aren't ready, you'll lose confidence and credibility.

# Chapter 19

# Managing Your Relationships at Work

"*I* cried every day for two years," one woman recalled.

"It was like she was being bullied in staff meetings," her coworker added.

Tears poured down faces and voices escalated as I (coauthor S. Renee) listened attentively to the issues resulting from miscommunication and poor relationship development that had haunted this team of 25 employees.

It's not unusual to see passionate, committed, and highly talented employees feel unappreciated, irritated, and fearful of being their authentically innovative, intelligent, and hard-working selves. Preconceived notions, lack of compassion, and poor communication are the typical reasons workplace distractions persist, health problems surge, and productivity falls.

Are these the core causes of confusion and frustration in the workplace? Is it possible to have people from different backgrounds, experiences, and skill sets effectively work together and genuinely like and value one another?

In this chapter, we provide answers to these complex questions. We also help you develop into a leader who knows how to break through barriers and build effective relationships and confidence in others.

# Building Effective Working Relationships

According to law enforcement, it's not uncommon for witnesses of a crime to express completely different stories about what happened and why they believe it happened. Is one lying and the other telling the truth? Does one person have more to gain by telling his version over another? Is malicious intent at play?

Conflict is the result of different versions of a shared experience. The innumerable amount of court hearings confirm this as fact. Is this definition of conflict applicable in the workplace as well?

Have you ever had a disagreement with a coworker or supervisor? Despite both of you being in the same place, at the same time, doing the same thing, your opinions of a given experience may be different. Is that what causes conflict? Of course it is.

Building effective working relationships requires your attention in three key areas:

- ✔ Understanding yourself
- ✔ Listening and responding to others
- ✔ Utilizing a strategy to sustain your mental and emotional well-being amid chaos

In this section, we ask you to reflect a bit on the current state of your relationships within your workplace. Then, we provide some strategies for improving your relationship with your employees, your company's leaders, and your peers. (**Note:** We aren't starting with understanding yourself because earlier chapters provide you with information and exercises that help you discover a lot about yourself. Refer to Chapters 11, 12, and 14 if you first need to spend some time learning to understand yourself.)

Building positive relationships in the workplace simply means listening and being authentically kind and supportive.

## Reflecting on your current work relationships

Before every workshop I (coauthor S. Renee) share with participants my intentions. My number one intention is always to get them to stop — to stop doing, thinking, strategizing, researching, moving — to simply stop. To shut down the noise. As I stand in front of the room, I observe people as they struggle to settle themselves into this unfamiliar state called *silence*.

Setting the expectation to "stop" assures that if I connect, engage, and present interesting content, I have a chance at beating my competition — family, friends, projects, community service, conflicts, unmet needs, and anything else that is going on in the hearts and minds of participants.

This directive isn't a miscellaneous tactic to feed my ego; it's a space creator for participants to take time to reflect on themselves and their relationships with others. It helps them to honestly assess where they are and unite with the unexamined place they want to be.

If you're willing to pause and reflect on your work relationships, start by completing this exercise. Because people's perceptions of you are based on how your behavior impacts their lives, make a list of the people whose lives you impact on the job. Think about what you say, how you say it, and what you do. Put yourself in their position and, as you say their name aloud, objectively answer the following question based on how you treat them: How do I make you feel?

You never know exactly how you're making a person feel unless you ask them; however, this exercise, which increases your consciousness of others, will put you in the right ball park.

You know how you make people feel based on how they respond to you. If you have problems assessing your impact, work backwards. Think about how the person acts when she's around you. If she's normally talkative but unusually quiet around you, that may indicate that she feels uncomfortable and lacks trust.

## *Improving relationships for leaders*

Regardless of what organization hires me, without fail, I (coauthor S. Renee) hear employees blurt one of the three following statements during a workshop:

> "I don't have to like them to work with them."

> "I don't care if they don't like me."

> "I have to make a living somewhere."

Unwilling at first to identify exactly whom he's referring to, the revelation comes later in the workshop, when it becomes evident there are ongoing misunderstandings between leadership and employees and among coworkers. Leaders are responsible for the confusion, but often prefer to ignore it. Leadership must set clear expectations for everyone to adhere to, and create a safe, fair, transparent culture to foster trusting relationships between leadership and staff and among coworkers.

Has anyone ever directed any of these statements at you or shared them with you? If so, what you were hearing was an employee who was fed-up with the difficulties and barriers that had been created and that were prohibiting him from doing his job.

As you were listening to the person making one or more of these statements, how did you feel? Did you intuitively know that the person was asking for help, encouragement, and direction? Were you unsure as to how to help?

In order to improve morale and increase productivity, you need to dig further to get to the root cause of the person's concerns. To better understand the challenges that person may be facing, you need to get him to tell you more. Check out Table 19-1 for some suggested responses to these common statements to help you get to the root of the problem.

| Table 19-1 | Coaching that Gets to the Core |
|---|---|
| *Statement* | *Coaching Response* |
| I don't have to like them to work with them. | Let me see if I understand what you're saying. You don't feel that it's necessary to like the people with whom you spend eight or more hours a day — is that correct? Tell me more about that. How did it come to be that you don't like your coworkers? What can I do to help? |
| I don't care if they don't like me. | You said, "I don't care if they don't like me," correct? Does that mean you believe that you don't need people to help you do your job? Do you realize that people help people they like? Because people promote people, what I hear you saying is that you don't care if you never grow beyond where you are right now. Is that what you're saying? |
| I have to make a living somewhere. | What I hear is that you only work here for the money. Is there something else you would prefer to be doing? Is there somewhere else you would prefer to work? What would make you happy? |

Have you ever had your concern met with: "Don't take it personally; it's just business." Why would anyone say that to his most valuable resource? What he's saying is "How you feel isn't more important to me than making a profit." People impact an organization's bottom line. Do you think that inspires greater commitment in employees?

Responding to an employee's concern with "Don't take it personally" dismisses his feelings and opinions, sending the message that he doesn't matter. It's paramount that you understand that people come from different cultures and experience life differently. Being a leader calls you to a higher level of thoughtful consideration of others and their workplace experiences.

When you listen and take the time to probe further, you'll be surprised by the responses you get. Most people aren't unhappy with what they do; they're unhappy with how they're being treated. Unsupportive organizational cultures and unproductive operational systems are what make employees say, "What's the use?"

Employee satisfaction is at the core of every successful organization. The role of a good leader is to provide resources and developmental opportunities to employees so they can effectively do the job that is expected of them. By doing so you increase productivity, advance executive leadership's agenda, and grow the business.

Here are additional things you can do to help build positive relationships with employees:

- ✔ **Model the behavior you want.** Set the goal for yourself that your employees will be able to look to you because you'll model the behavior you want to see in them. Never put yourself above your employees. Create opportunities for them to succeed and recognize them for doing so. Most importantly, show them that you care.

- ✔ **Use your listening skills more often than your directional skills.** Always remember who's doing the job. Your employees are on the front lines witnessing and taking notes on all the bottlenecks and faulty operational issues. *Listen!* And understand what is being said to you so that you can help them and the organization be more successful.

- ✔ **Set clear expectations.** Never take for granted that people know what to do. People need to be clear on what's expected of them. Ambiguous instructions create poor results, leaving people feeling like failures. This outcome lowers self-esteem, productivity, and job satisfaction. Your decisive directions help to build trusting relationships with your employees and better results.

- ✔ **Provide the necessary tools to do the job.** In accordance with the resources available, the job should get done with the least amount of effort. Give your staff the tools to be effective at completing assigned tasks. Remember, a series of successes builds confidence.

- ✔ **Be transparent.** Don't withhold information like you have a big secret. Change and the lack of information put people on edge.

- ✔ **Look for future leaders.** Seek direction from your workforce and reward people for great ideas. When you seek to find and develop leaders, people will look for ways to be the "chosen one."

- ✔ **Let others express themselves.** People are humans, not robots. They inevitably bring personal issues to the workplace. Give them time to express themselves. If you listen, they'll know that you care. It will also help you decide whether further help is needed. Sometimes by hearing themselves talk, they'll release themselves from the bondage of the situation, which will result in more productive employees. If you don't listen, a coworker will. Then you'll have two unproductive employees.

✔ **Find out what your employees really want.** Everyone is looking for something to satisfy her internal yearning. When I (coauthor S. Renee) ask workshop participants the question, "What do you want?" I get a blank stare, silence fills the room, and then they say, "I don't know." I respond, "You know what you want. Sometimes we are afraid of appearing selfish to leadership and our coworkers because so much emphasis is put on the word, 'team.' Instead of acknowledging our individual needs, we bury our true feelings and pretend they don't exist. Unmet needs are also at the core of our frustration in the workplace." When leadership creates a safe place for employees to express themselves, they're willing to share. As the leader, you may want to share your desires first to illustrate that it's okay for employees to have their own desires. By knowing and responding to your employees' core needs, you can improve their morale and your relationships with them.

For most people, a core desire is an internal yearning to be recognized in a specific way for the value they bring to the organization. Money is a means of making a living and creating a lifestyle; recognition confirms a meaningful existence.

✔ **Engage every employee.** Some employees are overlooked because they're shy or lack confidence. Within themselves they're thinking, "Everyone else sounds intelligent but me." They could be holding the best idea yet. Stop overlooking them by asking, "What do you think?" You may be surprised by what you hear.

✔ **Give employees the authority to do their jobs.** If you do your job properly by providing the necessary resources, development, and information to your employees, they'll be able to do their jobs correctly.

✔ **Don't act like the "big boss."** People won't talk to a boss who intimidates them, but they will talk *about* that boss. Don't sit in your office all day taking care of paperwork: Be among the people and for the people. You don't want to separate yourself from the people who provide vital information and opportunities to connect, engage, and grow your business.

✔ **Embrace change.** Doing the same thing the same way every day stagnates innovation and employees' desire to develop their intellectual property. Find creative new ways of doing old things to get the results you want. Some organizations — the military, for example — change management every two to three years to ensure that ideas, systems, and people stay fresh and on top of their game.

# Screaming for help

While giving a presentation, I (coauthor S. Renee) advanced to the next slide. It read: "Don't worry more about the mess you are in than the mess that you are." Out of my peripheral vision, I noticed a hand fly up, while these words decisively flowed out of a participant's mouth: "I don't agree with that!"

Walking over to where she was sitting, I looked her in the eyes and gently said, "Okay, can you tell me why?"

She said, "There are certain circumstances you don't have control over. They have nothing to do with you."

Intrigued by her response, but unsure of what she was really saying, I probed for clarity. "Can you give me an example?"

I won't dare to attempt to quote her extensive answer here, but she talked about her ex-husband's irresponsible behaviors and undiagnosed depression. She credited herself for supporting him despite his inability to value her support. She shared her struggles with health issues. In closing, she confidently declared that she hadn't created any of it.

Before speaking I weighed the following: the business environment we were in and the "I'm-the-victim" stance she was proudly taking.

Not wanting to go too deep in front of her colleagues, but hoping to give her a hand out of the ditch of despair, I asked with great care, "How long did you know your husband before you married him?"

"Five years," she responded.

"You didn't see any signs of these behaviors in five years of dating?" I asked.

"No," she said and diverted the attention to her husband and his ability to fool not only her, but his family and her family, and then she again started talking about her health issues.

In the coaching process, my first priority is to always maintain respect and preserve the integrity of the coach/client experience, so I excused myself from her personal space and turned to address the group.

This quick coaching exchange revealed to upper leadership why one of their middle-management leaders wasn't able to take responsibility for her actions. These are the kinds of life issues that employees have a difficult time understanding, processing, and overcoming. You don't see them during the interviewing process and you can't understand them during performance reviews, yet they show up in employees' leadership style and work performance, and during interactions with you, coworkers, and their staff. Pain shows up in different ways. In the workplace you often hear words such as "defensive," "bully," and "odd behavior." Providing this employee with counseling or a coach could help turn her life and work performance around. Leadership will never know what she needs if they don't ask the right question — which will leave everyone frustrated within the organization.

## Improving relationships with leadership for employees

Seeing a member of leadership walking toward you in the hallway can cause your heart to flutter. Being assigned to work on a special project with a member of leadership can trigger sleepless nights. Your expectation of their expectation of you can create doubt, fear, and ultimately silly mistakes.

Interacting successfully with leaders requires some simple but intentional decisions:

- ✔ **Look them in the eyes and give a firm handshake.** These gestures demonstrate confidence and show that you have nothing to hide.

- ✔ **Listen and let them lead the conversation.** Don't say anything unless you have something to say. Resist the urge to start talking and jump into nervous chatter. Instead, let them tell you what they're thinking.

- ✔ **Meet them at their level.** Don't be arrogant, but don't act like you're reaching up, either. Stand in your power and let them see your brilliance.

- ✔ **Find out whether something is particularly important to them.** Don't forget that leaders have needs too. By asking, you may discover a way to help and increase your exposure. Listen and ask questions when necessary.

- ✔ **Remember that you were invited.** You were invited to the table. This means that someone has vouched for you or has been watching you for a while. Impressed by what you do and how you do it, that person extended you the opportunity. Don't ever forget this: You were invited for one reason only — you have something they want.

There are times when everyone at the table isn't happy that you're there. If you feel unwelcomed or unduly challenged by someone in leadership, read the section, "Enduring the Difficult Boss Without Sacrificing Yourself," later in this chapter.

## Connecting with coworkers

You likely spend more of your waking hours in the workplace than in your home. In fact, you probably spend more hours with coworkers than you do with your spouse or other loved ones.

Because you spend so much time at work, we recommend that you preserve your sanity by deciding to genuinely get to know and get along with your coworkers. If you deal with many difficult people and situations in the workplace, you may believe that developing good working relationships is impossible, but it's not.

Building positive relationships in the workplace needs to be treated like anything else you consider worth doing — you have to make a decision that it's important to you and be open and willing to do the work to create the outcome you want.

Following is a list of suggestions you can use to build workplace relationships:

- ✔ **Live the golden rule.** "Treat others the way you want to be treated" is the only rule you need to follow to build successful relationships. We bet you've heard that before. It's a simple principle, yet difficult to follow. Think about how you treat others. What can you do to make them feel the way you want to feel when you interact with others?

  You can't understand someone else's pain until you stop thinking with your head and feel what that person is saying with your heart.

- ✔ **Define what you'll get.** Whatever you do, you expect something in return; otherwise, you're not motivated to do it. Admittedly, interacting with people can take a lot of energy. Despite its challenges, it's hugely rewarding. When you know what you get out of helping people, you're less likely to get discouraged when more is required of you than you expected.

- ✔ **Seek to understand people.** People have unique and varied needs. Some of these needs are simpler to see and understand than others. Meet the people you seek to understand where they are, and you'll discover more of who you are.

- ✔ **Trust that you and your coworkers want the same thing.** It can be difficult to see that you and a coworker want the same thing when you go about getting it in different ways. Communication can eliminate the confusion and create unity by allowing coworkers to know each other's intentions.

Everyone has core desires, which are driven by core needs. Most people are unaware of the messages they send to others. You can uncover what people want by attentively watching how they react and respond in various situations and by closely listening to what they say. Here are some questions to engage your coworkers in conversation that will help you to better understand them. Watch their reactions as they express how they feel about each question. You're listening for the emotion that drives the words.

- ✔ Did you think you would be doing what you're doing right now when you were young? What did you think you would be doing?

- ✔ Do you ever wish you were doing something different? What would you be doing?

- ✔ What do you like about this work?

- ✔ If you could be doing anything you want, what would you be doing?

- ✔ What satisfaction would you get from doing that?

Never use private thoughts, feelings, or experiences that a person has shared with you against that person. And don't ever share them with someone who can, which means don't ever share them at all.

# *Establishing a Plan for Change*

If you want to change your workplace experience, you have to be willing to change your behavior. It's easier to point the finger at other people and blame them for the state that you're in, but nothing new will happen without your permission and participation.

You don't have to have it all figured out. You just have to be willing to walk through new doors and know that by changing you're going to create a better experience for yourself and others. Some people thrive on change, while others struggle to understand the need to change. Stuck in the middle are those who would like to change but don't know how. Resistance to change is driven by fear, uncertainty, and lack of faith in oneself.

Change requires the following from you:

- **Faith:** You believe that you can handle whatever awaits you on the other side of change.

- **Courage:** You take the chance of doing something different because you know that if you fall, you'll have the strength and ability to get back up.

- **Confidence:** You know that you're capable of doing anything.

- **Personal accountability:** You're willing to take the heat, hindrance, and hype of every choice you make.

Are you still wondering, "But what do I need to *do* to change?" Follow the five steps that follow:

1. **Decide what you want to change.**

2. **Uncover why the change is important to you.**

3. **Identify what you'll gain and lose as a result of changing.**

4. **Take small, consistent steps toward change.**

5. **Measure your growth.**

Changing relationship dynamics will require you to dig deeper within yourself to find your "kind" spot. This isn't easy, especially if you believe someone has mistreated you and you've had a contentious relationship.

You're trying to get what you want, and they're trying to get what they want. You're not on opposite sides; you're on the same side, but in different positions, trying to be recognized for your individual contributions.

## Prove yourself

"Every day I would stand outside, wait for the buses to arrive, and greet every student with a warm smile and 'Good Morning,'" the assistant principal shared.

"I would do this day after day, but there was one student who would look me straight in the eyes and when I said, 'Good morning,' she would roll her eyes and turn her face."

"Months passed, and one morning, she looked at me and gave me half a smile. A few more months passed, and she smiled back and said, 'Good morning.'"

"One morning, I pulled her to the side and asked, 'Why did it take you nearly half the school year to give me a smile and say, 'Good morning?'" She said, "I just wanted to see if you really cared."

Here are some things for you to keep in mind so that you can grow even if the other person remains the same — for now.

- ✔ **Ego destroys.** Your ego will stop you from getting what you want. Don't focus on them: focus on yourself and stop trying to figure out who's winning.

- ✔ **Right is relative.** Who's right? You both are. Decisions are made based on personal value systems. The "right answer" is relative to the person who is making the decision. Once you understand that, you won't spend energy getting upset about things that you can't control and have little to do with you.

- ✔ **Don't expect miracles.** People don't change because you decide to change. Make the decision to be kind because it's what you define as the right thing to do. If the person never changes, that's okay, because you didn't change for them — you changed for you.

- ✔ **Don't give them what they give you.** You may not get the response that you expect at first, but keep showing kindness towards others. I (coauthor S. Renee) was presenting a workshop on branding for educators. To support my point about consistency, one of the participants, who worked at a school for troubled teens, shared the story in the sidebar "Prove Yourself."

Like in the example given in the sidebar "Prove Yourself," whoever you decide to be, it has to be because you care and you want to help create a different culture at work. People and situations can get on your nerves, causing chaos and drawing you into gobbledygook. Let distractions come, but don't get swindled into the mess.

## Socializing with coworkers after hours

You're a team player, and you want leadership to know it. This goal requires your attendance at fundraisers, golf tournaments, and holiday parties. Networking with leadership and your coworkers after hours is necessary to advancing your career.

Most people know the following rules, but ignore them. If you want to advance in your career, avoid these danger zones:

✔ Don't smoke, use foul language, or drink too much. Two drinks are more than enough; one is preferable.

✔ Don't join a gossip session. If you walk into one, keep moving.

✔ Don't talk about sex or have an affair with anyone you work with.

✔ Don't go too dramatic or sexy with your wardrobe.

✔ Don't join a clique — get to know different people from different departments within the company. You never know where your next opportunity may be.

✔ Behave like the company's leaders are always watching — because they are.

Here are some specific things you can do to stay on target to improve your workplace experience and your relationships:

✔ Stay positive. Memorize or post your favorite scriptures, quotes, or quips around your office.

✔ Set an intention. When I (coauthor S. Renee) present at corporations, I explain the difference between intentions and goals. A goal has tasks attached to it. An intention is a deliberate thought to create something in particular. You have enough work to do: Let your subconscious work for you by setting an intention every day for what you want to create.

✔ Commit to taking the high road in every situation — become an ego-free zone.

✔ Listen to music that motivates and inspires you.

✔ Let silence be your power.

# Enduring the Difficult Boss Without Sacrificing Yourself

*"No doubt I was dealing with issues that had nothing to do with you."*

That sentence was pulled from an email sent to me (coauthor S. Renee) by my supervisor 11 years after I was unfairly fired from my position as director of public relations.

She had bullied me for a year — humiliated me in front of my staff, described me as a prima donna, and told me I couldn't write. After seeking relief from human resources and the president of the organization, I was fired.

I have no doubt that the pressure and challenges she imposed on me to become a better writer contributed to my ability to write three popular books and co-write this one. However, as a result of constantly being degraded and embarrassed, I was diagnosed with depression and my self-esteem hit rock bottom. I spent years rebuilding my confidence and my life after that incident.

Some people are difficult to work for because of high expectations. Others are impossible to work for due to their issues. You have to be able to look at your situation objectively to know the difference.

To help you make that distinction, answer the following questions:

✔ Does the person make disparaging comments about you?

✔ Have you ever been physically attacked or threatened?

✔ Do other people in leadership compliment you on your work, while your supervisor often criticizes it?

✔ Does the person make demeaning remarks about you or your work in front of others?

✔ Does the person withhold pertinent information you need to do your job?

✔ Does the person use intimidation tactics to discourage you from offering your opinion?

If you answered yes to any of these questions and you feel shut down and out of the workplace experience, you're working for a difficult person. Unfortunately, if this type of treatment is permitted in the company culture, there's nothing you can do.

If you work for someone who is fearful, insecure, and wrestling to grasp her own brilliance, she'll do anything to dim yours. We advise that you find another place to shine.

## Communicating effectively with a boss who's difficult to work for

Some leaders have high expectations and hold their employees to standards that force them to expand their capacity for learning and success. Because these bosses are focused more on completing tasks, they forget that people need to feel appreciated and valued.

If you work for someone who lacks social skills but otherwise provides what you need to be a success, here are some communication strategies to help you survive the taskmaster:

- **Have a focused agenda.** When communicating with your supervisor, have a well-laid-out plan to avoid going off on time-wasting tangents.

- **Get clear direction.** Missing assigned targets only irritates task-oriented people, and they can be impatient listeners. To avoid mistakes, confirm what you hear the person say he requires of you. Consider following up with a written email confirmation for future reference.

- **Take the emotion out of it.** This is difficult for warm-and-fuzzy people, but to work successfully with someone who isn't, you have to step out of yourself and value what he brings to the table. This type of person is often firm, but fair. Being fair means he won't play favorites. Perform well, and it'll work in your favor.

- **Offer a solution.** Leadership means having the ability to think through complex challenges and provide a workable solution that builds the confidence of the team. As a member of the team, you can position yourself well by offering ideas that help move the agenda forward. Don't get discouraged when you share ideas and they aren't acted upon right way. It takes time for people to hear, see, and understand what you're saying. Or it just may not be the best idea at the time.

- **Consider the pressures your leader is under.** Take into account that some leaders transfer pressure they're getting from their leadership to you. Although this isn't the best way to inspire great work, it's not unusual due to the complex and competitive marketplace.

## Addressing disrespectful treatment

No one deserves to be mistreated by anyone under any circumstances. Mistreatment includes directly or indirectly demoralizing you privately or publicly. Some people refer to it as "politics." Good politics are necessary diplomacy to move an agenda forward. It's not lying, shaming, or dehumanizing you — that's bad behavior.

You have the right to stand up for yourself. The best way to address being mistreated is relative to who you're communicating with. Here are some suggestions for you to consider:

- **Connect on a human level.** Say, "I thought you viewed my work performance as . . . but I must have been mistaken. Could you help me to see it from your point of view?"

✔ **Be transparent and honest.** Leadership doesn't appreciate you whining about the amount of work you've been assigned or making an unreasonable number of mistakes. Leaders do appreciate you standing in your power and addressing any feelings of disrespectful mistreatment when presented in a focused, professional, non-accusatory way.

✔ **Decide whether it's best to communicate with human resources.** Poor treatment of employees is often a supported culture. If this is the case, human resources may not be a viable option. For example, if it is commonplace for employees in the organization to be mistreated and fired for speaking up about that treatment, more than likely, human resources will not be able to help you.

VISUALIZE

# Speaking and acting confidently with your coworkers

Sit or lie down in a comfortable position. Uncross your hands and feet and close your eyes. Now breathe in deeply and exhale. Breathe in deeply again and exhale. Completely relax.

Visualize that you're at work. You need to speak to a coworker about a problem that's been bothering you. It may be someone you supervise, a coworker, or your boss. Whoever it is, think about the person you have to discuss the problem with and what the difficulty is that needs to be talked about. Imagine that you ask for an appointment.

After you've made the appointment, you go home. See yourself writing down what you want to say. Now that it's written, hold it in your hand and visualize yourself practicing it at home over and over again. See yourself standing in front of your mirror practicing what you're going to say. As you practice, you notice that it gets easier and easier to speak. You get more and more confident and comfortable. Feel totally confident with a strong will that you can do this!

Now see yourself at work again. The time for the appointment has arrived. Before you meet this person, you take several deep breaths to

calm yourself. You rehearse two more times what you're going to say.

You walk into this person's office or this person walks into yours. Your body is sitting in a strong position; your tone of voice is friendly yet solid. You look the other person in the eyes, and you enunciate your words clearly. You speak a little more slowly than normal, and you gesture with your hands to make the points that are important.

See this person agreeing with you. This person now understands your point of view. This person gets up and shakes your hand, smiling at you because you'll be having an improved relationship and you both will make the workplace better.

Say goodbye and sit down at your desk, feeling perfectly satisfied with what has taken place.

Now it's time to come back. Know that you can communicate with people with strength and ease. Begin to come back gently. Become aware of your physical body. Breathe in deeply and exhale. Breathe in deeply again and exhale. Become aware of your hands and feet. And when you are ready, you may open your eyes.

# Chapter 20

# Presenting with Confidence

. . . . . . . . . . . . . . . . . . . . . . . . . . . . . . . . . . . . . . . . . . . . . . . . . . . .

. . . . . . . . . . . . . . . . . . . . . . . . . . . . . . . . . . . . . . . . . . . . . . . . . . . .

*I* (coauthor S. Renee) confidently walked up to the mic. I opened my mouth, but I didn't have an inkling of what was going to happen next. My mind went completely blank. Surprised by my mind's unfaithfulness and convinced it couldn't be true, I again opened my mouth to greet, in Spanish, the audience of approximately 350 people.

I couldn't believe it. I'd practiced for months, but my mind wouldn't cooperate. As I flubbed through the humiliating experience, I made a commitment to myself — this would never happen again.

I was 21 years old at the time but had been on stage since age 5. Over 15 years of experience standing in front of people hadn't changed the nervous, tingling feeling I would get. Neither did it let me get away with trying to present something that wasn't a part of who I was — fluently speaking a foreign language.

What I learned that day was that it doesn't matter how long you've been a public speaker or how many speeches you've given. Public speaking is an art that demands your thoughtful consideration, uninterrupted attention, constant respect, and genuine presence.

Whether you're an amateur or an experienced speaker, this chapter shows you how to present with presence, passion, and power. You find out how to identify what your audience is looking for and give it to them. You discover attention-grabbing techniques, and we give specific examples of what keeps audiences engaged.

If you want to look and sound like a pro when you deliver your next presentation, this chapter is for you.

# Exploring the Art of Public Speaking

Public speaking is a powerful vehicle that offers you an opportunity to influence the hearts, minds, and behavior of others.

Your ability to communicate effectively can increase profits, productivity, and work performance. You can use your words to inspire hope, restore love, and deepen spiritual commitment. You can even get people excited about rallying around your idea to stop pollution, find a cure for a deadly disease, or raise money for a favorite charity.

Public speaking is the visual and auditory expression of your exclusive creative style. No one thinks, sounds, or presents like you do. Even if you're a novice speaker, you have a speaking flair that is unique to you. Your job is to develop and perfect it.

This tremendous amount of power can deceive you into thinking that public speaking is about you. It's actually about what happens through you when all eyes are on you.

The art of public speaking is your ability to communicate ideas in a way that influences the audience to consider and accept your theory as a practical solution to a problem that interests them or that they wrestle with.

## Paying attention to what's important

This is an uncomfortable truth: No matter who you are, you must know that your audience will not automatically like you. They may be courteous, but that doesn't equate with liking, hearing, and desiring to act on what you say.

As a speaker, your number-one goal is to quickly create a trusting relationship with your audience. If you want them to listen, participate, value, and act on what you're saying, trust is essential.

You can't rely on your credentials to build trust. Your credentials form an impression upon your audience. However, your audience trusts what they see and sense coming from you — your personality, style, and character.

## Learning what your audience is looking for

Knowing what your audience wants isn't complex. All audiences want the same thing: helpful information from a *trusted* resource. The complexity of public speaking is in the delivery of the information.

The following sections discuss three things you can do to build trust with your audience.

### Connecting with your audience before your presentation

Arrive early and greet your audience as they walk through the door. Go into the room and have conversations with those who arrive early. If you don't know them, ask them their names. Ask questions such as, "What do you want to get out of this presentation?" or "What information would be most helpful to you?"

Remember a few people's names and talk about what's important to them from the stage. This makes them feel a part of the presentation, and it keeps everyone alert because they don't know what's going to happen next.

If you're presenting for a corporate meeting and already know people's names, ask those people for any ideas or questions they have about the new project — and always give them credit during the presentation. When you call out other people's names and acknowledge their valuable input, questions, or concerns, it gives your audience permission to participate, and you exhibit strong leadership skills.

Use phases such as, "While Amy and I were talking, she brought up a good point . . ." or "Justin expressed a great concern about the time frame on the deliverables. I think he has a valid point . . . let's flesh this out further."

The purpose of sharing someone else's conversation with you as the trusted resource is to engage, uplift, and create a safer environment for people to have a healthy exchange in. Never share confidential information or information that could make a person look bad.

### Being the expert, not the authority

If you are in a position of power, people know it. You don't have to flex your authority muscle — doing so is offensive and shuts people down. You are the expert. Experts understand that it's more than what you say; it's how you say it. It doesn't matter how much you know; it takes relationship-building skills to engage people around your message. Who wants to listen to a closed-minded Mr. Know-It-All?

### Validating people

If you can, make time for your audience to ask questions or share their opinions about the information and how they will use it.

It takes courage to stand up in front of a group of people and ask a question. For some, it takes all they have within them. They've asked you the question because they trust you. Never disregard that trust by being condescending or rude.

If someone doesn't agree with a point you shared, say, "That's an interesting way of looking at it; have you considered . . .?" If the person doesn't agree with you, let it go. Everyone doesn't have to agree with you. When people trust you, they're more likely to be open to further explanation and direction.

## Deciding how to set up your presentation

You can set up your presentation a number of ways. First, you must be clear on the following:

- ✔ **Expectations of the presentation:** If you're presenting for an organization, ask them the following questions: "Who is the audience?" "What are their challenges?" "When the presentation is over, what do you want them to walk away with?"

  If you're in leadership and putting together a presentation for your staff or colleagues, ask yourself these questions: "What do I want them to get from this presentation?" "What do I want them to do as a result of hearing the information presented?" "How is this information going to impact the team?"

- ✔ **Length of the presentation:** The amount of time you have to present is crucial because it lets you know how quickly you have to get to the point. Trust is built over time, and if you have a 30-minute keynote, you have to know what you're going to do to grab your audience's attention within the first few minutes.

- ✔ **The platform being used:** Knowing the platform being used tells you what mindset your audience will have the moment they see you. Is it a meeting, workshop, retreat, webinar, teleseminar, rap (question-and-answer) session, or keynote?

- ✔ **Room capabilities:** Don't ever show up to speak to a group without knowing what you're walking into. What kind of stage will you be standing on? Is there a podium? Is it inside or outside? What type of mic will you be using? Is there an area for movement? Can the system accommodate visual or audio needs, such as a PowerPoint with video?

- ✔ **Expected number of attendees:** Speaking at a graduation where 10,000 people are expected is different from speaking at a workshop with 50 people or a corporate meeting with 7 people sitting around a boardroom table.

After you know the basics, you can begin thinking about how to communicate your message. Based on what is expected of you, you can choose one or more of the following:

✔ A PowerPoint display to guide the presentation

People can read. Don't clutter your PowerPoint presentation with every word you want to say. Know your material and use bullet points to guide and focus your presentation.

✔ Props to engage different types of learners

✔ A video to emphasize a point and add an entertainment factor

✔ Stories that connect your audience to you

✔ Humor to relax your audience and create an opening to be heard

✔ A fill-in-the-blank handout to ensure that you don't lose your audience

✔ Bullet points you've either written on paper or memorized

Stories engage and stimulate greater interest from your audience. But how do you decide what story to use and when? How should you frame your story? How long should it be? What details should be included? Every good story should have the following four components. To begin crafting your story, fill in the information related to each of these components:

✔ Characters

✔ The problem

✔ An emotional touch-point

✔ The lesson

When the material is presented properly, the audience should

✔ Go wherever you take them

✔ Develop a mental picture of what you're saying

✔ Have an emotional response, humor included

✔ Be able to apply the lesson to their lives

Ten minutes or less is enough time to convey a good story. If you include too many details when communicating a story verbally, you can lose your audience.

You can successfully frame a story when you understand that the purpose of using stories is to capture your audience's attention. The primary goal of sharing your story is to communicate a message.

Not sure how to choose the best story to tell? Start with the end in mind. Decide what message you want to convey. Consider your audience. You can even set up the same story differently based on the audience and the message you want to communicate.

Be sure to include the following details:

- ✔ Identify the characters and their roles in the situation. Try to limit the number of main characters to three or fewer.

- ✔ Pinpoint the thoughts and behavior of the main characters.

- ✔ Determine how the main characters interact and respond to the situation.

- ✔ State what was done, the impact of what was done, and the lesson learned as a result of what was done.

## *Putting it all together*

You know who your audience is. You know the topic you're going to speak about. Now, you have to bring it all together by insuring that you, the presenter, make your presentation with presence, passion, and power.

- ✔ **Presence** is a combination of confidence, charisma, and character. Confidence comes from knowing what you're talking about. Charisma is what inspires others to like you, listen to you, and be loyal to you. Character is the expression of your integrity in how you treat others.

- ✔ **Passion** is the expression of your truth and your desire to share and experience it with others.

- ✔ **Power** is your ability to get people to act on what you're saying.

Keep in mind that becoming a dynamic speaker requires you to use your voice masterfully. Like a skilled singer or poet who uses her voice to create an emotional experience for her audience, you also have to learn how to control the tone and expressions of your voice.

Here are just a few techniques you can use during your next presentation:

- ✔ Practice and video-record yourself reading a children's book. By doing, so you'll be able to hear and see your facial expressions. As you practice, lift your tone up on questions and drop it down on statements.

- ✔ Use pauses to give your audience time to process how they're feeling in addition to what they're thinking.

- ✔ Silence is a powerful tool to create wonder and mystery. Lowering the volume of your voice can create concern and increasing it can trigger a warning.

Communication is a learned skilled, so we encourage you to practice before using these techniques in your presentation. Doing so helps you sense which ones work best with your personality and style.

Your nonverbal communication — dress, gestures, facial expressions, body language, and attitude — influence your audience's opinion of you more than your verbal communication does. Be sure that your verbal and nonverbal forms of communication are in sync.

# Shining During Your Presentation

You're the star to your audience, but don't think of yourself as the star.

As a speaker who helps develop other speakers, among the first things I (coauthor S. Renee) share with them is, "You're in the audience and you are on stage." What does that mean? In order to "shine" on stage, you have to understand what impacts the lives of the people who sit in the audience. This is the only way for you to connect with them, and them with you.

Here are some tips to help you shine in the eyes of your audience:

- **Be fully prepared.** Preparation requires thought and practice. If you sound too rehearsed, your words seem less genuine. Allow yourself to flow in the moment and trust that everything you know to be true will support you.

- **Dress accordingly.** Why would you create an unnecessary barrier? How you dress communicates to your audience how much you respect and appreciate them. If you're over- or underdressed, you may cause your audience to disconnect. When this happens, you have to work harder on stage to bring them back in alignment with you. Be aware of where you'll be speaking, who you'll be speaking to, and the type of event you'll be speaking at.

- **Be aware of your body language.** There are times when standing behind a podium is appropriate and necessary. But don't use it to protect you from your secret insecurities. You can't hide your undisclosed thoughts because they show up in your presence. Whenever possible, speak through a cordless or lavalier microphone and use your body movements to assist you in communicating your message.

- **Make eye contact.** Talk to people, not to the tops of their heads. Look them in the eyes to let them know, "I see you. I'm talking to you."

- **Laugh at yourself.** I (coauthor S. Renee) was speaking at a church in New York. While walking and speaking, I didn't see the air vent in the floor. My heel got stuck and my shoe came off. It was hilarious! I laughed, the audience laughed, and I used that moment as a lesson for all of us to remember that the unexpected would happen, and whatever happened, we'd be ready for it.

Those are the basics. But what is it that will *really* make you shine? What will make you a dynamic speaker who creates buzz, and what will help you grow in popularity on your job and in your business?

It's called the "it" factor. Everyone has an "it" factor. Your "it" factor is what attracts people to you. It's what makes them want to stay in your presence. Following is a short list to help you begin thinking about what factors into your "it" factor:

- ✔ Your sense of fashion and style
- ✔ Your unique way of moving
- ✔ Your eloquent way of speaking
- ✔ Your warm embrace of others
- ✔ Your intuitive connection to others
- ✔ Your ability to ask profound questions
- ✔ Your unexpected transparency
- ✔ Your service to others
- ✔ Your expression of compassion
- ✔ Your outrageousness
- ✔ Your sense of humor

To help you identify your "it" factor, ask yourself the following questions. If you have a difficult time answering them or feel that you aren't objective, solicit help from your family and friends.

- ✔ Why do people want to be in your presence?
- ✔ What makes you cry?
- ✔ What touches you on a deep level?
- ✔ What do you do that makes others feel good about themselves?
- ✔ What is the personality trait that you appreciate most about yourself?

You know you've identified your "it" factor if the answer to each question is the same or leads you to the same place.

When you know what makes you shine, you don't have to try to shine — "it" shines through you.

# Letting Go of Fear

Preparing to stand in front of a group of people and share your thoughts, feelings, and ideas can be nerve-wracking. An even greater feat is sharing *you*. Few people boast that public speaking doesn't cause their sweat glands to kick into action. Why is public speaking so challenging?

✔ Is it low self-esteem?

✔ Is it lack of information to share?

✔ Is it feelings of unease?

✔ Is it feelings of anxiety, fear, and uncertainty?

The fear that causes many people to shy away from holding a microphone is multidimensional. There are many mental and emotional aspects to public speaking. It's not necessarily linked to low self-esteem. Some people are introverts and are uncomfortable in front of or around groups of people. However, you can move out of your comfort zone and become a proficient public speaker.

Try this exercise to gather data in order to shake your fears:

1. **Assess where you are by asking yourself the following questions:**

   • "Do I trust myself?" List the evidence you have that proves you can trust yourself.

   • "Do I believe I have something to say of value that others want to hear?" State the information you share with people at work or in your inner circle that they appreciate.

   • "Do I believe people will like me?" Write down why people like you.

   • "Do I believe in what I'm saying about this subject?" Explain what you believe about the topic you're speaking about and why you believe it.

   Did you respond "no" to any of the questions above? If you did, examine your responses to determine where you're blocked. If you're unclear as to why you have a negative perspective of yourself, turn to Chapter 11.

   If you said "yes," continue to the next step.

2. **Determine why you're uncomfortable with public speaking by completing the following statements:**

   • I don't like speaking in front of small and large groups because . . .

   • I think that if I give a presentation, I'll . . .

   • Whenever I think about giving a presentation I feel like . . .

- My worst experience of public speaking was . . .

- The commitment I made to myself after my worst experience of public speaking was . . .

Because your fear comes from your anticipated outcome, you have to change your expected outcome to crush your fear.

3. **Gain some clarity.**

You should have some clarity as to why you don't like speaking in public. Outside of fear that you create intuitively to protect yourself from danger, fear is a lie. In this case, it's a lie because there's nothing you need to be protected from.

Whatever the fear that is causing you to resist, turn down, and dismiss opportunities to share valuable information with others, you have to determine whether what you're telling yourself is true. If not, what is the truth? Complete the following statements with the truth of who you are and what you are capable of doing:

- I can put together a great presentation because I am . . .

- When I present to a group of people, I am . . .

- When I present to a group of people, I will . . .

- The audience will like me because . . .

- When the presentation is over, I'll see that . . .

Creating a new belief about who you are, what you have to offer, and what will happen when you stand in front of an audience is the foundation that will support you as you stand in your power.

# Speaking Up Confidently in Meetings

You don't have to stand in front of a large group of people to get that feeling of butterflies dancing in the pit of your belly. You can get that feeling in the boardroom, courtroom, or classroom.

No one is thinking about you as much as you are thinking about you.

By communicating with others, you climb to the top of their mind. That's how businesses are built, products are sold, and fans are gained. Perhaps you never thought of it this way, but by sharing your intellectual property — your ideas — you're positioning and promoting yourself. That's how contracts are won and promotions are earned.

ANECDOTE

# Incarceration

I (coauthor S. Renee) was hired to develop a team that existed within a major corporation. By coincidence, the team was composed of all women. During the fact-finding phase (when I'm trying to uncover the challenges), the leader pushed the level of education and cohesiveness of the team. She bragged about their ability to effectively get the job done and create buzz about their department. Shocked by the unrealistic picture of perfection, I continued probing. "Can you tell me this?" I asked. "What is the one thing you wish your team would do that they're the least effective at doing?" "Being confident," she revealed. "When they get to the table, instead of speaking up, they shut down. They know their stuff, but we're an afterthought in everyone else's mind because we don't let our presence be known when we get to the table."

Have you ever wanted to raise your hand to share a point, but didn't because you didn't think what you had to say was important or would be received well? Did someone else raise his hand and say what you were thinking, and did everyone rally around the idea? Did you sit in silence, but mentally beat yourself up because you hadn't had the courage to share the idea first?

Failing to speak up because you're concerned about what everyone else will think of you is imprisonment. When you don't give yourself permission to be yourself, there are invisible bars between you and world.

Here's some advice to help you confidently and effectively communicate your thoughts during meetings:

- ✔ **Understand the culture in which you work and the people you work with.** Every organization has spoken and unspoken rules. If you want to be successful within the organization, you have to know, respect, and follow the rules. Knowing the various personalities that you work with is also important. Knowing what triggers people helps you to get more done with less effort.

- ✔ **Be clear.** Understand the purpose of the meeting. Know what constitutes success for all players in the room.

- ✔ **Know your environment.** Know the people at the table. Listen intently to gain an understanding of how they think and what's important to them.

- ✔ **Listen to what's being said.** You probably know a person who always has something to say, but her irrelevant tangent is pointless. Don't talk just to be heard.

✔ **Be observant.** If you're observant, you'll notice that, at times, people eye one another when someone is talking or right after a point is made. And you may notice shifts in body language. By being observant, you gain insight into who is at the table, who supports them, and what they support.

Don't ignore these nonverbal cues. Effective communication requires you to be present and to pay attention to every message. You can also sense these messages during conference calls. You'll notice a shift in the tone of others' voices, or a once-active speaker may become silent.

✔ **Listen to what's not being said.** People communicate with words and their emotions. Sometimes people are tied emotionally to their point. Listen. Positioning your thoughts from a compassionate point of view can help you improve your communication skills and relationships with others.

✔ **Jot down your points.** If it's difficult for you to stay focused or remember your points, or if you get nervous, jot down your ideas before talking.

✔ **Think partnership.** Recognize your strengths and where you sit at the table. As you listen, gain an understanding of what success means to individuals as well as the group.

✔ **Acknowledge what you're hearing.** In 10 to 15 seconds, acknowledge what you understand is being said even if there are different viewpoints.

✔ **Look for points of connection.** When you're in business meetings, it's good practice to offer and get agreement before you make your point. For example, "I agree with what Virginia said about . . . I would like to add . . ." If you don't agree with anything that is being said, you can say, "There have been a lot of interesting points shared. Here's what I'd like to offer . . . I think this connects to what you want to accomplish, Jack."

✔ **Be clear, concise, and deliberate.** Meetings can be long and tempers short. Many people are overworked and overcommitted. With so many things to do within tight deadlines, they guard their time — and rightfully so. You have the right to add value to the conversation without the pressure of feeling hurried. Organize your thoughts before you begin speaking. Know where you're going, how you want to make people feel, what you want to leave them with, and where you want to end.

VISUALIZE

# Being confident in meetings

Sit or lie down in a comfortable position. Uncross your hands and feet and close your eyes. Now breathe in deeply and exhale. Breathe in deeply again and exhale. Completely relax.

Imagine you are at work. See the place where you work and the people who work with you. See your boss. If you're the boss, visualize your employees. Imagine what they're doing and what they're wearing. Listen to the sounds at your workplace.

You look at your watch and realize that it's time to go to your team meeting. You gather your materials and head to the conference room where your team has already begun to gather.

When you enter the conference room, several of your teammates welcome you and one compliments you on an insightful comment you made at the last meeting. You feel confident and excited about this meeting. The team will be brainstorming about the project it has been given. You've already been thinking of ideas that you previously wrote down. You look at the folder for the meeting and bring out the agenda and the list of ideas for the brainstorming session. You reviewed the agenda yesterday, so you already know what's going to be discussed.

The team leader comes into the room and the meeting begins. There is an air of expectation and anticipation as various team members begin discussing the project at hand. You sit up and forward and lean in a little toward the table. You keep your hands on the table, and make eye contact with everyone around the table at least one time during the meeting.

After three of your teammates offer their ideas, you raise your hand and then offer the ideas you previously wrote down. You speak calmly

and with confidence, knowing that these are achievable suggestions. You enunciate your words clearly, breathing deeply and projecting your voice by speaking from the diaphragm. This gives your words more power and makes your voice stronger. You build your case and explain why these ideas would be useful in accomplishing the team's project. When you finish, you notice your teammates are looking at you with admiration.

Later, after the ideas have been brainstormed and your team is discussing each idea, as one of your teammates is speaking, you jot down a couple thoughts that come into your mind. As soon as he is finished, you speak up. You make your points, referring first to your teammate's suggestion. As you are speaking, you can see a few of your teammates nodding in agreement and smiling. They appreciate that you brought up these points. A different teammate turns to you to question one of your points. You answer, noting one of the statistics that crossed your desk last week. Your teammate is satisfied and now understands what you are saying.

At one point, after all the ideas have been discussed, you believe that one of them will not work. You say your opinion without belittling the person who had the idea. You point out a couple good points about it and then talk about why the idea is not the best one. Your teammates listen intently. When you are finished, several of them say they agree with you. They smile at you and you smile back. You know they respect your input. You feel proud of yourself.

The meeting is over and you get up to leave. The team leader comes over to you and thanks you for bringing up the important points you made today. She tells you that you're a valuable

*(continued)*

*(continued)*

member of the team and that the team is better because you're on it.

You go back to your office and sit down, smiling, almost laughing. You realize it's very easy to speak up in meetings and that you have much to offer your team. You turn back to your desk and begin to work on the next most important task for the day.

It's time to come back now. You have taken a wonderful journey in the world of work, and you remember the feelings of strength, confidence, and sureness you had all through your day. Keep those feelings within you as you go about your day and as you go to work. Know that as your self-esteem grows, your success at work will increase. Come back gently. Breathe in deeply and exhale. Breathe in deeply again and exhale. Become aware of your hands and feet. And when you are ready, you may open your eyes.

# Part VI
# Nurturing Self-Esteem in Others

## *Five Ways to Dig Deep to Forgive Others*

- ✔ Acknowledge your imperfections and recognize that you too have behaviors that need forgiving.

- ✔ Seek to really understand what drives the behavior of the other person.

- ✔ Come to terms with your hurt and know that you're not going to die.

- ✔ Realize that forgiveness opens the door for you to move your life forward.

- ✔ Recognize that forgiveness is taking your power back.

Loving those who hurt us is difficult — even when we're young. Check out a free article that discusses bullies and why they need love too at www.dummies.com/extras/self-esteem.

# In this part . . .

- ✔ Find out when enough is enough, when you should let go and move on, and whether you're obligated to be your brother or sister's keeper.

- ✔ Discover the step-by-step process of how to coach family and friends.

- ✔ Find out whether your children can build the confidence to avoid being swayed by their friends, misguided adults, and the media.

- ✔ Discover how to teach your children how to hear and respond to their own truth and how to develop them to be kinder, gentler, and more peaceful.

# Chapter 21

# Helping Family and Friends

## In This Chapter

▶ Becoming more understanding of others

▶ Coaching others effectively

▶ Helping others through tough times

There's a saying, "You can pick your friends, but you can't pick your family." This phrase is often used to explain the dysfunction of some family relationships.

Nothing is more cumbersome than family dynamics that don't work: when a mother doesn't meet the needs of her daughter or when a sister thinks she's better than her brother. What happens when the father suddenly hates the mother?

Where did it all begin? Did these characters meet by happenstance? Were decisions made that caused these individuals to be called family? Regardless of whether you believe that people make decisions to come together and procreate or that your family origin is connected to the big bang theory, you have to learn how to manage difficult moments and complex relationships.

We dive into this multifaceted subject and help you develop the tools needed to support, coach, and assist in the development of healthy family interactions. You find out why you have to dig deep within yourself and say the "f" word — "forgive me" or "I forgive you" — more often than you want to.

In this chapter we also answer the tough questions: "When is enough enough?" "Should I let go and move on?" "Am I obligated to be my brother's keeper?"

# Understanding Others and Their Life Journeys

Showing compassion toward others is the hallmark of maturity and a highly evolved person. It's what makes you love and appreciate others when they express compassion toward you. Their willingness to overlook your weaknesses with kindness and acceptance makes you feel safe, free, and loved unconditionally. Is there any greater gift?

It appears that accepting this divine gift is easier than giving it. When a person doesn't call you out or try to change you even though you know you have weaknesses, it's a constant reminder that you're okay.

Learning to give compassion requires you to understand this: Every person has his own lessons to learn and experiences to create. These lessons and experiences are what shape his uniqueness and help him to come into his own awareness of self-love and compassion. The unspoken agreement you have with your loved one is for you to be a witness and supporter of his growth.

This can be difficult when you're hurting from past interactions with this person or you know that he's living below his potential and capabilities.

Complete the following statements to get clear on your role in your family member's life and how to love and understand him. If you don't know the answer, complete this exercise with the person. Fill in the blank spaces with the person's name.

- _____'s greatest pain is . . .
- What _____ needs from me is. . . .
- I can offer _____ . . .
- _____'s perception of my role in his/her life is . . .
- My perception of my role in _____'s life is . . .
- The best thing I can do to meet _____ where he/she is is to . . .

# Understanding what's being said and what isn't

Oftentimes it's difficult to understand others and more difficult to understand yourself. The reason is this: You're dynamic and ever-evolving. As a result of the many experiences you're consciously and unconsciously creating, you're not the exact same person from one moment to another.

For example, say your mate always leaves home at 6 a.m., but suddenly, seemingly out of nowhere, you're bothered, even suspicious, of why your significant other is leaving home so early. Those strong feelings didn't suddenly show up one day — they had been brewing for a while. If you're not in touch with yourself, this missed awareness can create irritations that can cause you to react out of character.

That's why you have to know what you're feeling and make yourself aware of the situation first. Then share your feelings and ask non-accusatory questions to better understand the behavior of your loved one.

Building healthy relationships with family and friends begins with you understanding yourself and being confident and courageous enough to share your feelings with others.

You can't seek and be open to the answer and know it at the same time. This concept is important because your eyes can deceive you and your ears can fail you, but a pure heart will never mislead you. What you say and do in the midst of a tough moment can forever help or hurt your relationship. Establish a practice that works for you.

Here are a few suggestions:

- ✔ **Engage in self-reflection.** Take a few moments by yourself to think introspectively about the issue. Examine what you're thinking and feeling first. Ask yourself, "Why do I feel this way?" Then objectively consider the person's behavior. Give that person the benefit of the doubt before drawing a negative conclusion.

  You can't think for anyone else.

- ✔ **Talk to a confidant.** Talk to someone who has your best interest at heart and compassion for others. Talking to the wrong person can cause more harm than good. You'll know you're talking to the right person when she offers you advice that's free of judgment and moves you to an amicable solution without sending you through a cloud of conflict.

- ✔ **Read.** Reading positive information raises your awareness and elevates you to a higher state of being. This helps move you to a place of seeking answers rather than one of drawing conclusions.

- ✔ **Meditate or pray.** Seeking your highest self or having faith in something greater than yourself humbles you. When dealing with your loved one, you can't go wrong in the humble position. It says, "I care about you and our relationship."

When you approach the person, keep the following four steps in mind:

- ✔ **Respect.** Ask him if it's a good time to talk about something that's on your mind. If he says, "no," don't push and don't become annoyed. Ask for a good time to talk.

- ✔ **Share.** Begin by sharing what you know to be true about your relationship.

- ✔ **Explain.** In a nonthreatening tone and an organized fashion, explain your concern from the viewpoint of how his behavior makes you feel and why.

- ✔ **Listen.** Your answer will be found in his words and the emotions that give his words life.

The person who is listening is in the position of power. The listener is gathering information. The listening isn't the power. The information that is being shared is the power. It can help you make the necessary changes to help yourself and your loved one.

## Showing compassion and listening without judgment

Do you remember what it felt like when you were suffering? The times when you wanted or needed something but didn't know how to get it? The periods in your life when you knowingly made foolish decisions and didn't care that you did? Settle into that place for a moment. Does it make you shake your head and say, "Ugh, what was I thinking?"

Where were you at that time of your life? What were you thinking? What were you feeling? Do you recall that you were in a painful place?

Although you know that certain behaviors are indications of pain, it can be difficult to look at your loved one and see the pain taunting her. Your inability to see and understand it doesn't make it disappear, nor does it make it any less real.

Someone loved you enough to show you the way. Are you willing to do the same?

Trying to help a family member who is having a difficult time finding her way can be emotionally and mentally crippling. You have to develop the right mindset and skill sets to help her and preserve your own sanity in the process.

In addition to recalling your own frailties, remember the following three things to help you develop the right mental approach to support your loved one without wondering, "Why can't you get it right?"

✔ **Every person has her own journey.** You are called to help support the person, but you must understand that she has her own path to self-actualization. Some journeys are longer and more turbulent than others.

✔ **Every person is creating what she needs.** There are some things that you just can't explain or understand; neither can she. You just have to trust. Know that every situation is consciously or subconsciously being created to advance the person's development. Even if it doesn't look like it, she's trying to get it right, but because of the state she is in, she can't figure it out.

✔ **Everything is showing up to serve her.** It has been said that nothing is wasted. When you're in the midst of witnessing a loved one failing to live according to her potential, it can appear that she's wasting her life. It may appear that she isn't "getting it," but every positive word and every act of kindness you show toward her contributes to the love she feels that is helping to heal her hurt.

## Accurately assessing the situation

It's impossible to know the truth of what's going on in a person's heart.

A cross between watching a person's behavior and listening provides the best indicators of a person's heart message to himself and others.

People have become savvy in creating the image that they think will help them get what they want from you. Therefore, you have to build trust with the person to get him to relax and start talking. When he's comfortable, he'll intentionally or unintentionally tell you what's really in his heart.

Here's what to look for to assess what's going on with someone:

✔ **Consistency of behavior:** Authenticity automatically yields consistency.

✔ **Alignment of behavior and words spoken:** When a person says one thing and does another, believe what he does over what he says. You can have the right intention without the desire or skills to execute it.

Here's how to get people talking about themselves:

✔ **Be friendly.** This may sound like odd advice about how to treat a family member, but some people are less friendly to family than to strangers. This is often because of past experiences. If you want to help someone resolve a problem, forgive and focus on the possibility of your loved one having a happy future.

✔ **Find a way to connect.** Notice something about the person that you can connect with to encourage conversation: a recent accomplishment, an interesting hobby, or an upcoming event that may interest both of you.

✔ **Get the person talking.** Once you make a connection with your family member, let him talk uninterrupted. You'll learn what you need to know about him — his heart's message.

Knowing his heart's message helps you to more accurately assess where he is and put together a strategy to help him.

## Deciding how to best serve

Families face many complex challenges. Each family condition is unique and dynamic. A customized plan based on the culture, personalities within the family, and the problem is what best helps you. Therefore, this isn't the place to give specific advice.

However, we want to offer you these urgently important points:

✔ You cannot help your loved one if you are dying yourself.

✔ You must know the difference between empowering your family member to be responsible for herself and her behavior and encouraging an environment of dependency and immaturity.

✔ Family members who are helping another family member should be clear and in unison on how they are going to help. Like a child, a dysfunctional person doesn't have the ability to think beyond herself.

✔ Professional assistance should not be off limits if the issue is adversely affecting the family member's life and the problem persists.

✔ The amount and type of support offered should be in direct correlation with the person's willingness to be accountable to herself.

# Coaching with Care, Purpose, and Impact

I (coauthor S. Renee) have coached hundreds of people in the last few years. Yes, I have had the honor of coaching family members. What I've learned is that the only reason a person seeks assistance from a coach is because he's stuck. He wants to improve in some area of his life but doesn't know how.

The key is that the person is seeking to find an answer. If he isn't seeking and is resisting your help, and he's over 18 years of age, you have to respect his decision and find other ways to help him until he's willing to accept your help.

Coaching isn't counseling or therapy. It's exceptionally unique work that gives the person the opportunity to discover more about himself, his power, and his capacity to create the life he wants.

The person will typically seek you out, or a family member may request that you help. Either way, you are perceived as a trusted, wise resource who is capable of helping.

Coaching family demands more from you because you have to separate yourself from what you think, know, and feel about the person. As a coach, you create a safe place to support, guide, and provide positive feedback. Judgment, preconceived notions, and secret opinions will contaminate the process.

If you are asked to coach a family member who shared the same parents and household growing up, it may lead you to feeling disgruntled over the energy the person is robbing the family of. Keep in mind that no two people interpret any experience the same. He sees his experience through his eyes, not yours. Try the following step-by-step process to assist you in meeting him where he is and in helping you to help him develop the tools to move himself forward. Your job is to ask more questions than give answers because the answer lies within him.

Every coach is different, bringing a unique style to the process. You'll find your own method of effective coaching. This is my (coauthor S. Renee's) preparation and actual coaching process:

1. **Prepare ahead of time by doing the proper research on the person.**

   Visit his social media page to see what's important to him. If necessary, reach out to him and have brief conversations. Don't talk long or too much. Keep it simple. The purpose of doing this is for you to better understand what you'll be walking into more objectively.

2. **Prepare yourself by ensuring that your heart is open and you are in a place of unconditional love.**

   I meditate and ask for divine guidance and support, and for the knowledge of what's in the best interest of the person as we take this intimate journey together. Use whatever method works for you to connect on a spiritual level. Set an intention for your meeting. To learn more about intention, read Chapter 13.

3. **Set the tone of the session to be upbeat and positive by establishing a point of connection with the person before beginning the session.**

   Consider recalling a funny story from the past or a moment you shared. Recall something he did that will make him feel fabulous again.

Regardless of the issue, everyone has something amazing about him. It could be his humorous personality, smile, or kindness.

4. **Ask the person what he'd like to accomplish during your time together and why it's important to him.**

   Listen to understand where he is and to see his potential and capacity to move beyond his current state.

5. **Ask follow-up questions that give him an opportunity to explain his thoughts, feelings, and ideas.**

   The purpose is to get him to hear himself and to rediscover his own truth.

6. **Summarize what you hear him saying.**

   Give him the opportunity to clarify anything that you didn't understand. Ask, "How do you see yourself moving forward?" and "How can I help?"

7. **End the conversation on a positive note.**

   Affirm the person's greatness and remind him that you believe in him.

Coaching requires acute listening skills. You'll also use your intuition to guide the process. To begin developing your skills, get a partner to help you practice through role play. Your partner should have the ability to improvise and express emotions with words. He doesn't have to be an award-winning actor.

Have a friend write down three or four scenarios. Each situation should have a suggested ending that would help the person. It's for his eyes only. Have your partner randomly select a scenario. Don't ask questions about the scenario. He's to act out the feelings and experience of the situation. Follow the seven preceding steps to coach him and help him find his own solution. Spend about 30 to 60 minutes on each scenario. Although it's not required, we strongly suggest that you practice via the telephone. This will further strengthen your listening skills. Record the exchange. Listen to it later to hear your strengths and weaknesses.

# Believing in others when they don't believe in themselves

Seeing people for who they're created to be versus where they are isn't for the faint of heart. It's a humongous task. The journey is unpredictable, the time commitment is boundless, and the energy investment is draining.

Believing in someone who doesn't care about her life and doesn't see any worth in who she is and the value that she brings to the world isn't "a dance on the river." It's a dive into the ocean to help her find her treasure, which can only be found within her by her.

While she's searching, you are standing in a space by yourself, holding a light and giving love so that she can see herself through her dark place of undiscovered truth.

There aren't any perfect paths or best practices that we can recommend. Many families have watched helplessly as their loved ones suffered with substance abuse, eating disorders, sex addiction, or other self-defeating behaviors in search of healing their hearts, and the answer isn't simple and does not come easily.

Here are some things you can do to support yourself and your loved one while standing up for her until she can stand for herself:

✔ Take care of yourself first by renewing your mind daily with prayer, meditation, and affirmation.

✔ Be clear on what you want to offer your loved one. Set the intention and don't allow yourself to be taken off course because of her pleading or manipulative behavior.

  You aren't feeding the pain; you're helping her find her purpose.

✔ Seek the support of others who will support you in prayer, with conversation, and with random acts of kindness.

✔ Find a safe place for yourself to release any guilt, hurt, and disappointment that attaches itself through your being around the negative thoughts and actions of your loved one.

✔ Join a support group or seek professional help. This will assist you in better understanding the mystery of your loved one's issue.

## Knowing when you've done all you can

The invisible cord of unconditional love that binds a parent, sibling, and spouse to a loved one is awe-inspiringly beautiful. Letting go can be devastatingly painful. Some situations turn pain into torment. How do you know when you should step back?

When you begin to lose yourself in the situation, you start saying to yourself:

✔ I don't care about how I look and feel.

✔ I feel weak, sick, and depressed.

✔ I don't care if I live anymore.

✔ I'm willing to die fighting for my loved one.

✔ I'll lose everything to save my family member.

When you've done all you can and need to retreat, find ways to regroup and replenish — connect with friends, return to hobbies that you enjoy, and indulge in self-care programs. For example, schedule massages, manicures, pedicures, or find a great book to read.

# Teaching Others How to Handle Challenging Times

Challenging times come, and they force you into a new "normal," regardless of whether you want to accept it or not. If you resist, you'll feel the friction of your choice — creating a hostile environment for you to attempt to survive in. When you don't accept change, it's difficult for those around you to move on. The best way to teach others how to handle challenging times is to properly handle the issue yourself first. Here are some tips on how to do so:

✔ Acknowledge what has happened. Ignoring the truth only causes it to find other ways to move you to accept it.

✔ Accept your role in creating what has happened.

✔ Empathize with the other person or people involved by looking at it from their perspectives.

✔ Get in agreement with what's happening and give it permission to teach you what you are to learn.

After you've appropriately handled the change, you can show others how to do the same. Consider the following as you support others in handling challenging moments:

✔ **Meet them where they are.** Their interpretations of the situation are how they see it. Don't try to change their opinions. Help them to accept what they feel at the present moment. As they grow, they will discover a new truth.

✔ **Allow them to express negative emotions.** Negative emotions don't lead to bad behavior. Unexpressed negative emotions and criticism of negative feelings do. No one should be chastised for feeling what he feels. Help others to process their feelings in a healthy exchange, and the negative feelings will dissolve on their own.

✔ **Create a safe place to keep talking.** Situations happen, people talk about them, and then silence comes. Keep engaging your loved ones by talking about the situation until they have processed it and can talk about it without the pain controlling them.

# Grappling with broken relationships

Marriages fail. Siblings fight. Friends argue. When vows are violated, commitments are broken and expectations are shattered, and people shut down and check out. Wrecked relationships represent lost credibility. The message is "I don't trust you."

When trust is violated or perceived to be disturbed, you immediately feel that harm has come upon you. When you no longer feel safe with yourself or another person, the red light flashes in your head, cautioning you to stop and chronicle the event. Instantly, perceptions shift and the relationship dynamics change.

Days, months, and sometimes years pass and the spear of unfaithfulness that is lodged in your heart reminds you, "I don't trust him."

The foundations of healthy relationships are trust and transparency. If the issue isn't worked through, the relationship is doomed — even if it endures a slow death for 10, 15, or 20-plus years.

Most relationships are broken before they break down. Insincere interactions, mysterious wounding behaviors, and deceptive tactics are the culprits that creep into relationships, strangling the life out of them.

What should you do when someone deceives you? What do you say when that person has deliberately tainted your trust? What is the best response to the manipulative tactics of those you put your faith in?

✔ Be thankful that you discovered the truth.

✔ Decide how you want to respond to the truth. Never ignore what you've discovered.

✔ Move forward, trusting and being faithful to yourself first.

✔ Most importantly, forgive the other person — and yourself.

# Digging deep to forgive others

You can't get caught up in the dysfunction and self-hate of others. People who lie, manipulate, and deliberately go behind your back and do things that they know will offend or could destroy you are suffering. They are in deep agony.

Although you're hurt, disappointed, and perhaps pissed off, you have to forgive them for your own benefit. What does this mean?

Forgiveness is letting go of anger by cancelling the obligation that a person has to you. There are spoken and unspoken obligations, and unwritten contractual agreements among family and friends.

When a person doesn't satisfy his obligation according to your expectations, you are intensely hurt. The hurt turns into anger because of what did or didn't happen. When you release the person from the obligation, you're actually releasing yourself.

Here's why: The moment the person violated the agreement, he cancelled his contractual agreement with you and rewrote the boundaries and expectations of your agreement. You are now the only one still expecting the original commitment to stand.

Not forgiving is the hope that a nonexistent agreement will be upheld by the person who has already communicated to you that he no longer wants to be obligated to you based on the previously negotiated boundaries and expectations.

This requires you to dig deep to forgive. Follow the steps to extract the spear from your heart, stop the bleeding, and move on to creating healthy relationships with healthy people.

1. **Accept the truth for what it is.**

   You can try to explain it, but the facts remain the same. Writing down the facts may help you to accept what has happened. Don't add your opinion. There's a difference between an error of judgment and a character flaw. If there are events that lack transparency, it's called deceit.

2. **Stand in integrity.**

   Your power is in the decision to responsibly uphold faith in yourself and maintain the integrity of your personal space. Don't be swift to react to nonsense. Be wise and sensible.

3. **Shut down the noise.**

   Your mind wants to figure it out, and your aching heart wants to blame you. Take responsibility for anything that you may have done in error, such as sharing too much information, trusting too soon, or failing to acknowledge signs of dishonesty. When the voice keeps pounding in your head, go back and read the facts of the case.

**4. Think of it as a cancelled contract.**

Forgiveness releases you from remaining committed to an unenforceable agreement. As with a contract that has been violated and taken to court, there are consequences. In this case, you won't go to court, because you don't have to. This planet has its own laws and rules of accountability. The law that applies here is that whatever a person sows, he'll reap. It's called karma. Your job is to acknowledge that the agreement no longer exists, wish the person well, and accept that the consequences of dishonoring and disrespecting you and himself are not your call.

## I never thought

I (coauthor S. Renee) had a client I'll call Alex. Alex was married with three children. His job required him to travel, but when he was home, he spent his time with his family whom he deeply and loyally loved. While home, he focused his attention particularly on his kids. Because his wife stayed at home, they'd agreed that when Alex was home she was entitled to some fun with friends — at least that was what Alex thought.

After ten years of marriage, she was caught in a five-year affair. Alex was devastated. The five-bedroom house on three acres of land no longer held the same value. Jet-setting didn't equal more money, fancy trips, and boastful conversations with family and friends anymore. The equation had changed. He'd learned that bad decisions plus neglect equaled divorce.

It took Alex years to accept the fact that he'd made a bad decision 13 years earlier when he'd started dating his wife while she'd been living with another man. He couldn't see that he'd picked up where her boyfriend had left off, feeding her pain with material goods that weren't making her happy. Clearly, she'd needed to mature and develop her self-esteem. She'd wanted someone to love her — she'd needed him.

Because he didn't see what his laser-sharp focus on his personal ambitions was costing his family, he lost the marriage, and to his own dismay, contributed to the destruction of the family structure. He hardened his heart, and with his mouth he made a covenant with his heart — he would never love again.

As his coach, I couldn't help him break that vow because he continued to refuse to see and accept responsibility for his role in the broken relationship. People create their happy endings according to their ability to look at and deal with their pain.

His happy ending is filling the hole in his heart with the relationships he has with his children.

# Chapter 22

# Helping Children and Teens Achieve Healthy Self-Esteem

*W*ho doesn't want to be cool and accepted? Even you love to hear the call of your name when you travel in your social circles. It reminds you that you're important. Is the innate desire to be loved, appreciated, and valued a blessing or a curse? How can you raise a child to satisfy his needs in a healthy and constructive manner?

All human beings come into the world with their own unique, designated call to action. You may have heard it called "life purpose." Parents, mentors, community leaders, and friends share the responsibility of helping young people see, understand, and move toward their designated calls to action. When we fail to accept and do our part, young people become lost, confused, and angry. This failure creates a selfish society full of violence, cruelty, and anger.

Can your children build the confidence to avoid being swayed by their friends, misguided adults, and the media? Can you teach your children how to hear and respond to their own truth? Are your children the answer to a kinder, gentler, and more peaceful world?

In this chapter, we explore these questions and their answers as we share how to develop self-esteem in children and teens.

# Helping Children Develop in Complex Societies

Tattoos. Nose rings. Plastic surgery. In some societies these practices are a rite of passage, while in others they're perceived as a choice of rebellion. Regardless of where you live or what your cultural mores are, raising children in a world driven by uncensored access to information about anything and everything is a challenge.

Is the proverb, "It takes a village to raise a child" still relevant? Do you need to think and care about people who live on the other side of the world, but who can come into your home via the Internet? Technology has changed the rules of nearly every industry imaginable — creating as many complexities as opportunities.

Raising children isn't an industry; it's a responsibility that also has been profoundly impacted by the rate of change within cultures. The Internet isn't the only cause. Perhaps young people's levels of exposure to adult troubles have become the low cost of entertainment, but the high price of overexposure to problems they can't properly process.

Reality television and hip cartoon characters aren't the only villains. Some parents believe talking to their child as a friend is an appropriate way of dealing with personal issues. But is it? The rise in blended families also presents unique challenges without obvious solutions.

## Helping your children to understand who they really are

Daily your children are having experiences that are shaping their psyche. These experiences are shaping how they see themselves and how they see where they fit in the world. How can you protect and raise your children to believe in themselves and live from a centered truth of love and respect when chaos, corruption, and perplexity seem to have a grip on the world?

Consider the following tips to help you provide guidance to your child in a complex society:

- ✔ **You have the greatest influence.** Recognize that, as a parent or mentor, you have the greatest influence on your children's lives. They trust you first. Whatever you say and do tells your child, "This is how to get it done."

- ✔ **Find the beauty.** It's unfortunate that some people are suffering from anger, hate, and an ego takeover, but great beauty and brilliance are also shining through. If your child is exposed to outrageousness, show your child the opportunities that are being presented to resolve the conflict instead of focusing on the craziness of the situation. Jobs are created because problems persist. This strategy will help your child to begin to think about becoming a problem-solver in the world.

✔ **Protect your child.** Years ago when I (coauthor S. Renee) hosted and produced a television talk show, we produced an episode on protecting your children from Internet predators. I distinctly remember this advice: Put the computer in a room where everyone has access to it (no computers in your child's bedroom), purchase software that blocks specific sites, and know who your child is communicating with. There are also apps that can monitor or block your child's activity on her cellphone. Because information changes so fast, we don't want to offer specific sites here, but a quick search on the Internet will bring up the most current information you need.

✔ **Give your child the tools to choose friends wisely.** As your children get older, their friends will increasingly influence their decisions. If you don't give them the tools to stand in their own power, they'll succumb to peer pressure. Continue reading to discover what those tools are and how to develop them in your child.

## Believing in your children and those you mentor

Nothing feels better than knowing that the people you trust and love the most will love you regardless of how many mistakes you make. When a child doesn't feel unconditional love and acceptance, he's less likely to develop authentic self-expression, self-acceptance, and self-trust.

Like you, your children or those you mentor will err. There will be moments when their behavior will shake the trust you have in them. Your job description requires you to stand by them and believe in them regardless. Your belief in them will sustain them until they can believe in themselves.

When you were a new parent, your child believed in you when you had no idea what to do next and trusted that you'd figure it out. No one is perfect in the parent/child relationship. It's a journey of two people learning, discovering, and teaching one another how to be their best.

However, when you want your child to know that you love her unconditionally, you can't leave it to your child to figure that out. She doesn't have the capacity to do so. New clothes, trips to amusement parks, and a night out at the movies don't tell a child that you love her unconditionally. It's the words you speak. It's how you respond to her when she spills milk on the floor after you just scrubbed it. You have to learn to say, "It's okay; we all make mistakes."

A good portion of self-esteem is built on the understanding that you're okay despite your imperfections. Using this strategy lets your children know that you believe in them irrespective of the outcome they create. It requires you to be conscious and in the present moment. Blowing it is easy when time is limited and more work has been created as a result of an accident.

Committing to the following can help support you as you prepare yourself for unexpected tense moments:

- ✔ **See yourself in your child.** Don't view yourself as the person who has power over your child. Your child is you and you are your child. You both are called to help each other grow and evolve.

- ✔ **Don't multitask when interacting with your child.** You brought your child into the world with the intention of loving and developing him. You want the best for him, right? Give him your best. It's easy to become overwhelmed, frustrated, and even violent when you're trying to work, talk, or text on your cellphone, think through complex issues in your relationship, and take care of your child. It's better to stop, acknowledge your child's request, and tell him that you'll address his needs later than to haphazardly interact with him.

- ✔ **Recognize that death, disease, and divorce are the biggies.** In Chapter 11, we talk about the cycles of life: the good, the bad, and the ugly. Your attitude can be dictated by the state you find yourself in or by the gratitude you have in the midst of your circumstances. You get to choose. Whichever you decide, your child will be directly impacted.

# Creating a Safe Place for Children to Share Their Feelings

Have you ever been sharing something important with a friend when his attention was drawn to something else? How did it feel? What did you begin telling yourself about yourself? Did you say within yourself, "I'm alone. No one cares about what's important to me"? Children aren't any different. They know when they're being ignored.

Love, trust, and respect come when you create a safe place for your child to communicate her thoughts, feelings, and ideas. Here are ten things you can do to create a safe place for your child:

- ✔ **Listen attentively.** When children are young, they'll say things that'll make you laugh, and when they become teens, they'll say things that don't make any sense — in your world. But they don't live in your world, they live in their world. Without judgment, listen to your child. Additional tips on how to listen are listed in the next section, "Listening attentively."

✔ **Exercise compassion.** Because you've had more experiences, you know more than your child. Be honest, though — there's a lot you don't know. There are even things that you don't realize you don't know. Being honest about this fact humbles you and helps you develop compassion for the times when your child does something that makes you say, "What the heck were you thinking?"

✔ **Protect your child.** Be mindful of who you trust with your child. And if a conflict arises, don't automatically take the other person's side because you "know your child." Be open to hearing both sides of the story. Teach your child how to work through conflict instead of blaming him for it.

✔ **Give your child permission to be herself.** Every child comes into the world with her own unique, designated call to action; help your child to discover hers by freely letting her explore options.

✔ **Don't let looks influence your love.** I (coauthor S. Renee) have heard horror stories from clients who were treated indifferently and some-times meanly as children because they looked like a parent that the other parent hated or because they didn't meet a perceived standard of beauty. You'll destroy your child's self-esteem if you love him according to how he looks.

✔ **Don't let your child's size fool you.** Children mature physically at dif-ferent rates. People have an unconscious tendency to expect more from a child who is taller, bigger, or more developed than one who is shorter, thinner, or more fragile. There's brain development and there's physical development — don't confuse the two.

✔ **Don't stoop down to your child's level.** There will be moments when you'll be tempted to get into a back-and-forth verbal argument with your child. Don't get pulled in. Your silence allows your child to hear her own insanity.

✔ **Speak to the behavior, not the person.** Name-calling and speaking vicious words to a child are off the table — at all times. Speak to your child about his behavior. Connecting the behavior to the child redefines who he is.

✔ **Believe in your child's capacity.** You had to grow into yourself. And you're still growing. Your child has to do the same. Never stop believing that there is greater capacity for expansive thinking within your child.

✔ **Give your child plenty of hugs.** Hugging your child at any age is a price-less gift of silent safety. Do it often.

## Listening attentively

It's been said that every person wants to know: "Do you see me? Do you hear me? Do I matter?" When you care enough to listen to your children, they know how important they are. Listening is a developed skill. It requires you to listen to the words and emotions — and what these bring up for you — in order to create a connection to and understanding of where your children are and how they feel.

Looking at your pain and accepting responsibility for where you are and how you ended up there isn't easy. Like Debra in the sidebar "Emotional hunger," it's easier to blame others and tell a story that allows you to be the victim, but that will get you nowhere. This type of mentality begins at a young age and should be identified and dealt with in a safe place that gives your children permission to understand and express their feelings.

Many adults can recall unpleasant feelings of being treated differently by their parents, other adults, or siblings. Through observation and experience, they learned early what was valued in their homes, schools, churches, and communities. You have no way of knowing how your child perceives his experiences unless you ask him. When you ask, give him permission to share without judgment or penalty.

---

# Emotional hunger

As a coach, I (coauthor S. Renee) listen for a living. Every client I've ever served has called my office claiming that he needed something external to get his needs met. Clients ask for a strategy to make more money, an improved image for increased recognition, or better communication skills to enhance their chances for a promotion. Rarely is their want the same as their need.

What I've discovered is that at the core of an external desire is an unfed emotional hunger. I had a client I'll call Debra. Debra claimed, "I need a mentor to write my book." It didn't take long to discover that the lack of a mentor wasn't the problem; she was struggling with rejection, anger, and low self-esteem.

I asked, "Tell me why you think you need a mentor to write a book?"

I listened attentively as she talked about all the workshops and conferences she'd attended. She mentioned coaches she'd hired to help her. With sadness in her voice, she shared that she'd had zero success.

I followed up with the question, "Why do you want to write a book?"

She began explaining, "I was born into a well-educated family. My father is an Ivy League graduate and my mother is a highly regarded medical professional."

She paused. I remained silent.

She continued, "All my siblings have high-profile, successful careers in law and engineering. They even married successful companions. I'm divorced and although I'm educated, they treat me differently because I don't have any money."

I asked, "How do they treat you differently?"

She answered, "When they talk to me, they're condescending and mean. I'm an outsider. But if I write this book, they'll respect me because I'll be accomplished." As her story continued to unravel, we discovered that as far back as she could remember, she'd felt like an outsider.

Practice the following listening techniques to improve your listening skills and create a safe place for your child to share his perceptions and opinions with you:

- ✔ **Set an intention.** Set a well-defined intention for the interaction so you're clear on what you want to create with your child. This intention helps to sustain you while you try to remain in the present moment.

  The purpose of setting an intention before a conversation isn't to control the experience; it's to be deliberate in creating a positive interaction and outcome.

- ✔ **Ask open-ended questions.** Avoid questions with yes-or-no answers — get your child talking.

- ✔ **Ask your question and stop talking.** Don't fall into the trap of believing that because your child is sitting quietly, she's listening to you. More than likely your voice is drowning among the images and voices she sees and hears every day, all day. Let your child talk. A pause doesn't mean she's done saying what she wants to say.

- ✔ **Ask follow-up questions.** Ask follow-up questions relevant to what is being said. When necessary and appropriate, ask questions that require your child to think. Again, don't give answers; let your child hear himself talk.

- ✔ **Hear with compassion.** As your child is talking, find that place within yourself that relates to your child. This tactic helps you avoid judgment.

- ✔ **Don't exhaust your child.** When you sense your child disconnecting, stop the conversation regardless of how important it is to you. Once one of the two people in a conversation mentally checks out, the conversation is over.

Positive communication with your child teaches him to respect rather than fear you. The reward you get for taking the time to listen to your child is a child who loves himself and you. A worthy investment, wouldn't you say?

## Assessing your child's needs

Every household has a culture that includes values, rules, expectations, leadership, and specific ways of getting things done. Despite the highest perceived vision for the family, each person is an individual and should be treated according to her unique, designated call to action.

Assessing your child's needs requires your utmost attention. Long-gone are the days when you could pat yourself on the back for providing food, clothing, shelter, healthcare, and other physical necessities. Not to belittle the value of a parent's hard work and monetary investment, the fact is that prisons can provide that humanitarian service. Your child needs emotional connection, engagement, and support.

Some emotional needs are obvious, while others require you to work at understanding and assessing your children's unique patterns of operation. Examine your children's fundamental needs first:

- ✔ **The need for love:** Your children need to feel and deserve to know that you love them and that you're elated that they're here with you.

- ✔ **The need for a role model:** Your children innately learn by observation and emulation. Be the person you want your children to imitate. It's inevitable that their behaviors will mirror yours.

- ✔ **The need for fair treatment:** Treat your child the way you want to be treated. You and your child are in a partnership to help one another grow. Understanding the value of this partnership and honoring it are imperative.

- ✔ **The need for developmental assistance:** Develop your child. We deliberately chose the word "develop" versus "train." You train animals; you develop people. Development requires teaching, testing, and assessing the evolutionary process.

- ✔ **The need for exposure to a variety of experiences:** Expose your child. Exposure increases curiosity and builds the capacity for expansive thinking and greater acceptance. Create opportunities for your child to see and do new things often.

All of these needs are universal. Your child has more distinctive needs that are unique to his personality. You're not a genie, so you have to listen and watch for signs that your child gives you about who he is, what he needs, and how you can help him identify his designated call to action. Keep the following caveats in mind:

- ✔ **Listen.** It's not always what your child is saying that matters — it's what she's not saying too. Your child has top-notch sensors that tap into your emotions and relate to you even when she can't or won't communicate what she's feeling.

- ✔ **Watch.** Your child tells you his needs based on his actions. When you see specific behaviors, don't ignore them. Test different responses and watch how your child reacts to them. Putting effort into understanding how your child processes his experiences and his internal world helps you pinpoint his needs.

- ✔ **Nurture.** Don't try to change your child according to your preconceived expectations; nurture your child's natural, instinctual responses.

If you're willing to watch patiently, your child will identify for you what her needs are and tell you how to meet them.

# Relating your values to your child

Your child learns what's important to you based on what you do. The decisions you make, the people you affiliate with, the organizations you choose to be involved in, and even your occupation communicate your values. They all say, "This is what works or does not work in the world."

Wanting your child to be successful is only natural. But if you don't provide a day-to-day example of what is required to live a successful life, in the eyes of your child, it will be a fantasy rather than an obtainable reality.

Communication is also essential to relating your values. Helping your child understand the "why" of what you do is paramount in getting buy-in and personal ownership from him, thus inspiring your child to want to share in your values.

It's also important that you expect, encourage, and reward behaviors that'll help your child be successful. Suffering the consequences of violating the values is just as important as receiving rewards for living them.

Consequences help your child develop an understanding that for every action there is a reaction. By holding your children to this standard, they'll learn early that there's a penalty for violating the values you are trying to instill.

# Teaching your child to be responsible

I (coauthor S. Renee) started reading self-development books at age 13. I was being teased and bullied at school and was secretly looking for a solution. At some point, I read about or heard *responsibility* defined as "your ability to respond in any situation." This idea spoke to me.

Although you may think you can save yourself time and your child heartache by solving your child's problems yourself, it's paramount that you stop and ask yourself, "Is this in the best interest of my child?" Parenting is preparing your child through education and development to enter, survive, and happily live in the world. When you require your child to be responsible, he develops the tools to live successfully in the world.

Here are some quick tips on how to prepare your child to be responsible in the real world:

 ✔ **Relational responsibility:** Building and sustaining relationships are imperative to success. If you nurture your child with love, respect, and support but don't expect them in return, you send the message that your child is the only one who's important in the relationship. The end result is a selfish husband or wife, friend, colleague, and neighbor. You'll also regret failing to teach relational responsibility when you are on the receiving end of your child's self-centeredness. Demonstrate to your child how to give and receive love, respect, and support.

✔ **Emotional responsibility:** Your child will experience a wide range of emotions based on events that occur in her life. She has to learn how to acknowledge and manage her emotions. If you allow your child's emotions to control her instead of helping her to understand and channel her emotions properly, your child will be headed in the wrong direction. Teach her how to respond to the emotional highs and lows of life.

✔ **Mental responsibility:** Thoughts will strangle you if you don't learn how to choose the right ones wisely. You can tell what your child is thinking by watching his behavior. Explain to him how to make good decisions. Talk to him about short- and long-term impact. Share how his decisions affect those of others.

✔ **Educational responsibility:** Teaching your child the importance of education and lifelong learning is paramount to her livelihood and the survival of her family. We're not talking just about grades — educational responsibility involves more than that. Teach your child interpersonal skills such as being flexible, resilient, innovative, and team-oriented.

✔ **Professional responsibility:** Your child will grow up and have to work in a variety of cultures. As a professional, he'll have to know and understand how to step into different aspects of his personality at appropriate times.

✔ **Fiscal responsibility:** Poor management of finances has been shown as the number-one reason for divorce and the main culprit leading to stress and other health complications. Teaching your child how to earn and budget her money is critical to her wellness.

✔ **Social responsibility:** Society is an integrated group of people who have various needs and responsibilities to one another. Showing your child the importance of helping to uplift, encourage, and inspire his community is good citizenship.

## Showing children how to handle disappointment

Life happens. And when it does, it can be difficult for you and your child. With everything from failing to earn a spot on the cheerleading team to the passing of a loved one, the range of possible disappointments is endless.

There aren't any easy answers, and every situation demands great thought and consideration. You won't always hit the mark, but when you do your best, share your heart, and make decisions for the good of your child, your love will supersede the disappointment. The tips outlined in this chapter can help. Here are a few additional suggestions to think about:

✔ **Give your child time to process his own feelings.** Respect is giving a person time to figure out his own feelings before being asking him to share them with others. Every child is different. Some children have an immediate response while others take a few days. If you've built strong communication with your child, he'll let you know when he's ready.

✔ **Have a conversation about what happened.** Even if your child doesn't appear to be affected by an event, never dismiss any disappointment as unimportant or think that it will automatically resolve itself.

✔ **Ask questions according to the situation.** Here are a few to consider: "How do you feel about . . . ? What do you think this has taught you about your-self? What would you do differently next time? How can I support you?"

When you ask a person, "What do you think?" you're asking her to tell you what's going on in her mind. When you ask a person, "How do you feel?" you're asking her what's going on in her heart.

# Preparing Teens for Success

Teens are in between being a child and becoming an adult. They've learned a lot, but don't know enough. For seven years, from ages 13 through 19, your child is likely to face his most difficult struggles to design his own identity, fulfill undisclosed personal expectations, and grasp an understanding of what it means to stand at the edge of taking full ownership of his life.

Unaware of the full impact and consequences of their choices, teens wobble between two worlds. While teenagers face many difficult, life-altering deci-sions, they aren't always aware of how these decisions will affect their psy-chological advancement and stability.

## Monitoring your child and helping him make good decisions

If you don't build a loving, respectful, and supportive relationship with your child from the beginning, it'll be hard — although not impossible — to start during his teenage years.

Trying to control your teen by telling him what to do only builds anger, resentment, and retaliation — an "I'll prove you wrong" mentality. To avoid that happening, we recommend asking questions to help guide your teen to the right answer. Will he still make obvious mistakes? Absolutely. Will you cringe when he falls? You sure will. But if you let your teen trip over small things, he's likely to learn lessons along the way that will stop him from fall-ing over big things in the future.

From birth through age 12, you're preparing your child through development. During ages 13 through 19, you're overseeing and monitoring how your child is processing and using what she's learned. At age 20 and beyond, although you're still the parent, your relationship evolves into a friendship.

How do you oversee your child's choices? Take the following actions:

- ✔ **Talk to your teen about goals.** Find out what's important to her and what makes her happy. Set goals to engage your teen in sports or activities that she'll enjoy and help her achieve her ultimate goals.

- ✔ **Set expectations.** Ask your teen what he expects and work together to find a place of agreement. This strategy encourages teamwork and relationship building, and it offers a measurement of success.

- ✔ **Monitor progress.** Have monthly meetings to give your teen the opportunity to assess how she's doing. It's also good to talk about your relationship and assess whether more or less support is needed.

- ✔ **Require new learning.** Talk to your teen about areas where you can see the need for improvement, even if he doesn't agree. Engage your teen in helping to make decisions on how he'll improve in that area. Ultimately, as the overseer, feel confident about moving forward.

Here's how you can help your teen understand your point. If he plays a sport, talk about the coach's job of supporting the team by knowing the strengths and weaknesses of each player. You could say something like: "You play in the position of your strength, but you're still required to improve on your weaknesses to grow as a player. It's the coach's job to see, understand, and help you maximize your potential. As your parent, I have the same responsibility."

## *Staying positive when dealing with a difficult teen*

Unfortunately, following the preceding advice doesn't guarantee that you won't encounter any glitches. What it does provide for you is a framework for developing and overseeing the personal success of your child. As we mention earlier, children are vastly different. What works for one may not work for another. That's what makes parenting so challenging and enjoyable.

When times get difficult, you can reflect on the mistakes of your own adolescent years and appreciate that you made it to the other side. If you didn't have the same difficulties, think of someone who did and made it through okay.

As a parent or mentor, you're naturally intuitive and connected to your child. You have the answer. Perhaps there's too much noise to hear it. When times become seemingly unbearable, steal time away for yourself to become centered and open to hearing what your teen needs. Complete the following exercise to help you understand and reconnect with your child on a deeper level.

*VISUALIZE*

# Nurturing self-confidence in others

Sit or lie down in a comfortable position. Uncross your hands and feet and close your eyes. Now breathe in deeply and exhale. Breathe in deeply again and exhale. Completely relax.

You see a blue light within your heart. Blue is the color of power and determination. You feel potency, strength, and force. You know you are confident. You feel confident, self-assured, and worthy. You are entirely infused with these qualities.

You look around you and see adult members of your family. Some are strong and some are not. Identify two or three who are not very confident, and pass the blue light from your heart to their hearts, filling their bodies, emotions, and minds with the attributes of power and self-reliance. They know they are capable and that they can accomplish anything they strongly desire to attain. They are delighted to be related to you because you are an example of how a person with healthy self-esteem speaks and acts. You are an inspiration to them on how to become stronger and more effective as a person.

Now visualize children you know who need more strength in their personalities. Send the blue light from your heart to their hearts, seeing it expand throughout them. You imagine they can master their subjects in school and their relationships with their peers. You see them succeeding in their lives, developing their skills and talents, and becoming happier and achieving more than they ever dreamed possible.

Next, you see your coworkers. You may see your boss, people you work with on an everyday basis, teammates, subordinates, or employees. Think of a few who could use more skills in being confident.

Imagine the blue light extending from your heart to theirs, and see the blue light increasing to envelop them. They begin to have a self-assurance you haven't seen in them yet. They know their value to the organization, and they work hard to both do an excellent job and have satisfying relationships with their coworkers. They respect themselves, and they respect their coworkers too. See them being determined to do better at their work and courageously doing whatever it takes to get the job done. They are so happy to know you and work with you.

Now it's time to come back. Begin to come back gently. Become aware of your physical body. Breathe in deeply and exhale. Breathe in deeply again and exhale. Become aware of your hands and feet. And when you are ready, you may open your eyes.

Try this exercise to help you control yourself when your teen loses his mind. Take a deep breath in and release it. Repeat this three times. Without guilt or trying to figure out an answer, feel what you need to feel about your child and what's happening. Relax in that space for a moment. Tell yourself, "It's going to be okay. This is only temporary." Now, within yourself, call your child's name and ask, "What do you need from me?" Whatever comes up, write it down. Next ask, "How can I support you with (fill in the blank)?" Fill in the blank with whatever came up when you asked "What do you need from me?" Wait patiently for the answer.

By doing this exercise, you come into alignment with the truth that your child has a designated call to action and that you're open to guiding him to it.

Don't get discouraged or ever give up because of what you see or experience. There is always another day — and it does get better!

# Part VII
# The Part of Tens

Head to www.dummies.com/extras/selfesteem for a free article that details the ten qualities that will be yours when you create a unique personality with a strong sense of self-esteem.

# *In this part . . .*

- You're not the only person who has had to deal with self-esteem issues. Even famous and accomplished people have had to overcome hardships in their lives and make inner changes. Find out about the lives of ten prominent people who became triumphant in achieving that all-important healthy self-esteem.

- People with a sense of strong self-worth strive for excellence. Explore ten different strategies to help you attain excellence in all areas of your life.

- It's time to get started making crucial transformations in your life! Discover ten tips to quickly help you on your journey.

# Chapter 23

# Ten Famous People Who Raised Their Self-Esteem

················································································

**In This Chapter**

▶ Describing individuals who overcame hardship

▶ Celebrating the accomplishments of these strong men and women

················································································

*I*n this chapter, we introduce you to ten famous people who had substantial difficulties to deal with, but who overcame these problems and flourished. All of these famous people could have let a sense of low self-worth keep them down. But they chose to prevail over the negative events and feelings they had. They triumphed over their problems, and so can you.

## Helen Keller

Helen Keller (1880–1968) was born in Alabama. She had perfect sight and hearing until she was about 1½ years old. She contracted an illness that is now believed to have been either scarlet fever or meningitis. Thereafter, she had no sight or hearing. For the first few years of her life, she used only signs to communicate with her family, so she was considered to be unintelligent.

Because she couldn't see or hear, Keller was very fearful, clinging to her mother's skirts. She ended up being an uncontrollable child, frequently throwing tantrums, kicking, and biting when she didn't get her way. When she was angry, she smashed anything she could reach on the floor or against a wall. At meals, she walked around the table, helping herself to food off other people's plates. More than one family relative suggested she be put into an institution because she was so unruly.

Everything changed when her teacher, Anne Sullivan, arrived when she was 6 years old. Sullivan tried to teach Keller how to communicate by spelling words into her hand. Because Keller didn't understand that every object had a word, she got frustrated with this and broke the doll Sullivan had brought for her. One month after her teacher arrived, they were getting water at the well, and Sullivan spelled the word "water" into Keller's hand while the water ran over her hand. Keller realized for the first time that the movements her teacher was doing in her hand represented the word for "water." With this sudden awareness, she spent hours that day learning the names of the objects in and around her home.

From there, Keller started to blossom. At age 7, she attended the Perkins Institute for the Blind. Later, she and her teacher moved to New York so she could attend a school for the deaf. She became proficient in reading Braille, using a typewriter, and reading sign language with her hands. She could read people's words by touching their lips as they spoke.

When she was 14, she entered The Cambridge School for Young Ladies, and at age 20, she started at Radcliffe College. She graduated from Radcliffe, cum laude, at the age of 24 as the very first deaf and blind person to earn a bachelor's degree.

Keller learned to speak, and with the aid of Sullivan, she traveled the world as an adult. She became a world-famous speaker, campaigning for world peace, civil rights, labor rights, women's rights, and birth control. In addition, she was the author of many books and essays on these topics. At the age of 35, along with George Kessler, she founded the Helen Keller International organization, which was devoted to research in vision, health, and nutrition. At age 40, she helped establish the ACLU.

In 1964, she was awarded the Presidential Medal of Freedom by President Lyndon B. Johnson. And the following year, she was elected to the National Women's Hall of Fame at the New York World's Fair. In 1971, she was inducted into the Alabama Women's Hall of Fame.

# Thomas Edison

Born in Ohio and growing up in Michigan, Thomas Edison (1847–1931) went to school for only three months. His teacher felt he was intellectually disabled because he couldn't relate to how Edison's mind worked. In addition, Edison's health was fragile as a child.

Because Edison's mother was a teacher, she taught him at home, and Edison felt that he needed to please her. He began to read insatiably, and at the age of 12, he started going to the local library. He became fascinated with chemistry, electricity, locomotives, and railroads. Because of this interest, he spent much time at the machine shop operated by the Grand Trunk Railroad in Port Huron, Michigan.

As a young teen, he sold newspapers and candy on the Detroit-Port Huron train. He used his profits to buy laboratory equipment and assembled a laboratory in the baggage car of a train where he performed experiments. One day, a jar of phosphorus fell from the shelf and created a fire, so he was forced to take all his equipment out of the train.

Around this time, an incident happened that affected Edison for the rest of his life. He was lifted by his ears into a moving train, and he started going deaf. It got worse throughout his life to the point that he could hear only if someone shouted at him.

At age 15, Edison pulled a stationmaster's son from in front of an oncoming train, and the stationmaster rewarded him by teaching him how to operate the telegraph, the principal means of communication at the time. For the next several years, he made good money by traveling to different communities and working as a telegrapher.

Edison patented his first invention, an electric vote-recording machine, at age 21. He next made two inventions for gold and stock traders. He earned enough money from these inventions to set up his own engineering firm at 23. His firm manufactured his stock ticker, and he invented the mimeograph machine and improved the typewriter and the telegraph.

He was so successful that he built a large industrial research laboratory in Menlo Park, New Jersey, at the age of 29. Thomas's goal was to produce a new invention every ten days, and during one four-year period, he averaged a new patent every five days. His lab was so prolific that he was nicknamed the "Wizard of Menlo Park."

Edison's laboratory invented such things as the phonograph, the motion picture, and the incandescent light bulb. To prove this last invention, he gave a public demonstration on New Year's Eve in 1879, lighting up both his laboratory and a half mile of streets in Menlo Park. Thousands of spectators were amazed as the streets lit up. In addition to the light, Edison invented an entire system for generating and distributing electricity from a central power station. Eventually, his electric business became known as the General Electric Company.

His worst financial disaster took place at the age of 43. He invested $2 million into developing a process for producing iron from ore using magnetic separation. Although Edison's machinery worked, cheap iron ore was discovered in Minnesota, so his machinery was no longer needed. He fell deeply in debt, but he eventually paid off his creditors.

After that, Edison continued to develop new inventions, including a new type of storage battery that worked in trains and ships. He also improved the manufacture and use of concrete and different office machinery. In 1914, a fire destroyed most of his laboratory. During World War I, he did research on equipment and weapons for the U.S. Navy.

# Harriet Tubman

Harriet Tubman's maternal grandmother was transported on a slave ship from Africa, probably from what is now Ghana. Her mother was a cook for the Brodess family in Maryland. Tubman (around 1822–1913) was the fifth of nine children.

When Tubman was 5 or 6 years old, she was hired out as a nursemaid to a woman in another household. She was told to keep watch on the baby as it slept. When the baby woke up and cried, Tubman was whipped. She had these lash marks on her body for the rest of her life.

She worked for a different planter checking muskrat traps in the marshes near his house. She had to do this even when she was sick with the measles. She became so ill that she was sent back to the Brodess household. Shortly after she was well, she was hired out again. Over time, she worked in the fields driving oxen and plowing.

When she was a teenager, she was sent to a store for supplies. While she was there, another slave had left the fields without his overseer's permission. As the slave ran away, his overseer threw a 2-pound weight at him, hitting Tubman's head instead. She lost consciousness and was bleeding heavily, so she was moved to her owner's house where she laid for two days without medical care. Still bleeding, she was sent out to work in the fields again. She soon started having seizures and seemed to be asleep and couldn't be wakened. She had these seizures and headaches for the rest of her life as well as strong visions and dreams.

Tubman and two of her brothers escaped from slavery when she was 27. Her brothers returned and forced her to return with them. Shortly after that, she escaped again to Philadelphia, Pennsylvania, without her brothers, using the Underground Railroad, an informal, well-organized system of free blacks, slaves, and white abolitionists.

A year later, the U.S. Congress passed the Fugitive Slave Law that heavily punished anyone who helped slaves escape, even in states that outlawed slavery, and forced law enforcement officials in all states to assist in the capture of slaves.

Tubman spent the next 11 years returning to Maryland to rescue family members and friends, a total of 70 slaves in 13 trips. She took the slaves to the Province of Upper Canada where slavery had been outlawed. Neither Tubman nor the slaves she led were ever caught. She also provided instructions for 50–60 other slaves to escape to the north.

During this time, Tubman also gave talks to abolitionist audiences. She was a popular speaker who was in great demand.

Throughout the Civil War, Tubman worked for the Union Army, first as a cook and nurse and later as an armed scout and spy. She was the first woman to lead an armed expedition in the war, liberating over 750 slaves in South Carolina into three steamboats. Although their owners came with handguns and whips, they couldn't stop the escape of their slaves.

In her later years, Tubman traveled to New York, Boston, and Washington, D.C., to promote women's right to vote. She attended meetings of suffragist organizations and worked alongside Susan B. Anthony. At the founding meeting of the National Federation of Afro-American Women, Tubman was the keynote speaker.

# Theodore Roosevelt

Theodore Roosevelt (1858–1919) was born to a wealthy New York family, but he was a sickly child. He had severe asthma that was debilitating to him. He had sudden asthma attacks at night where he could scarcely breathe, and these attacks terrified him and his parents. In addition, he was nervous and timid. His father helped him by emphasizing the qualities of courage and tenderness.

Roosevelt accompanied his family on tours to Europe, Egypt, and the Alps. He discovered that physical exertion helped his sick body. With his father's encouragement, he began exercising, and eventually, his father hired a boxing coach for him. In addition, he read about courageous men, and he had a deep desire to be like them.

He was mostly home-schooled by his parents and tutors and entered Harvard University at age 16. Geography, history, and biology were easy for him, but he did poorly in math and the classical languages. When he was 21, his father died, and Roosevelt tried harder in school. He was active in rowing and boxing, and he was the runner-up in a Harvard boxing tournament. When he graduated from college, a doctor gave him a physical examination and diagnosed him with heart problems. The doctor recommended that he avoid demanding physical activity, and Roosevelt promptly ignored the doctor's advice.

He went to Columbia Law School, but he dropped out because he decided to run for public office. He was elected as a Republican to the New York state legislature between 1882 and 1884. He was a strong activist during those years, writing more bills than any other legislator.

He got married on his 22nd birthday, and his wife died four years later after the birth of their daughter. Only 11 hours later, his mother died in the same house. He was so distraught that he put his baby in the care of his sister and became a rancher in the Dakotas to grieve. When blizzards destroyed his cattle, he returned to New York. He took custody of his daughter when she was 3 years old.

In 1886, Roosevelt was the Republican candidate for mayor of New York City, but he lost a three-way race. In the 1888 Presidential race, he campaigned for Benjamin Harrison, who won. President Harrison appointed him to the U.S. Civil Service Commission, where he served for six years. He then became President of the Board of New York Police Commissioners, and for two years, he radically reformed the police force.

In 1897, Roosevelt was appointed Assistant Secretary of the Navy by President William McKinley. The Secretary of the Navy was more interested in the pomp and ceremony of his position, so Roosevelt made the majority of the decisions. When Spain and Cuba declared war, he resigned from the Navy and formed the First U.S. Volunteer Calvary Regiment (the "Rough Riders"), taking part in the war.

He then became the Governor of New York in 1898, and he was Vice President when President McKinley was killed in 1900. Roosevelt became the youngest person to be President, and he won in a landslide in 1904. As President, he concentrated on breaking up corporate trusts and monopolies, raising corporate taxes, promoting better labor relations, and conserving natural resources. He greatly expanded the national parks and national forests, built the Panama Canal, and pushed Congress to pass the Meat Inspection Act and the Pure Food and Drug Act.

# Albert Einstein

Born in Germany, Albert Einstein (1879–1955) was considered a slow learner and may have had dyslexia. He was shy and quiet. He started speaking at age 2, and he rehearsed what he wanted to say, which was interpreted by some people as an indication of stupidity. Even after he started school, he continued to speak slowly. Because of these speech patterns, Einstein's teachers thought he was a slow learner.

They also thought he was slow socially. Instead of playing outside with the other children, he enjoyed spending time by himself doing jigsaw puzzles and playing with a steam engine his uncle had given him. Einstein's parents hired a tutor when he was 5, but the tutor quit shortly thereafter because of his student's temper tantrums. Einstein was frustrated because all his teachers and tutors wanted him to do was memorize material and focus on rote learning, with no opportunities to investigate what really interested him.

At age 9, he went to high school, where only 3–4 hours a week were spent on math and science, which is what Einstein excelled in. The rest of the time, he studied Latin and Greek. He began to question some of the ideas that were being taught, and his teachers interpreted this behavior as not respecting them and challenging their authority.

It was only at home that Einstein could learn what he wanted. His uncle taught him algebra and the Pythagoras theorem. A medical student his family knew gave him a series of math textbooks, and they discussed math and philosophy. By the time he finally got to study physics in school, he had already learned all the concepts covered in the course and wasn't interested in what the teacher had to say. He eventually either was asked to leave high school or dropped out.

He applied at Zurich Polytechnic in Switzerland, and while he passed the science and math sections, he failed the general section. Instead he went to Cantonal School, where he flourished because he participated in hands-on activities and conceptual thinking. He applied again to Zurich Polytechnic and was accepted. Again, he was expected to do rote learning, and again he questioned the conventional wisdom. He started to cut classes and passed his exams only because his friend took good notes that he could study.

His first job was at the Swiss patent office, judging the worthiness of patent applications that required physics to understand. He eventually obtained a Ph.D. After learning that he was targeted by the Nazis in Germany, he moved to the United States at the age of 33 and took a position with the Institute for Advanced Study at Princeton University.

He developed the general theory of relativity in physics and created the formula $E = mc^2$ to explain the relationship between mass and energy. He received the Nobel Prize in Physics in 1921 for his discovery of the law of the photoelectric effect.

In 1946, he helped found the Emergency Committee of Atomic Scientists that worked to control the atomic bomb. In addition, he actively campaigned for civil rights in the United States. He published over 300 scientific papers and over 150 nonscientific works.

# Mahatma Gandhi

Mohandas Gandhi (1869–1948) was born and raised in a Hindu merchant caste in India. At the time of his birth, India was ruled by England. He was a timid and shy boy, and he was afraid of the dark. A friend told him that the English were powerful because they ate meat, which Hindus did not do. Especially because he was a thin and weak boy, he began to eat meat. In addition to feeling shame for deceiving his family, the meat made him sick, so he stopped shortly thereafter.

Gandhi's family had him get married at age 13 to a girl one year older. He believed a husband should have authority over his wife, so he told her what to do and who to see and when. She rebelled against this strong control, and the more he tried to control her, the more she resisted. They often argued and didn't talk to each other. He still needed to sleep with the light on at night because of his fear of the dark, but he couldn't tell his wife why because of his embarrassment.

He barely passed his entrance exam for Samaldas College in western India, but he was not happy there and moved to England to study law. After passing the bar, he returned to India to practice law. Unfortunately, he was too afraid to speak at his first court case to cross-examine a witness, so he was hired by various law firms to do research and writing for them. He accepted an offer from a Muslim Indian firm to travel to South Africa to advise on a lawsuit for a year.

It was there that he experienced racial injustice when he was thrown from first class on a train because he was an Indian, even though he had a valid ticket to be in first class. He witnessed racial bias by his countrymen both in South Africa and in India. He founded a political movement and, after reading spiritual texts and various authors, he believed that nonviolent civil protest was the correct political stance.

He encouraged oppressed people to improve their circumstances and led peaceful protests and strikes. He was arrested six times in South Africa and six times in India, and he served various time in prison between 1908 and 1942.

Gandhi returned to India in 1915 and led the movement to break away from England. He published the Declaration of Independence of India, making the case for Indian self-government.

In 1930, he led tens of thousands of people to the Arabian Sea, where they disregarded the law by making their own salt. Salt was used for preserving food, and Indians were prohibited from producing or selling salt independently and were forced by law to buy expensive, heavily taxed salt from the British. Most Indians were poor and could not afford to buy it. At the time of the march, protests broke out across India, and over 60,000 people were arrested, including Gandhi.

Largely because of Gandhi's efforts, India gained independence from England in 1947. Two countries were created against Gandhi's advice, one for Hindus and one for Muslims. Gandhi died in January 1948 when a Hindu nationalist shot him for being too sympathetic to the Muslims.

# Ralph Waldo Emerson

Ralph Waldo Emerson (1803–1882) was born in Massachusetts. Three of the eight children born to his parents died in childhood. His father died right before Emerson's eighth birthday. He was raised by his mother and other women in the family.

At the age of 14, Emerson went to Harvard College, but he was not a very good student and graduated in the middle of his class of 59 people. He had poor health, so he moved first to South Carolina and then to Florida to regain his health. He took long walks on the beach and wrote poetry.

He first worked as a schoolmaster in Massachusetts, and then went to Harvard Divinity School. His brother Edward's health deteriorated and he suffered a mental collapse, so he went to a mental asylum and died later of tuberculosis. Two years later, Emerson's brother Charles also died of tuberculosis.

Emerson got married at age 24, and his wife died three years later. He was very affected by his wife's death, and he visited the grave every day.

He was the junior pastor for the Second Church, but he began to disagree about the worship service, public prayer, and communion. He resigned and toured Europe.

After returning to the United States, he started giving lectures. In all, he gave over 1,500 public lectures and wrote dozens of essays on individuality, freedom, and the ability of people to accomplish anything.

# Abraham Lincoln

Abraham Lincoln (1809–1865) was born in a log cabin in rural Kentucky. His family was forced out of their home, and he had to work at age 7 to help support his family. His mother taught him to read and write, but she died when Lincoln was only 9 years old. His sister died ten years later.

He had only one year of formal education by a number of traveling teachers, but he educated himself by reading books. As a young man, he worked as a boatman, clerk, merchant, postmaster, and surveyor. He believed he had an important purpose to fulfill.

When he was 23, Lincoln ran for the Kentucky legislature and lost. He bought a small general store that same year, and it failed. He tried to get into law school, but he couldn't. He studied law on his own and had a successful law practice.

A year later, he ran for the Kentucky legislature and won. He served four successive terms. He voted to expand the vote to all white men, whether they were landowners or not. After being in the legislature, he returned to his law practice, taking both criminal defense and civil cases.

Lincoln's fiancé died before they were to be married. He had a nervous breakdown and was bedridden for six months. He was a sad, almost depressed, person most of his life. He married Mary Todd at age 33.

He tried to become Speaker of the Kentucky legislature and was defeated. He ran for the U.S. Congress when he was 35 and lost. When he was 37, he ran for the U.S. Congress again, and this time he won and moved his family to Washington, D.C. Two years later, he ran for reelection to Congress and lost. Shortly thereafter, his son died.

When Lincoln was 45, he ran for the U.S. Senate and lost. Two years later, he sought the Vice Presidential nomination and got less than 100 votes. Two years later, he ran for Senate again and lost again.

He was against slavery and also against having the new Western states become slave states. He helped create the Republican Party.

In 1860, Lincoln ran for President and won. After his election, the South seceded from the Union and the Civil War began. He preserved the Union during the Civil War, put an end to slavery, and strengthened the federal government. He helped strengthen the American economy by modernizing banks and instituting protective tariffs to encourage the building of factories and railroads.

# Frederick Douglass

Frederick Douglass (1818–1895) was born a slave in Maryland. He was separated from his mother at the age of 7 and then lived with his grandmother. Later he was separated from his grandmother.

He learned to read when he was about 12. It was illegal for slaves to learn to read, so he had to do most of his learning secretly. He believed that the knowledge he gained from reading would help him move from slavery to freedom. When his owner hired him out to another family, Douglass taught the slaves on that plantation to read at their weekly Sunday school. When other plantation owners found out, they came with clubs and stones to break up the group, and they didn't meet again.

When Douglass was 16, his owner sent him to work for a farmer who was a slave breaker, a person who whipped slaves regularly to make them suffer physically and break them psychologically. It almost worked on Douglass, but after Douglass fought back, the slave breaker never tried to beat him again.

Douglass tried to escape twice before he succeeded. When he was 19, he met and fell in love with a free black woman in Baltimore. She provided a sailor's uniform for him and money to cover his travel costs. He also had identification papers that he had gotten from a free black seaman. It took him less than 24 hours to take a ferry, train, and steamboat to New York City and freedom. He worked as a steward, Sunday school superintendent, and sexton.

He began attending abolitionist meetings, and at one, he was unexpectedly invited to speak. He was nervous, but he forced himself to speak. He was so eloquent that he was encouraged to become an anti-slavery lecturer. A few days later, he spoke at the Massachusetts Anti-Slavery Society's annual convention. Joining other speakers, he traveled for six months throughout the eastern and Midwestern United States lecturing for the American Anti-Slavery Society. At one lecture in Indiana, an angry crowd chased and beat him, breaking his hand. His hand never healed properly, and it bothered him for the rest of his life. He also lectured in Ireland and Britain for two years.

The first of three autobiographies was published in 1845. After returning to the United States, he published his first abolitionist newspaper.

Douglass lectured against slavery and in favor of school desegregation during the Civil War. Thereafter, he spoke in favor of women's right to vote.

# Eleanor Roosevelt

Eleanor Roosevelt (1884–1962) was the niece of Theodore Roosevelt. Her mother was a beautiful socialite, whereas Eleanor was anything but. She had buckteeth, wore simple clothes, and wasn't pretty at all. Because of her plain looks, her mother insulted her by calling her "granny," and she considered herself an ugly duckling. She was insecure about her relationship with her mother, timid, awkward, and starved for affection. Her mother died when Eleanor was 8 years old, and her younger brother died the next year.

She had a wonderful relationship with her father, whom she adored. But her father was an alcoholic who was confined to a sanitarium. He died when she was 9 by trying to jump out of a window followed by a seizure. Because of these childhood losses, Eleanor was inclined to be depressed throughout her life.

She lived with her maternal grandmother where she was privately tutored. When she was 15, she went to a private finishing school outside London, England. There, her personality flourished as the headmistress took a special interest in her, took her shopping for fashionable clothes, and encouraged her to take command of the itinerary during their travels.

After she returned, she was active in the New York Junior League and taught dancing and calisthenics twice a week to poor people on the East Side. She joined the New York Consumers' League that highlighted the harsh working conditions for women and children.

She married Franklin D. Roosevelt when she was 21. After a honeymoon in Europe, they moved into a townhouse that her husband's mother Sara gave them. From the beginning, the relationship was contentious between Eleanor and Sara because Sara wanted to run both households and control the raising of the children.

At the age of 34, as she unpacked her husband's suitcase, Eleanor discovered a collection of love letters between Franklin and Lucy Mercer, Eleanor's social secretary. After that, although they stayed married, the relationship was more a political partnership. Eleanor became more active in public life. She joined the League of Women Voters and the Women's City Club.

Three years later, Franklin was stricken with polio, and his legs were permanently paralyzed. His mother wanted him to retire and become a country gentleman, but his wife argued that he should stay in politics. Franklin took his wife's advice, and from then on, Eleanor separated from her mother-in-law's control.

After Franklin contracted polio, Eleanor began to stand in for him, making public appearances for him and speaking to groups of people. She didn't like speaking in public though. Because she had a shrill, high voice, she was coached by Franklin's political advisor. She also spoke for the Women's Trade Union League to raise funds for the 48-hour work week, minimum wage, and the abolition of child labor. She was increasingly active in the New York State Democratic Party and campaigned for various candidates, including her husband. Franklin was elected Governor of New York in 1928, and they moved into the Governor's mansion. While he was in this position, Eleanor traveled throughout the state, gave speeches, and examined state facilities, reporting back to him what she found.

Her husband was elected President in 1932, and Eleanor became even more active. She held press conferences, toured the country, wrote newspaper columns, and appeared on radio. She spoke up for the rights of minorities, the poor, youth, and the unemployed.

In 1945, Eleanor was named as the U.S. Delegate to the United Nations. She chaired the committee that wrote the Universal Declaration of Human Rights in 1948. And in 1961, she was appointed by President John F. Kennedy as the Chair of the Commission on the Status of Women.

# Chapter 24

# Ten Approaches to Pursuing Excellence

*E*xcellence is performing at your highest level. Whether it's raising your self-esteem, doing well at your job, having satisfying relationships, or improving your physical body, engaging in excellence means you carefully think through your goal and make logical plans, you take the time to do your best, and you work hard at achieving what you desire.

Pursuing excellence begins with a decision you make, an ideal you envision. Once that vision is in place, you do whatever is necessary to make it a reality. This chapter details ten different strategies to use that will help you attain excellence in your life.

## Take Pleasure in What Brings You Satisfaction

Imagine reaching your full potential by becoming your best self. Imagine being happy and living the life of your dreams, growing and achieving in all aspects of your life.

You have the power to succeed in creating a life that works for you and to set and reach goals to improve your life. There are two types of people: those who succeed because they do the things that help them realize their highest potential, and those who are disappointed because they neglect to do what is required for success. And when you succeed, you have more power to do even more.

Striving for self-improvement and the desire to continue to grow and develop are often natural for people with healthy self-esteem. By identifying what aspects of your life you want to improve in order to be more satisfied, you'll become more aware of what plans you need to construct in order to make the necessary changes. Then it's time to develop strategies to attain excellence.

# Commit to Do What Is Required to Excel

After you make a plan to reach your goal, your commitment to do everything that's required to reach it is essential. This commitment involves having a high level of dedication and self-discipline.

Being committed is persevering through all the ups and downs that happen, persisting in the face of any obstacles that appear before you, and continuously striving to do your best.

The most effective way to carry out your commitment is to make a detailed plan to reach your goal with all the steps needed to be completed. Then, at the beginning of every day, review your list and identify exactly what you need to carry out that day to bring you closer to accomplishing your goal.

Years ago, I (coauthor Vivian) worked for a nonprofit organization dedicated to increasing recycling in four states. I was the manager in my state, and part of my job was to travel around the state and assist the residents in rural communities to either begin or expand recycling programs. I introduced this project at a conference of recycling coordinators with a slide show of the different recycling programs already existing in rural communities throughout the state. I read the descriptions of the programs, and it was very boring. A couple people even got up and left. I decided right then and there that things had to change. Before I went to my first community to give the same presentation, I memorized every slide and what to say with each one. I wrote out phrases on 3-x-5-inch cards, and then I practiced over and over again until I had my talk just right. I also made sure that the night before each presentation, I practiced one more time to be certain I was confident of my ability to do my talk well. I was committed to doing whatever I needed to in order to excel in this task.

# Use Your Knowledge of Yourself and Your Goal

Personal excellence requires that you evaluate your strengths and weaknesses. Your strengths are those things that are easy for you to do and what you do best. They are your natural talents and skills. You may not even notice them because they're so instinctive to you. Your strengths may or may not be what you like to do. They can be, but that's not always the case. Consider these characteristics that describe strengths:

- ✔ Kind
- ✔ Creative
- ✔ Positive
- ✔ Disciplined
- ✔ Visionary
- ✔ Focused
- ✔ Intelligent
- ✔ Motivated
- ✔ Analytical
- ✔ Flexible
- ✔ Sociable
- ✔ Energetic
- ✔ Patient
- ✔ Responsible
- ✔ Communicative

Just as important as identifying your personal strengths is recognizing your personal weaknesses. Realize that everybody has weaknesses. No one is perfect; it's normal. Weaknesses are qualities that create negative situations in your life. Consider these traits that represent weaknesses:

- ✔ Closed-minded
- ✔ Fearful
- ✔ Self-centered
- ✔ Impatient
- ✔ Lazy
- ✔ Controlling
- ✔ Temperamental
- ✔ Undisciplined
- ✔ Antagonistic
- ✔ Prejudiced
- ✔ Negative

> ✔ Offensive
>
> ✔ Sloppy
>
> ✔ Complaining
>
> ✔ Inflexible

What should you focus on the most when creating an excellent life? It's best to concentrate on using and enhancing your personal strengths and on controlling and minimizing your weaknesses.

The next step is to expand your knowledge in the area of your desired growth. By reading this book, you're taking a giant step in becoming more knowledgeable about the various means to increase your self-esteem. Reading, taking courses, and attending seminars are all ways to grow in knowledge.

# Have Enthusiastic Feelings That Lead to Creativity

In order to achieve excellence, you need to have a keen interest in accomplishing what you desire. Without these deep feelings of enthusiasm, you won't have much motivation and you'll stop partway through without completing what you started.

Your enthusiasm about your goal engenders creativity, and this creativity then generates even more enthusiasm. As you inspire yourself and others to take the steps that are needed to reach your goals, your passion increases even more.

Being fervent inevitably spills over to other people. When you talk to your friends, family, and peers about what you desire, your excitement helps push you in a positive direction.

You may find that some people don't support you in reaching your goals, no matter what they are. Some people have to see you living your vision before they will encourage you. Don't continue to seek their approval. Realize that you can reach your aspirations without their support. You can't please everyone, and it's most important to please yourself. If you wait for everyone to agree with your dreams, they may never happen. They are your dreams and not theirs. So you can't wait for them to approve before you take action.

Instead, do your best to be around people who encourage you in what you're excited about and want you to succeed. Look for friends, colleagues, and peers who can share in your enthusiasm and cheer you on.

Life is all about growing and improving yourself. When you do this every day, getting better and better, you build intensity to develop your skills and talents in whatever you're focused on. Bear in mind that your energy goes to wherever your attention is. And your intention takes form as you focus your thoughts and feelings on what you want to improve. The more enthusiasm you have, the more energy you put into your goal and the greater attention you put into creating it. That's when you'll actually reach your goal.

## Maintain an Upbeat Attitude About Yourself and Your Goal

To attain excellence now, remind yourself of past triumphs. Congratulate yourself on what you've accomplished and the good you've already done.

Fill your mind with positive thoughts. Read inspirational books, listen to beautiful music, and talk with people who help uplift you and make you feel good about yourself and what you're achieving.

Remind yourself that any important goal takes a lot of work and that most things are possible if you try hard enough.

When I (coauthor Vivian) was in junior high, I had a long poem to perform before an auditorium full of parents and other students at a Christmas show. In the middle of the poem, I forgot where I was, so without missing a beat, I started the poem all over again. The second time through, I completed it. Interestingly, everyone clapped with smiles on their faces, and my parents told me they had no idea I had made a mistake. Sometimes you just have to carry on, no matter what errors you've made.

## Stay Focused on What You Want

Maintaining a constructive focus on your goal keeps you applying your efforts in a positive direction. If you get frustrated because your goal isn't turning out as you first imagined, don't let yourself fall into the trap of being a victim.

Think about exactly what has gone wrong and gain from it. Reflect on what you did well as well as how you can improve in the future. Concentrate on working on those particular points. Consider different options to overcome these obstacles and choose one or more that make the most sense.

It's crucial to regain your focus, keep doing constructive things, and realize that the negative situation will pass soon enough. Understand that impediments do happen and that they're normal. See them as minor bumps in the road and remember that your main path is still moving you forward toward accomplishing your goal.

# Be Willing to Share Your Feelings with Others

Everyone experiences obstacles reaching goals, and these setbacks can lead to annoyance and frustration. Keeping these emotions inside can lead to stress and damage your physical well-being. Pent-up emotions can cause tension in your neck, back, shoulders, and jaw. They can also produce long-term problems like frequent headaches, high blood pressure, and stomach ulcers.

Sharing your feelings can go a long way in relieving your stress and aggravation. Take these steps in opening up:

1. **Identify your feelings.**

   Ask yourself these questions:

   - What am I feeling?

   - When did I start feeling this way?

   - What is this feeling trying to teach me about the situation?

   This chart can get you started. As you go down the list, the emotions become more intense.

   | *Sad* | *Angry* | *Scared* | *Confused* |
   |-------|---------|----------|------------|
   | Disenchanted | Displeased | Unsure | Undecided |
   | Drained | Annoyed | Anxious | Disorganized |
   | Demoralized | Humiliated | Alarmed | Troubled |
   | Depressed | Agitated | Overwhelmed | Flustered |
   | Hopeless | Furious | Desperate | Directionless |

2. **Choose someone to share your feelings with.**

   This can be your partner or significant other, a family member you're close to, or a friend whom you trust. Or, if someone caused you to feel these emotions, communicate with that person.

3. **Decide on the method to express your feelings.**

   Consider how to best articulate what you're feeling. If you're opening up about events that happened while trying to reach your goal, talking directly with the person you chose in Step 2 is best, whether it's in person or over the phone. This way you can get immediate feedback. If you're discussing your feelings with the person who caused them, this interaction can take place verbally in a face-to-face encounter, or it can be in a more indirect manner such as by writing a letter or an email. The latter methods allow you to think about how to best make the person you're addressing understand your point of view. Be open to hearing this person's point of view too.

4. **Open up and express your feelings.**

   If you're going to face in person someone who caused your emotions, practice several times what you're going to say. Make sure you don't say, "You made me feel . . . " because this is an accusation. Rather, state, "I feel . . . " and describe your feelings.

Sharing your feelings will help you figure out what to do about the situation. You'll be able to release negative energies within you so you feel better, and you'll be more capable of identifying how to improve the situation and the problems you're faced with. If you're communicating with a person who caused the emotions, the two of you will be able to discuss how to deal most positively with your relationship.

# Accept People for Who They Are and Look for the Good in Them

Although it's important to speak up when your feelings have been hurt or you see a problem, it's also essential to respect others. So consider this question: Do you believe that everyone is here to serve your personal happiness? In order to live a life of excellence with more happiness, it's better to accept people for who they are rather than try to change them. This includes people who are involved with you in meeting your goals.

The first step is to stop seeing the world in black and white, with you always being in the right and others as being in the wrong. It's important to understand other people's point of view. Perhaps they had a poor upbringing or difficult situations to deal with throughout their life. Perhaps they honestly see things that you don't see.

Everyone has had various life experiences that form who they are. Everyone's experiences have been different from yours, and those differences are what make us all unique.

Trying to make someone into someone they're not is exasperating and wearisome. Realize that just because your way of doing things works for you doesn't mean it will work for others and that you have to force your way on them. When you try to change people, you're in essence saying that you're better or smarter than they are.

The second step is to turn the situation around. Ask yourself how you would feel if someone were judging you and refusing to accept your point of view.

However, if you don't enjoy being around certain people, move on to be with people you're more compatible with and who share the same interests that you do. Spend time being around people who enjoy being with you. If you do this, you'll have much more energy and concentration for the goals you're trying to reach.

If you're like most people, you're more likely to notice qualities that annoy you than ones that you admire about other people. When you do this, you naturally feel less safe and less disposed to be generous with others. Seeing the good in others helps you be happier, more confident, and more productive.

All of us tend to filter out information that doesn't reinforce our beliefs and to look for information that supports our beliefs. When you look for the good in others, you're likely to find it. Identify anything that supports this belief.

Appreciate the abilities other people have. Notice when others are good at their jobs, excel in certain specialties, and demonstrate good relationships with others. Look for others' positive virtues such as being helpful, inspiring, courageous, trustworthy, and determined.

You may hear a third party say something kind about a person, or someone you respect may see something positive in that person. Pay attention to these things and be open to what you hear.

When you see the good in people, they naturally feel a greater connection with you. This connection creates more excellence in their lives as well as in yours.

# Have Flexibility and Balance in Your Life

Don't be a slave to your goal and feel that you have to accomplish it a certain way. Flexibility is having the willingness to adapt and try something different if something isn't working as you thought it would. Be very aware of your environment and the people in it. If things aren't going as you originally planned, make changes until you find what works.

Along with flexibility, it's vital to have balance in your life to allow time for the other important people and activities in your life. Although you may need to devote extra time to your project, it's best not to totally immerse yourself in one area of your life to the exclusion of all others.

Make a list of everything and everyone that's in your life, including all the goals you're working on. Note how much time you feel is appropriate to give to each one during a typical week.

# Stick with Your Goal Until It's Completed

To truly reach excellence, it's crucial to persist with any project until it's completed. Giving up halfway through will diminish your self-esteem quickly.

If you're unsure which direction to go, spell out exactly what steps need to be taken to finish your goal and brainstorm all the possibilities you can think of to move you through these steps.

If you lose your motivation before the project is finished, make yourself accountable to another person. Take the steps you've created and write down what is required. Tell the other person exactly what you're to perform and the date and time by which you should complete it. Be open to being responsible to this person for accounting for each step you are to take.

Fear is the adversary of excellence. When fear rules your life, you never complete your goals. To conquer fear, you must practice courage more than you desire protection. To be courageous, you have to be daring and forsake holding onto what makes you feel safe.

If you're fearful about completing your goal, write down exactly what it is you're afraid of that keeps you from finishing it. Then indicate whether each fear is unreasonable or prudent. If it's unreasonable, do your best to ignore it because it's not worth your attention. If being cautious is prudent, write down exactly what to be watchful for and how to deal with any problems that may arise.

Also note whether what you fear is outside of your control. If it is, record what steps you can take to adapt if it actually does happen. Then put your paperwork away and forget about this fear because you've done everything you can at this time. Continue to work on your goal. If what you fear is within your control, take a deep breath, prepare yourself, and then do the thing that's worrying you.

If your problem in completing your goal is being unable to prioritize your tasks, make a chart designating these four time frames:

- **Immediate priority:** These tasks should be done immediately.

- **High priority:** These tasks should be accomplished as soon as possible.

- **Medium priority:** These tasks should be started as soon as the immediate and high priority tasks are done.

- **Low priority:** These tasks can wait until all the other tasks have been completed.

In addition, you can prioritize your goals according to how much effort they require. Look at the goals you've labeled as immediate, high, medium, and low priority, and within each category, note whether each goal takes high, medium, or low effort to accomplish.

Once you've completed your goal, celebrate! Honor yourself and your strong commitment to see it through to the end. You've earned it.

Striving for excellence is one of the most important things you can do with your life. It helps you achieve all your goals and raises your self-esteem to its healthiest level.

# Chapter 25

# Ten Tips for Quickly Improving Your Self-Esteem

**D**eveloping your self-esteem doesn't necessarily have to take a long time. There are many fun and pleasurable things you can do to improve your opinion of yourself and enhance your outlook on life.

In this chapter, we feature ten different things you can do easily and quickly to boost your sense of self-worth. Some are short and to the point, and some we describe in more detail.

## Become Proficient at Something You Enjoy

Find an area that interests you, something you naturally excel in, and put your focus on learning everything you can about it. This venture takes some hard work and dedication, but it's well worth the effort. You need a willingness to work at it and a determination to succeed.

You can gain expertise by reading books, interviewing people, and learning from websites and courses. You also need experience in the real world.

To become proficient quickly, you need to practice often. As you perform in your area, make adjustments and improvements to get even better. This increased competency will be a source of satisfaction and achievement for you.

# Read Websites, Books, and Articles That Uplift You

If you have a habit of thinking poorly about yourself, you can lift your spirits by reading materials that make you look at the brighter side of life. You can improve your mood just by taking control of what you put before your eyes.

Watching television shows and movies with violence and disrespectful behavior as well as looking at commercial advertisements can go a long way in making you feel like a victim and that you're not good enough. Your self-esteem can easily take a nose-dive if that's what you frequently look at.

When I (coauthor Vivian) was a girl, I loved to read biographies of famous women that I got from the local library. Even at night when I was supposed to be asleep, I would snuggle under my blanket with a flashlight and read books about women who did amazing things. I especially remember reading about Helen Keller and Joan of Arc. Some were shorter children's books, and some were more complex adult books. I was thrilled to read about these strong women and felt that someday, I could do amazing things too.

Reading uplifting material can give you inspiration to live a better life. Look for materials that emphasize self-improvement, motivation, and fun and interesting ways to raise your mood.

# Review Three Things Every Evening That You Did Well That Day

Ending the day with thoughts of what you did well helps build your self-respect. Set aside a few minutes to review the events of the day. Close your eyes and relax. In your mind's eye, go through what happened. Begin with the morning, then move to the afternoon, and finish with the evening. Observe the events that took place, the people who were in your life during the day, any decisions you made, and any successes that took place.

Be thankful for all the good things that happened and that you accomplished. Notice at least three things that were successful for you or that you did well that day. Be grateful for everything that you felt good about, big or small. You can also note the things you'd do differently next time.

An evening review helps you identify everything good that happens in your life as well as how you can improve in the future.

# Eliminate Behaviors That Waste Your Time

Do you spend a lot of time watching television? Playing video games? Surfing the Internet? All of these are time wasters that don't add to your sense of self-esteem. Either stop doing them altogether or reduce the time you do them. Fill those hours with constructive, creative, and positive ways to spend your time. Ask yourself these questions:

- What gets you excited?

- What do you enjoy doing or what are you good at doing that's useful?

- What accomplishments do you want to achieve?

The answers to these questions will provide you with direction.

# Make a List of Your Accomplishments

Whenever your thoughts about yourself are low, making a list of your accomplishments can change your focus. Get more than one sheet of paper and a pen or pencil, or create a blank screen online. Set a timer for at least 15 minutes. Then start writing out all your achievements both as a youth and as an adult. Include everything — big or small — that you can think of, not only what you've done for yourself, but also what you've done for your friends, family members, neighbors, and complete strangers. Include such things as:

- Being loving to animals

- Planting a garden or caring for houseplants

- Sending a card to a good friend

- Doing some sort of artwork

- Getting good grades

- Finishing housework

- Helping a stranger across the street

After you make this list, read it over several times, give yourself a pat on the back, and allow the pride you take in carrying out all these accomplishments to sink in deeply.

When I (coauthor Vivian) made my list of accomplishments, one of them was teaching in college classrooms. I had no training to teach, but I did have the confidence that I could. After I earned my master's degree, I contacted all the people I knew about positions they knew were open. I talked to a friend who worked for our local community college about an opening in the administration, and he said that although there were no openings in administrative work, the sociology department was looking for an instructor. Sociology was my major for my bachelor's degree, so I decided to apply. I was hired by the head of the department because of my enthusiasm for the subject. I had about two hours of training by the woman who taught a similar class at the college and that was all. I diligently studied the material and practiced what I would teach until I had it thoroughly memorized. The classes went very well, and I taught two or three classes every semester at that college for ten years before beginning to teach at another one.

# Ask Others to Go Out

Good friends like you for who you are and provide companionship. Having a fun time together can bond your friendship, so asking them out helps the relationship grow.

But where can you go? Here are some ideas:

- To a movie
- To a store or the mall to shop
- To the park to play Frisbee or just walk and talk
- To an ice- or roller-skating rink
- To a bowling alley
- To get a meal or even just a treat
- To another friend's party
- To the gym
- To get a massage

# Offer to Teach Your Skills to Someone Who Wants to Learn

When you teach others, your own self-confidence increases because you have the opportunity to expand your student's knowledge and understanding of the topic. You can be a positive role model and teach your student not only what to do but also what to avoid.

Teaching someone interested in your skills means sharing your experiences and insights. Sharing what you've accomplished, as well as your mistakes and what you've learned from them, helps your student be aware of the challenges and how to build resilience.

Self-confidence is having the belief that you can accomplish something. If you have self-esteem, you respect yourself and believe you have worth, no matter what you accomplish. By both providing feedback to your student to gain further insight into developing specific skills as well as acknowledging your student's achievements, you build your student's self-confidence and self-esteem too.

# Plan an Exciting Trip or Escapade to Do Something Fun

When you plan a trip, it's for excitement, adventure, and fun. It's something different to do, and just the planning gives you a sense of purpose.

Here are some tips for planning an excellent trip:

- ✔ Talk to friends who like to travel to find out where they had a great time. Research online to browse for photographs and videos of real people sharing what happened in their travels.

- ✔ Consider the types of recreation the place offers, such as historical places, beaches, and museums. Also consider whether the transportation facilities and restaurants are sufficient.

- ✔ Look for places with weather conditions you'll enjoy.

- ✔ Make a list of the places you want to visit and things you want to do, but don't create a schedule that's too hard and fast. Things rarely go as planned on vacations, so keep your schedule fairly loose.

- ✔ Leave space in your luggage for things you'll be bringing home.

And have a wonderful time!

# Volunteer for an Organization with a Worthy Cause

There's nothing like helping others to make you feel good about yourself. Not only do you feel more connected to others and have pride in what you're doing, but volunteering also offers you a chance to give back to your community.

Volunteering has many benefits. Here are some of them:

- ✔ It helps you make new friends and contacts.

- ✔ It gives you the opportunity to practice and develop your social skills.

- ✔ It increases your self-confidence that you're accomplishing something important and worthwhile.

- ✔ It leads to greater happiness for you and those you assist.

- ✔ It provides the opportunity to try out a new career.

- ✔ It teaches you new skills you can use when seeking a new job.

When you're considering where to volunteer, don't limit yourself to just one organization or type of volunteer work. The smartest thing to do is to visit several organizations, learn about the opportunities that are available, and see whether you connect with the staff and other volunteers.

Also, your local newspaper may carry information about volunteer openings, and some communities have an organization dedicated just to providing volunteers to organizations. So take advantage of these if they're available in your community.

You can find volunteer opportunities in a variety of organizations: Youth organizations; sports teams; after-school programs; historical places; national, state, county, and city parks; libraries; senior centers; service organizations such as the Lions Club or Rotary Club; and museums are just a few.

As you're considering different places to volunteer, ask yourself these questions to make sure there's a good match between what they need and what you have to offer:

- ✔ What type of mission is important to you?

- ✔ What skills do you have?

- ✔ How many days do you want to volunteer, and for how long on those days?

- ✔ Do you prefer to work alone or as a team member?

- ✔ How much responsibility are you willing to take on?

Once you find a volunteer position that is mutually beneficial, you can generally remain with it as long as you'd like. The advantages of volunteering are great, so if you have the time and inclination, do look into it.

# Get Started — It's Time for You to Begin Your New Life!

After you've read this book, done the exercises, and discovered what you need to change and how to make those changes, go do it!

Start implementing some of our easier suggestions today, and you'll see small benefits start taking shape almost immediately. As you see these benefits increase, one after the other, you'll continue to have a positive attitude that change is possible, and your self-esteem will improve all the time.

Don't expect to make a complete change overnight though. Have some patience and realize that it takes time to be the person you desire to be. As you increase your self-esteem and self-confidence, you'll experience exponential growth that will lead to great joy in your life. Carry on!

# Index

# *About the Authors*

**Vivian Harte** has taught assertiveness skills to over 10,000 students worldwide through the ed2go.com online course "Get Assertive!" From being a shy child, she developed her own self-esteem. She earned a bachelor's degree in sociology and a master's degree in public administration with a specialization in energy policy. She was instrumental in writing the City of Tucson Energy Plan. In the mid-1990s, she was the chair of Concerned Arizonans for Renewable Energy that took solar and energy legislation to the Arizona legislature, and most proposed bills were passed into law. She was a commissioner on the Tucson-Pima County Metropolitan Energy Commission that advises the Tucson City Council and Pima County Board of Supervisors. She also was the chair of the Arizona Solar Energy Association, which is a chapter of the American Solar Energy Society, and she has educated many people in the public about solar energy.

She was the Arizona manager for the Southwest Public Recycling Association, assisting rural communities around the state to begin recycling programs, hosting workshops for Arizona recycling coordinators, and writing the state's manual on recycling. She also hosted her own radio and television shows for many years in Colorado Springs, Minneapolis, and Tucson.

Vivian has 14 years of experience teaching in the college classroom — four years at the University of Phoenix and ten years at Pima Community College, where she taught "Women in Society" classes, which included working with students to improve their self-esteem.

Find out more about Vivian at www.self-esteem-course.com.

**S. Renee Smith,** a nationally recognized self-esteem and branding expert, image consultant, and motivational speaker, has worked with over 50 clients across eight industries including healthcare, banking, education, retail, nonprofit, state, government, legal, and religious organizations. Some of her clients include Cigna, Wal-Mart, Bank of America, University of Delaware, Alabama State University, and the National Black MBA Association.

S. Renee is endorsed by and shares platforms with such well-known international speakers and leaders as *Chicken Soup for the Soul* originator Jack Canfield, *ABC* journalist and author Byron Pitts, and winner of *The Apprentice,* entrepreneur and author Dr. Randal Pinkett.

With over 20 years of image development experience, she launched her speaking business in 2005. She is the author of three popular books, *There Is More Inside; The Bridge to Your Brand: Likability, Marketability, Credibility;* and *Our Hearts Wonder: Prayers to Heal Your Heart and Calm Your Soul.* She is also a resource to the media.

S. Renee serves on United Way of Delaware Women in Leadership Council and the Commission on Early Education and the Economy. She is honorary commander of the Department of Defense Charles C. Carson Center for Mortuary Affairs, a commissioner on the City of Dover's Human Relations Commission, and serves on the board of Delaware's largest philanthropic organization. Among many recognitions for the impact she has made on others' lives, July 17, 2010, was declared *S. Renee Smith Day* in the City of Buffalo.

A former QVC model, television talk show host and spokesperson in Philadelphia, and public relations director, she has worked for Fortune 500 companies in marketing and management. Find out more about S. Renee at `www.srenee.com`.

# Dedications

**From Vivian:** I dedicate this book to my parents, Jeanne K. Swearingen and Robert Swearingen, who encouraged my self-esteem, even when I was down on myself. One of my mother's favorite phrases while I was growing up was "You have so much going for you!" My mother was very excited about me writing this book, but she passed away before it was published. Mom and Dad, thank you so much for your love and deep belief in me. (Dad gets a copy of the book!)

**From S. Renee:** In honor and gratitude to my parents, William J. and Reverend Shirley M. Smith, Sr. Your unconditional love, patience, and support have given me the wings of faith. Because of you, I really believe that I can fly.

# Authors' Acknowledgments

**From Vivian:** I wish to thank my 4th grade teacher in Galion, Ohio. Mrs. Stella Ertley chose me to be part of a trio of girls, and she took us to sing in churches and on the radio. Because of Mrs. Ertley, I gained confidence in my voice and performing ability and I learned how to present myself before an audience.

I'm also indebted to my ex-husband Clay Adams, who increased my belief in myself as we performed on many stages together. In addition, he introduced me to the man who was instrumental in arranging for my scholarship for my master's degree. That degree enabled me to become a college faculty member, which then led to this book. I also would like to acknowledge my current husband Toby Schneider for supporting me in writing this book and listening to my adventures in creating.

Thanks to the sociology department at Pima Community College — West Campus and to `ed2go.com` for believing in me so I could touch a chord in my students.

My special thanks to you, our reader, for the courage and strength to open yourself to your journey ahead. Because you're reading this book, you're ready to become the eagle you truly are and to soar.

**From S. Renee:** I am thankful for every person who took this journey with me. The lack of space to name you individually doesn't lessen the greatness of my gratitude. I'm thankful to God for the gift of being a change agent on the planet. My brother, Mark, encouraged, challenged, and took every step with me.

My wisdom givers — my parents, William & Shirley; my brother, Joseph; and my uncle, James Smith. My prayer warriors — my mother and my aunt, Joan Draine-Burris. One of my secret inspirations — my aunt, Alice Smith-Coleman. We are in this together William Jr., Wanda (Thaddeus), Van, Renae, William III, Virginia, Jakeem, Julian, Tamia, Amir, Zariyah, Kirra, and Phyllis. I love each of you for who you are and where you are.

Steve Harrison, you valued me and my work and invited me to your platform. The exposure led to my being seen, heard, and asked to coauthor this book four months later. Many people hear God, but few listen and respond. Thank you for being you. Vivian, it's a pleasure to meet and work with you.

When teachers believe, respect, and support your learning experience, they make a difference — Mrs. Greta Fountain, the late Dr./Rev. Charles E. Drummer, Jr., Mr. Lacy Myers, Mrs. Virginia Carson, Mrs. Alice Carter, and Dr. Raymond Grandfield — thank you.

And last but not least, my inner circle, church family, networks, and social media friends, clients, readers, and new readers: I hold with great appreciation and integrity — your trust.

**From both:** Thank you to the staff at John Wiley and Sons, Tracy Boggier, and Chrissy Guthrie, for their encouragement and support in writing this book, and to Margot Maley Hutchison, our agent at Waterside Productions, for working with everyone involved regarding all the many details.

## Publisher's Acknowledgments

**Senior Acquisitions Editor:** Tracy Boggier

**Project Editor:** Christina Guthrie

**Copy Editor:** Christine Pingleton

**Technical Editor:** Matthew Grant, Psy.D

**Art Coordinator:** Alicia B. South

**Project Coordinator:** Patrick Redmond

**Cover Image:** ©iStock.com/GlobalP ©iStock.com/Studio-Annika